EMMELINE'S LOVING COMRADE, RICHARD MARSDEN PANKHURST

EMMELINE'S LOVING COMRADE, RICHARD MARSDEN PANKHURST

THE MAN WHO INSPIRED THE SUFFRAGETTE LEADER

JOANNA M. WILLIAMS

PEN & SWORD HISTORY

AN IMPRINT OF PEN & SWORD BOOKS LTD.
YORKSHIRE – PHILADELPHIA

First published in Great Britain in 2026 by
Pen & Sword History
An imprint of
Pen & Sword Books Ltd
Yorkshire - Philadelphia

ISBN 978 1 03619 499 4

Typeset in INDIA by IMPEC eSolutions
Printed and bound in England by CPI Group (UK) Ltd, Croydon, CRO 4YY

The Publisher's authorised representative in the EU for product safety is
Authorised Rep Compliance Ltd., Ground Floor, 71 Lower Baggot Street,
Dublin D02 P593, Ireland.
www.arccompliance.com

For a complete list of Pen & Sword titles please contact:

PEN & SWORD BOOKS LIMITED
George House, Units 12 & 13, Beevor Street, Off Pontefract Road,
Barnsley, S71 1HN, UK
E-mail: enquiries@pen-and-sword.co.uk
Website: www.pen-and-sword.co.uk

or

PEN AND SWORD BOOKS
1950 Lawrence Rd, Havertown, PA 19083, USA
E-mail: Uspen-and-sword@casematepublishers.com
Website: www.penandswordbooks.com

In loving memory of Ken

Contents

Acknowledgements viii
List of Figures ix
Abbreviations xi
Introduction xii

Part 1: Life Before Emmeline, 1834–79

Chapter 1 Origins 2
Chapter 2 Man About Town 14
Chapter 3 A Social Conscience 27
Chapter 4 The Ultra-Radical Emerges 45
Chapter 5 Women's Suffrage to 1880 60
Chapter 6 Married Women's Property 77

Part 2: Marriage and Children 1879–93

Chapter 7 An 'Ideal Marriage' 86
Chapter 8 Parliamentary Candidate 96
Chapter 9 London Adventure 110
Chapter 10 'The Four Pillars of My House' 126
Chapter 11 London Campaigns and the Emergence of Emmeline 137

Part 3: Final Years in the North, 1893–98

Chapter 12 The Family in the North 149
Chapter 13 ILP Candidate – The Gorton Election of May 1895 162
Chapter 14 Maintaining the Family Income 177
Chapter 15 Final Years 183
Chapter 16 Legacy 194

Conclusion 201
Notes 207
Select Bibliography 230
Index 234

Acknowledgements

I am deeply indebted to many who have helped me in this endeavour, particularly my publishers, Pen and Sword, and Amy Jordan who has been unfailingly responsive and supportive. My editor, Paul Middleton, has proved patient and professional in helping me to clarify the manuscript. The staff at Manchester Central Library; the John Rylands University of Manchester Library; the Women's Library at the London School of Economics; the British Library; the National Library of Australia; the University of Liverpool Library; the International Institute of Social History, Amsterdam. Rachel Kneale and Otto Smart, the archivists at Manchester Grammar School, Alfie Jenkins at the Royal Statistical Society, the Reverend Jo Jarratt at St Luke's Weaste, Maurice Barratt and Allan Edgar have all provided invaluable assistance in accessing their records or providing images. Should there be any unknown copyright holders of sources I have used unwittingly, they should kindly make themselves known to me.

Many individuals have given generously of their time to make suggestions and answer my questions, and I would like to thank particularly Janet Douglas; Alistair MacLeod; Anthony R. McGarel-Groves; David Bebbington, Emeritus Professor of History at the University of Stirling; and Sandra Stanley Holton, historian and author. Most especially I am indebted to June Purvis, Emeritus Professor of Women's and Gender History at the University of Portsmouth, who provided materials and was kind enough to read the manuscript and to offer much valuable advice. My sincere thanks also go to Helen Pankhurst, great-granddaughter of Richard Marsden Pankhurst, who provided me with material, read through the manuscript, and supported my efforts throughout. My friends have been wonderful in their help and interest in my work; most especially Pam Dawes, who read the first draft, and Susan Sinagola, who checked the proofs. Both provided invaluable feedback and suggestions. My family have been brilliant, and I could not have completed this biography without their love and belief that I could get there.

List of Figures

1. Emmeline c.1880
2. Richard Pankhurst
3. The Delves School
4. Owens College in Quay Street
5. Solicitor's qualification
6. Lincoln's Inn
7. Richard Marsden Pankhurst the barrister
8. The Manchester Brasenose Club
9. A young and confident Richard Pankhurst
10. The Free Trade Hall
11. JS Mill and Helen Taylor
12. Richard Pankhurst
13. Ernest Jones
14. Lydia Becker in 1873
15. Jane (Sophie) Quine/Craine
16. St Luke's Church, Weaste
17. Christabel Pankhurst
18. Sylvia Pankhurst
19. Adela Pankhurst
20. Harry Pankhurst
21. Campaign poster 1885
22. Annie Besant
23. Elizabeth Wolstenholme Elmy
24. Alice Scatcherd with other women's suffrage campaigners
25 Lorne House, 4 Buckingham Crescent, Victoria Park, Manchester
26. James Keir Hardie
27. Leonard Hall
28. Fred Brocklehurst
29. Katherine Glasier
30. Bruce Glasier

31. 1895 election poster
32. ILP conference 1898
33. Richard Pankhurst late in life
34. Smedley's hydro, Matlock
35. Clarion Club shares
36. Valewood Farm
37. Richard Pankhurst's grave in Brooklands cemetery
38. Emmeline in middle age
39. Emmeline Pankhurst's grave in Brompton cemetery
40. Detail from Emmeline Pankhurst's grave

Abbreviations

BAAS	British Association for the Advancement of Science
ESPP	E. Sylvia Pankhurst Papers
ILP	Independent Labour Party
JRUL	John Rylands University Library
LL	Labour Leader
LSE	London School of Economics
MC	Manchester Courier
MCL	Manchester Central Library
MCN	Manchester City News
MEN	Manchester Evening News
MG	Manchester Guardian
MNSWS	Manchester National Society for Women's Suffrage
MWP	Married Women's Property
NAC	National Administrative Council
NAPSS	National Association for the Promotion of Social Science
NRU	National Reform Union
SA	Staffordshire Advertiser
SDF	Social Democratic Federation
TSM	The Suffragette Movement
WFrL	Women's Franchise League
WSJ	Women's Suffrage Journal

Introduction

The name of 'Pankhurst' evokes in most Britons that great iconic figure of the early twentieth century, Mrs Emmeline Pankhurst, leader of the Suffragettes. Fighting unstintingly for the women's vote, she springs to the mind's eye in photographic images: the feisty street speaker, the diminutive figure carried off to prison in the arms of a burly policeman, the frail woman in bed recovering from hunger strike. In her home city of Manchester she has been commemorated in a life-size statue and in the artwork of Mancsy. Her two elder daughters, Christabel and Sylvia, who made their own contributions to the women's cause and individually went on to become campaigners in other fields, have become likewise renowned.

But the question arises: who was the husband and father who shared the celebrated name of Pankhurst with this phenomenal family? Richard Marsden Pankhurst has long been in the shadows. A noted public man in Manchester during his lifetime, it was remarkably claimed in 1895, perhaps somewhat tongue in cheek, by the *London Evening Mail* that 'Karl Marx and Keir Hardie pale into insignificance beside Dr. Pankhurst.' Yet he often operated behind the scenes in the early women's campaign. His profession as a lawyer, supporting, advising, representing in court cases, and drafting legislation rendered him vital to the cause, but also somewhat out of the limelight. Moreover, his death in 1898 meant that when the long-standing campaign for women's suffrage became 'militant' in the early twentieth century, in the guise of the Suffragettes, he had been forgotten in the public mind.

However, this book argues that his influence lived on through his family. He deliberately inculcated them with his ultra-radical, later socialist, ideals and aims, and his impact featured strongly in their thinking long after his death. Emmeline, only twenty-one when she married him, was to a considerable extent moulded by him, as were his children. They worked for the causes he espoused firstly as a partnership, then quite soon as a family. And many historians agree that the Suffragettes, in their focus and methods, reflected his commitment to principle without compromise. It is true that in the long run only his second daughter, Sylvia, remained a permanent disciple of his beliefs, throughout her life reinterpreting them in new circumstances. Nevertheless, his approach and methods underpinned the work of his widow and other children in their devotion to causes and their uncompromising application of strategies and tactics.

Richard Pankhurst was a Victorian visionary with aspirations and beliefs ahead of his time. He espoused ultra-radical causes such as the abolition of the monarchy and the aristocracy, the nationalisation of the land, the empowerment of the poor, and Irish self-government, and from a very early date he was an active proponent of women's social, economic and political rights. Although in early life he followed the religion of his father as a non-conformist, by mid-life he was openly agnostic, and was claimed by some to be privately an atheist. Initially a promising young lawyer, such challenging views made him an unacceptable 'firebrand' in the eyes of many contemporaries.

It may therefore not surprise us that by every conventional measure of success, Richard Pankhurst was also a failure. As a barrister, he failed to progress to the more important law suits and appointments which might have been expected to come his way. As he focused on those cases that chimed with his passionately pursued crusades, defending trade unions and attacking privilege, lucrative briefs went elsewhere. He did not live up to the expectations of those called to the Bar, that he should make a good living and support a family in style. He allowed his wife, Emmeline, to go into trade in a vain attempt to improve the family fortunes, something that no normal self-respecting middle-class gentleman would countenance. And when he stood for parliament on three occasions he was dismally unsuccessful.

While there is a lack of personal papers, with very few of Richard's letters and other documents extant, the dearth is to some extent mitigated by the writings of his wife and daughters. Understandably, these furnish very personal views and need to be handled with some care and circumspection. Yet they provide unique and controversial insights into his role as a husband and father, as well as a public figure. Emmeline, in *My Own Story*, continues to be the devoted wife with nothing but praise for her inspirational spouse. Christabel's short account of the early years in *Unshackled* praises both parents for their work and displays sympathy and understanding for her mother, with whom she was on good terms for the rest of Emmeline's life.

Sylvia's account, the most detailed and widely read, has become the most influential of them all. It affords an encomium of her beloved father's life and career. She followed his example and teachings unquestioningly for the rest of her life. This, and the fact that she and her mother became estranged, means that the shortcomings in the upbringing of the children are attributed by Sylvia largely to Emmeline, who often seems unfeeling and uninterested in her offspring except in so far as they could be a useful adjunct to the campaigns in which their parents were engaged.

Adela's contribution to the family history is the least known; her emigration to Australia has meant that her papers, titled 'My Mother', are now in Canberra. Like Sylvia, she ended up on bad terms with her mother but unlike her, in her writings she took the latter's part. Indeed, she avows that the reason she wrote 'My Mother' was to provide a sympathetic account as a riposte to Sylvia's hostile memoir. It is her father, Richard, whom she believes was fundamentally to blame for what she perceives as the neglect of the children, particularly the younger ones, herself and Harry. Indeed, she dramatically cites her father's influence even after his death as a reason for Emmeline's failure to nurse Harry in what became his final illness, leading to his premature death aged 20. Adela did not pull her punches where Richard Pankhurst was concerned.

The lack of personal papers may explain why Richard Marsden Pankhurst has not received the attention from biographers that we might expect. It might have been anticipated that he would appear in the studies that have examined the role of men in the women's rights campaigns, such as Richard Symonds' *Inside the Citadel,* where indeed there are a couple of brief nods in his direction. Sylvia Strauss's *Traitors to the Masculine Cause* includes some basic information, but that is the full extent of his recognition.[1]

In the 1950s ex-suffragette Theresa Billington-Greig attempted to collect information for an account of the Pankhursts from those who knew them, or whose parents may have done so. The replies to her enquiries, held in the London School of Economics Women's Library, demonstrate that she did not get very far beyond the writings of Sylvia as far as Richard's personal life goes. She complained to Emmeline's niece, Enid Goulden Bach, also an ex-suffragette:

> Sylvia gives both a very full record of his public work and suffrage activity and of his character as a beloved father – and there are the Liberal and early Labour papers – but apart from Sylvia and grateful suffragist letters – no one speaks of him personally, and his photograph (the only one I have seen) is in no sense enlightening – indeed it sets up new queries! I have always felt that he has not received adequate recognition from the suffrage movement – and that only Sylvia of the militants has indicated his part in the early campaign and the possible part his spirit and character may have played in the creation of militancy.[2]

As far as Richard's public persona is concerned, Billington-Greig drew her own, pithily expressed conclusions. She described him in her notes as 'a radical, passionately interested in social reform ... of the angry fervour type – nothing was too outrageous. He attacked all established institutions, associated in radical extremism with Joseph Chamberlain and Sir Charles Dilke and Bradlaugh – formed the Manchester Republican Club.' She also noted that 'he was regarded as an undesirable advocate by many older suffragists'. This may have been because, as Billington-Greig held, he was 'too exuberantly verbose and tactless', but it was likely even more due to his extreme political position.[3]

The main resource for Richard's public life is the press; news reports often include large parts of his speeches, quoted word for word. The extreme radicalism of his republicanism and later religious agnosticism was too strong even for most radicals, and his daughter Sylvia acknowledged that he was 'vilified and boycotted', and that contemporaries 'caricatured, lampooned and abused' him in the press as a result.

Yet it is true that Richard did attain a certain popularity in his home city of Manchester, being often nicknamed 'our learned Doctor' in the contemporary liberal press.[4] He was hugely respected as a man who put principle and personal integrity above all other considerations, even by those who considered him too radical to be taken seriously. One letter in the Billington-Greig collection from a 1950s Mancunian Liberal recalls, 'My late mother met him, I think only once, and I have heard her speak of him as a very fine man indeed.'[5] He was known for his vocal support of causes to benefit the people, such as freedom of speech, universal suffrage and the alleviation of poverty. As Sylvia noted he 'was a standard-bearer of every forlorn hope, every unpopular yet worthy cause then conceived for the uplifting of oppressed and suffering humanity'. She concludes that he was 'the most outstanding public personality in his native city'.[6] It is not clear whether this somewhat partial assessment was her own, or perhaps even conveyed to her young and impressionable mind by the man himself. Certainly there is little evidence that he expressed much in the way of self-doubt, and this assessment of his prominence may well have chimed with his own self-presentation.

Sylvia's description of his physical person is similarly partisan, in that the surviving photographs of him fail to convey the suave image she portrays: 'Younger in looks than his youthful years, graceful and vivacious in bearing, wearing his red beard pointed like a Frenchman ...' Later she adds:

> Wonderful father, the lodestar of our lives, like a bright sunny morning, brimful of energy. His hair was always grey in my memory of him, but at first it was a dark iron grey, later a bright, clear silver, very soft and fine. His skin was clear and ruddy, his head beautifully shaped. His hands and feet were slender and sensitive; his nails like no others I have seen. If he let them grow ... they clove to the fingers, curling over the tips.[7]

Usually a mild-mannered and cultured man, others note that he delivered his message with violent rhetoric, expressed in an unusually high-pitched voice that presented an opportunity for hostile newspapers to report his sallies with mockery and derision.

Yet his wife and elder daughters idolised him as a paragon of virtue and self-sacrifice and the influence he exerted over his family was entirely active and intentional. He repeatedly told his children that their role in life was to do good: 'If you do not work for other people, you will not have been worth the upbringing.' It can even be argued that Richard Pankhurst worked out his destiny through his family. His *modus operandi* as a husband and father, unconventional and idiosyncratic as it was, both moulded and allowed latitude to the remarkable Pankhurst women, who have made an indelible stamp on the history of this country.

In the long run, many of the ideals to which Richard Pankhurst aspired have either been achieved today or are now accepted as mainstream common causes: the alleviation of poverty and political rights for the poor, equality for oppressed groups, the adoption of peaceful methods of conflict resolution in the world. These are all widely accepted principles, where once they were considered unacceptably ultra-radical. In his lifetime, Pankhurst may have felt he had achieved little, but his influence has added to the great stream of idealism that has helped to change society, and is still doing so. He is surely worthy of recognition as a thinker, a campaigner and to a large extent the creator of the celebrated Pankhurst women.

PART 1

Life Before Emmeline, 1834–79

Origins

An Obscure and Inauspicious Beginning

What were the influences that formed the idealistic young man who was ostensibly just an unconventional and struggling barrister? Contrary to common belief, his family origins were very modest, verging on deprived at times. When his father moved the family to Manchester in the mid-1840s, it was to find a new start after economic disaster. It paid off: ten years later he was building up a business as an auctioneer and valuer and was able to send Richard to Manchester Grammar School, which set him up for a career with very respectable prospects in the law. But it was not a happy family. Of their four children, Richard was the only one with whom his parents, Henry Francis and Margaret, were in accord. And even that harmony was threatened by Richard's forays into the women's rights campaign of the 1860s and '70s. A picture begins to emerge of a struggling and divided family, with parents who made uncompromising demands that their children could or would not fulfil. It is here that the early formative influences on Richard Pankhurst may be found.

In contrast to his egalitarian principles, Richard was apparently proud that his Kent forbears pre-dated the Norman conquest. Christabel noted in a letter of 1953 that 'he valued his pedigree'. He apparently possessed a copy of the family tree, which may have been in the large Bible in which the family was recorded in the time-honoured way.[1] There had been a rapid decline in the family fortunes when his grandfather Francis James sold the family land, moved to London, and then lost his money in ill-advised speculation.[2] It may have been in an attempt to escape the opprobrium which this incurred that he changed the family name from Penkhurst to Pankhurst. He made a new start in 1822 as the headmaster of the newly founded Delves School at Walgherton in Cheshire, where he earned a living supporting his thirteen children, dying at 71 in 1857. He had become a respected member of the community, demonstrated in the reporting of his funeral at Wybunbury church. He was

> for more than forty years the exemplary, high-minded, and beloved master of the Delves's School ... The procession was preceded by the boys of the school singing a funeral hymn, while the body was supported and followed by the friends and relatives of the deceased. Over the procession, as it moved along, were borne the plaintive sounds of the singing of the boys, and the measured tolling of the bell, carried sadly though sweetly on the wind, speaking future joy and peace amid present sorrow and tears. The body was interred beneath the sombre shade of the venerable yew tree, the only tree in the graveyard near which the good old 'master' was often heard to wish to find his final resting place.[3]

The burial record is unusually detailed in that it notes he lay '4 feet south of Breeze's stone below yew tree'. His death notice added that he had 'passed in the faithful discharge of his duty a worthy life, in character and conduct irreproachable, in walk and conversation beyond rebuke'.[4] The relatives mentioned would surely have included his son, Henry Francis, and his grandson, Richard Marsden, who, if the claims about Francis James' character are true, perhaps inherited that gentleman's moral probity and high aspirations.

Richard's father, Henry Francis Pankhurst, though born in Clerkenwell, London, on 3 September 1809, apparently grew up in Cheshire, where the family moved before he was 8 years old. Nothing is known of his early years. In 1830 in Great Budworth church he married Margaret Marsden, daughter of Richard Marsden, a tailor and draper in Wigan. They were noted in the parish marriage record as both residents of Great Budworth, and according to the licence Henry Francis was from the nearby village of Witton by Twambrooks, but Margaret was noted to be from Liverpool. The ages of both were given as 21; this seems to indicate only that they were over 21 and therefore of age, as in fact Margaret was 26. Henry Francis apparently came to be living in Witton by virtue of his role as a schoolmaster, but how he met his bride is unclear. She was presumably impressed by the attractiveness of his person: 'ardent and eager in his affections', he was described by Sylvia as 'tall, blond, strikingly handsome and vivacious' and he was especially impressive on 'his great black horse'.[5]

It was perhaps around this time that Henry Francis abandoned the Church of England into which he had been born and became a baptist. The children came quickly; in the following year, Harriet Emma was born in Hough, Cheshire, though baptised at the Particular Baptist Chapel in Blackburn. Soon after, the young family moved across the border into Staffordshire to nearby Stoke and in 1832 a son arrived, significantly named John Calvin. Again the trek was made to Blackburn for his baptism. After a more respectable gap of two years, Richard Marsden was born probably in 1834, and the family was completed in 1836 with Elizabeth Mary.[6] It is unknown where or whether these later siblings were baptised; it seems that their parents did not make the journey to Blackburn as the records are extant and do not mention them.[7]

The move to Stoke seems to have marked an end to the schoolmastering, and Henry Francis set up as a grocer and tea merchant. They settled in Wheatly Place, Shelton, a market town that was part of the Hanley area of Stoke, the centre of pottery manufacture, and in fact just near the Etruria villa, hamlet and works earlier built by the great Josiah Wedgwood. Directories of the time indicate that Shelton in general featured 'well-built' houses; it was clearly an area favoured by the respectable working classes.[8]

In 1835, the business was operating in Liverpool Road and Henry Francis placed a large advertisement in the *Staffordshire Advertiser* of 25 July informing the public that the 'Pottery Tea and Coffee Warehouse' had opened recently. By the following year, it was offering new lines in beverages and general groceries. The most expensive tea was 'Gunpowder' at a costly 8s per lb. The advertisement also cautioned against mixing coffee with root of endive, clearly a common local practice. It seems that trade was good, as an apprentice was also wanted, who 'will be treated as one of the family'.[9]

However, by the end of the 1830s all was not well. Henry Francis's fortunes crashed, and in 1840 he was in the debtors' prison in the county town of Stafford; his debts must have amounted to at least £20, a not insubstantial sum.[10] His bankruptcy was announced in papers across the country, such as in the *Reading Mercury* on 13 June. By this time Richard was a little boy of about 6, who would perhaps have become dimly aware of the privations and social difficulties with which his parents were dealing. By 1842 Henry Francis was in court for failure to pay his church rate, which he argued was invalid, presumably partly because he was by now a non-conformist.[11] But this may have masked the fact that he was in any case unable to afford it. In 1843 he was again declared bankrupt, according to the *London Gazette*. Richard was about 9 by now and may have been more affected by events. Certainly, later in life as a lawyer Richard made bankruptcy law one of his specialisms.

By 4 May 1844, Henry Francis had begun an auctioneering business, as he was selling property in Hanley at the Sea Lion public house.[12] One of his clients was Francis Wedgwood, of the famous pottery company, who later on, in 1848, provided a letter testifying to Henry Francis Pankhurst's respectability and business-like methods.[13] Again though, all does not seem to have been going well, as an advertised sale of houses and other property in Eccleshall had to be 'postponed for the present' on 5 September 1844.[14] On the other hand, only a couple of weeks later, Henry Francis had contracted to auction off in Newcastle-under-Lyme part of a consignment of guano imported on a large scale direct shipping from Ichaboe (an island off modern Namibia) by an enterprising Mr Cummings of London.[15]

It may be that Henry Francis's wife, Margaret, persuaded her Marsden relatives to help him out financially. Later, in the mid-1860s, Margaret was pursuing her brother's executors, including his widow, in a claim concerning an annuity he had bequeathed her in fulfilment of their father's wishes. The widow's Wigan solicitors argued that the arrears due to her were forfeit in payment of a debt owed to the estate by her husband, but Margaret contested that there was no such debt still owing, implying that it had in fact already been repaid.[16]

It is possible that the opportunities for commercial expansion, coupled with escape from the opprobrium of bankruptcy, persuaded Henry Francis and Margaret to move away at some time around the middle of the 1840s to the rapidly expanding town of Manchester. It was sufficiently distant and populous that they would be able to use their anonymity to start afresh. And clearly the formula worked: when they appear in the 1851 census Henry Francis is established as an auctioneer and valuer. Indeed, as early as 14 April 1849 he features in the *Manchester Guardian* classified advertisements auctioning off household effects at his premises, The Mart, 60 Great Jackson Street, which also provided a home for the family in the respectable working-class district of Hulme. Their neighbours on either side were artisans and businessmen – an engraver, a chemist and druggist, and a grocer who employed a warehouseman and a servant.

By November 1850 Henry Francis was sufficiently invested in this community to attend a vestry meeting of about a dozen people who met to revise the street layout of the suburb. He was even so bold as to present a resolution to a further ratepayers meeting opposed to the local powers being taken over by the Manchester Council. On 16 July 1851 his respectability was established enough for him to be a member of the jury sworn in for a coroner's inquest into a suspicious death. This was sealed by his attendance at a meeting of the electors for the Manchester Council in St George's ward, where he spoke up to support the successful nomination for the candidacy of Mr Greig.[17]

Henry Francis was certainly establishing his credentials as a solid citizen of Manchester, and it was perhaps from his example that his younger son, Richard, grew into a profoundly public-spirited man. In February 1852 Henry Francis was active in a Hulme ratepayers' meeting that resolved to petition parliament to force poor law unions to adopt a policy of productive employment for able-bodied paupers, with a view to encouraging self-sufficiency and thereby hopefully reducing the rates. He had also become the secretary of the Manchester House Owners' Guardian Society, which provided insurance. The following October, he took a further interest in a council seat for St George's when he questioned a candidate about the provision of a rate to provide education for the poor.[18]

The next year, Henry Francis took over the auctioneering business of a Jasper Fletcher, by an agreement with the latter's widow. It was situated at a prestigious, city-centre address, York Hotel Buildings on King Street. A fortnight later he was advertising his services at this address, as a moneylender of substantial loans of £50 upwards. New premises were found by December 1854, when the business had moved to another central position at 28 Princess Street.[19]

Meanwhile, Richard was registered as a scholar in the 1851 census, and this is confirmed in the records of the Manchester Grammar School which show that a 13-year-old Richard had been enrolled there on 18 February 1847 by his father, who is noted as a share broker.[20] This may indicate that Richard demonstrated precocity and was thought worthy of an academic education. Sylvia recounts, presumably from Richard himself, that as a child he 'would creep under the table and read for long, delightful hours ...' By contrast, his older brother, John Calvin, who was aged 19 at the time of the census, was working as his father's assistant; he had not apparently had the benefit of much formal education. The free education that Richard acquired under High Master Nicholas Germon was of a traditional nature, consisting largely of Classics and Scripture, with possibly some French and Mathematics. There was apparently no sport at all. Whilst some of the school's pupils only remained until their mid-teens, Richard had aspirations to continue his education and remained until he was at least 18. When in 1903 the school held a prestigious anniversary dinner to say farewell to the High Master, Mr J.E. King, about seventy old boys attended, of whom one, John Kendall, recalled his time there in the later 1840s:

> The late Dr. Pankhurst was one of Mr. Kendall's schoolfellows, usually occupying the top of the form, whilst the narrator was at the bottom. Jocularly reminding Dr. Pankhurst of this in later years, he replied, 'My dear fellow, you simply turn a handle and the sovereigns flow out,' and then, striking his forehead with a characteristic dramatic action, he exclaimed, 'With me it is brains, brains, brains.'[21]

By 13 October 1856 the family had moved to 28 Clifford Street in Chorlton-on-Medlock, where they may or may not have taken advantage of an amenity then in vogue, the Turkish Baths, next door. They were also able to employ a servant by 1861.[22] Henry Francis continued to participate in local affairs in his new home, supporting efforts by the local ratepayers' association to reduce the poor rate by curtailing unnecessary expenditure by the guardians on a workhouse, which was claimed to have a grand staircase 'not much short of Chatsworth'![23] He continued to appear regularly thereafter in this august body.

He bolstered his Liberal credentials on 1 February 1858 when he featured prominently at a meeting to establish a Manchester Reform Association in support of an electoral reform to allow some of the better-off working-class men to vote.[24] This was followed up in August when he spoke at a gathering of Liberal electors called to discuss the nomination for the next election, and successfully backed the more liberal Mr Bazley against Mr Fairbairn.[25] And as the reformers got the bit between their teeth, Henry Francis appeared on the platform with prominent Manchester Liberals at a large meeting in the Free Trade Hall on 17 March 1859.[26]

He had come a long way since the days of Stafford debtors prison, but there may have been some continuing insecurity as to his social status. Having moved to 4 James Place, Stretford by the Census of 1871, as late as 1873 there was a formal challenge of his right to vote in the South-Eastern division of Lancashire based on 'the nature of his interest in the qualifying property'.[27]

The census of 1861 showed that by then Henry Francis and Margaret's elder son, John Calvin, was no longer living at home or working as an auctioneer's assistant, and this seems to have been as a result of a serious argument with his father. On 20 January 1853, 20-year-old John had married in Blackburn a Martha Ann Railton from the same town. The bride may have been pregnant, as the following July they had a son whom they named after his grandfather, Henry Francis.[28] Tragically, the baby died before he was 6 months old, and it is possible that his mother also did so, as only a year after his first marriage John married again, this time to Elizabeth Grimshaw, the illiterate daughter of a brewer.

However, the odd circumstance that he is described on the second marriage certificate as a bachelor rather than a widower suggests that there may have been some murky dealing here; perhaps John, now a 'mariner' was concealing his previous marriage. No evidence has been found to show that Martha had died. And he and Elizabeth may have been living together before their marriage as they are both recorded on the certificate as living in Back Acton Street.

In *The Suffragette Movement* Sylvia Pankhurst refers to a quarrel between John and his father, which resulted in his travelling to America. Indeed, this seems to have been mythologised in the family; Christabel refers to his being 'a legendary "Uncle John in America"'.[29] The real tale may have been much less glamorous. Henry Francis's non-conformist religious principles may well have been outraged by his elder son's lifestyle, possibly co-habiting with a woman who was not his wife. Marrying her was scarcely an improvement as she lacked even the education to write her name on the marriage certificate, suggesting that she was well below him in the social scale. He and Elizabeth arrived in Canada with their first child in 1856. Sylvia met her Uncle John in his old age, shortly before his death in the USA in 1912:

> His [Henry Francis's] elder son, John, as a mere lad, left the parental roof on account of some youthful peccadilloes and a marriage which aroused a father's displeasure, and sailed with his young bride for America never to return. There he encountered most terrible hardships. When I saw him, a tall, gaunt old man in Chicago, more than half a century later, John Pankhurst still spoke resentfully of those bitter days and of his little baby lying dead of privation on a bed of straw.

Henry Francis was scarcely less judgmental towards his younger daughter. Sylvia describes how Elizabeth, known as Bess, also married 'in face of her father's anger'. Her parents did not attend her wedding in 1868 at Manchester Cathedral to John Cavanah, a poor, young man 'noted for the beautiful white neck he displayed when appearing in women's parts at the Manchester Athenaeum Dramatic Society'. Perhaps he was the 'good looking fellow' Bess met when away with her father in the Isle of Man in August 1865; certainly she seemed 'a good deal taken' with him, and he paid her 'a great deal of attention and sticks to her like wax'.[30] The rift was healed by the agency of Richard, her brother, and the sister of Henry Francis, Aunt Mary. The latter set up the 'stagestruck' youth in a hatter's shop, at which he failed; he eventually achieved success as the manager of an Aberdeen theatre. Attaining happiness in his calling, he turned out in the end to be a good husband and father, well under the thumb of his strong-minded wife, Bess, who was described by her niece, Christabel, as 'loyal, affectionate and extremely firm'.[31]

The eldest child of Henry Francis and Margaret was Harriet Emma, noted by Christabel to have been Richard's 'guide and confidante, rejoicing in his success at school …' She also made an ill-advised marriage to an unnamed 'ne'er-do-well musician' who was the editor of a music journal, which according to Sylvia was actually run by Harriet, as well as maintaining their home. The husband was abusive and Harriet's ill health caused her family much sadness. A slow-growing cancer, which was thought to have been caused by one of her husband's blows, occasioned her death in 1881 at the age of 50.

The Child of Promise

In huge contrast to the other siblings, Richard Marsden was the great hope of the family, and he seemed set to repay his parents' aspirations. Indeed, Sylvia records that there was 'never a jar' between the parents and this favoured son, a claim that was probably somewhat exaggerated.[32] He was seemingly devoted to them and lived in the family home until after their demise, when he was 45. He claimed that he never went out without telling them where he was going and when he would return. Sylvia does admit that at times Richard's ultra-radicalism went too far for his father but describes how 'the latter would only shake his head and warn him kindly: "You are making the steep road harder."' She relates how Richard spoke 'constantly' of his father to his children, and with 'a fervent affection and the thrill of a poignant loss ever new'.[33] The absence in Sylvia's account of any comment on Richard's mother may suggest that relations in that direction were less affectionate. Lydia Becker in 1868, a decade before he met Emmeline, reported that Richard expressed antipathy towards women, and it may be that he struggled with ongoing issues with his mother.[34]

Having left the Grammar School, probably in 1852 or 1853 at the age of 18 or 19, Richard had continued his education at Manchester's newly opened Owens College during its early days in Quay Street, in the former home of Richard Cobden. His options for this stage of his education were considerably reduced by the fact that Oxford and Cambridge did not accept non-Anglicans, however at Owens he was able to gain London University degrees. Much later, in 1876, the *City Jackdaw* retrospectively described the distinguished citizen as a young man:

> Dr. Pankhurst was one of the earliest of a succession of Nonconformist students who attached a reputation for sheer hard intellectual and sound learning to Owens College, before that useful and highly-superior seminary had become fashionable and churchy, or itched to puff itself up into being thought a university [it later became the University of Manchester]. He was, perhaps, the most brilliant of the group who went to continue their laborious days, begun in Quay Street in the unceasing grind, at London University ...[35]

The bachelor's course was largely traditional, with Classics and Mathematics predominating, though it also offered some modern content such as History, Political Economy, Chemistry, Natural History, French, German, and Jurisprudence. Richard was an able and promising student. He gained an honourable mention in the 1853–54 classes of Mental and Moral Philosophy, and certificates of merit (though not a prize) in Languages and Literature of Greece and Rome (5th place), and Greek Testament studies (3rd place).[36] The next year he won first prize in Logic, Mental and Moral Philosophy, with papers in which Principal Scott noted he 'excelled, and the absolute merit of the papers was remarkable'. Furthermore, Professor R.C. Christie awarded him the first prize in Political Economy.[37] In 1856 he took first prize in Language and Literature of Greece and Rome, coming in for special praise by Professor Greenwood, and a prize in French. So it was that in 1856 he was one of a small elite at the college who were awarded a London BA in the second division.[38]

It may well have seemed that the young man was destined for a career in academia, but it would appear that Richard was so taken with the delights of leaseholds and copyholds, which made up a considerable part of the content of the Jurisprudence curriculum, that he opted to continue his studies and become a lawyer, and no doubt attended the extra lectures that Professor Christie offered on the principles of general jurisprudence, arranged at a time to suit the students![39] By 1858 he had become honorary secretary of the Manchester Law Students Society and was delivering a lecture to the Law Students Mutual Corresponding Society in London on 'Educational Requirements in Relation to the Study of the Law'. His 'legal friends' were so impressed that they had the text published, aiming to 'promote a higher standard of general cultivation amongst the members of the legal profession'.[40] By this time he had also joined the recently formed Athenaeum Discussion Society, which focused on social and political topics; on 6 October at the annual meeting he became a vice-president of the club.[41] His growing prominence gained him invitations elsewhere, such as the dinner held by the Huddersfield Law Students Debating Society in September, where he showed off his oratorical skills by delivering 'an eloquent and able address' expounding the virtues of such societies, and regretting a lack of textbooks on some areas of law, to the detriment of the students' learning.[42] This was a lack that he was later to address himself by lectures and writings.

Indeed, the study of law was in a state of change during this period, and only recently had it been mooted that it might be desirable to follow a curriculum at university before entering law courts and chambers. Until the mid-century, lawyers learned 'on the job' as an apprentice to an established practitioner, as exemplified in Dickens' *Bleak House* and the training of young Richard Carstone. The Inns of Court had long abandoned the old professional training, and it was claimed that 'Dining in Hall was the only survival, and it was almost literally true that a man ate his way to the Bar'. It is a staggering fact that no judge in England before the mid-century had formal legal training. As late as 1883 this was still the route favoured by the older lawyers, who themselves had been thus instructed.[43]

In the early 1850s, however, the Inns of Court and the universities instituted new courses of legal study, and by 1853 the first legal examinations were taken by seven candidates. But not until 1872 was the examination made compulsory for call to the Bar. Many senior lawyers served as lecturers and examiners, and later Richard Pankhurst played his part in the novel exercise of educating young lawyers in the secrets of their profession. He also added to the number of a new genre of textbook, devoted to the exposition of legal principles and written specifically with students in mind.[44] The appearance of the *Law Quarterly Review* in 1884 emphasised the importance of this new approach to learning the law.

In 1859 Richard gained an LLB (second division) with Honours in Principles of Legislation, and he also became an Associate of Owens College. This entitled him to continue to attend lectures, use the library, and even to dine 'occasionally' at the college table, as if he were still a paying student or a professor. Indeed, it seems likely that it was at this point he began to teach elementary Latin in the pioneering evening sessions for the lower classes.[45] He was apparently unpaid for this duty, which Sylvia relates was carried out not only within the college, but also throughout Lancashire.[46]

Even at this stage in his late twenties, Richard demonstrated his lifelong desire, richly evident in the way he later brought up his children, to preach high ideals. The elementary Greek examination papers of Mr Watson required the translation of such prosaic sentences as 'It is the duty of the soldier to fight for the citizens', 'The bird sings' and 'The bolt fastens the door'. On the other hand, the Latin paper of Mr Pankhurst set an altogether higher moral, as well as linguistic, bar in the sentences set: 'It is better to obey God than to be great among men', 'He is neither prudent nor learned, but he wishes to seem to be endowed with virtue' and perhaps most revealingly 'They must admit that we have need of such zeal, if we are in these times to live nobly and act rightly'.[47]

Acquiring his attorney's diploma on 3 May 1860, it may be presumed that it was much to the gratification of his parents that by the 1861 census, as a solicitor with a Bachelor of Law degree, he was on his way up the social scale, operating his law practice at 3 St James' Chambers on South King Street in Manchester from at least September 1860.[48] On this occasion, he was solicitor for the trustees of John Marsden, of Orrell near Wigan, a screw and bolt manufacturer, perhaps a relative of his mother. Marsden was bankrupt, and the trustees were liquidating the business; a sale was held only two weeks later.[49] This was only the first known of a series of bankruptcies with which he dealt, and indeed a branch of the law which he embraced, since he produced a book on bankruptcy reform.[50] It seems likely that his early experiences in Stoke may have sparked a desire to understand and improve this corner of the legal system. His portfolio expanded into property law by the end of 1861 when he acted for the seller of a beerhouse, two shops and some houses.[51] He also undertook to advise his mother on her claims against the executors of her brother William to the effect that she was owed a huge £1,000 in arrears, and brokered a compromise to which both parties, apparently grudgingly, agreed in 1866.[52] The impression is that he was a bookish young man who was admired and consulted as a legal authority in the family.

He attained a London University LLD in 1863, with the highest distinction of a gold medal worth £20. From this date he became known locally as 'the Doctor', or even 'the good Doctor'. New distinctions were reflected in his practice; the recently established Manchester Benefit Building Society appointed him as its solicitor.[53] Yet his ambition went further, and he opted to train as a barrister. Having entered Lincoln's Inn on 18 November 1864, on 11 June 1867 he was called to the Bar and began to establish himself on the Northern Circuit and in the Lancaster County Palatine Court of Chancery.

He and his father continued to show keen support for both Manchester Grammar School and Owens College. Henry Francis corresponded with the *Manchester Guardian* in 1863 in support of retaining a large number of free places in the grammar school, fees having been proposed by the trustees. As a true dissenter, he also hoped that attendance by the pupils at the Anglican cathedral might be ceased.[54] Richard, later in life, was also engaged in supporting his old school; at the eighty-eighth annual dinner at the Queen's Hotel on 17 October 1882 he was a steward. However, the occasion was not well attended and a correspondent to the *Manchester Guardian* complained that at 25s the cost was too high for those who were not 'rising barristers' and could not 'all be associated with that most lucrative of professions'.[55]

On 1 February 1867 Henry Francis attended a meeting at Manchester Town Hall to approve and arrange fundraising for an extension of Owens College with the new buildings that still today form the core of the University of Manchester. Richard himself became Chairman of the Associates; he tried to use his position to modify the college rules to support those at the time excluded, including women. At the meeting he chaired in 1873, it was recommended without success to the Governors that they should wherever possible institute mixed classes.[56] Pankhurst also took an interest in the institution of a memorial to the engineering magnate, Sir William Fairbairn, which, as well as a statue, would establish a chair of mechanics in Owens College.[57]

When in 1880 the college was subsumed by the new Victoria University, Richard was a member of the Convocation and successfully advocated a committee to oversee the running of the university, to which he then was elected. It is a measure of the regard in which he was held by the institution that on 1 November 1881 it was proposed to elect him as the first chairman of the Convocation. But there was another candidate in the person of Professor H.E. Roscoe, who in the end won the vote at 39 to 11. Richard did not accept his defeat very graciously, in that he objected to the fact that Roscoe already held seven university offices, and also that all the key positions were held by teaching staff. Trying perhaps to turn his disappointment into a matter of high morality, he declared he had only allowed his nomination to go forward because it was a matter of principle that 'those who teach and train ought not to govern and examine, and fill all the positions in the University'. In the end, he had to bow to the inevitable, and resumed his lower-profile position as, with Dr Greenwood, the person connected for the longest period with the institution.

In 1882 Richard joined the 'annual committee' set up to sort out degrees to be conferred on the Associates of Owens College so that they could also be members of the new university. He only attended one of their four meetings, and did not continue on the committee thereafter. In his defence, he was then living in London, but it is also perhaps true that his enthusiasm was dampened by his failure in the election the year before.[58]

His commitment to his *alma mater* and other educational bodies can be viewed as one aspect of a much wider campaign to establish his position in Manchester through participation in the major institutions patronised by the city's great and good. This began soon after he achieved his LLB. It may have been driven by his realisation that to succeed as a lawyer he needed to develop a network of influential connections. On the other hand, even at this early date he was clearly an idealist who wanted to change the world, and this may have been an even more significant motivation. What he probably did not perceive was that in the long run, these two interests were set to clash as he became more prominent; powerful citizens were not inclined to offer legal briefs to a political agitator who was trying to overthrow the power structure that underpinned their own position.

CHAPTER 2

Man About Town

Clubland

The young man who was becoming a prominent public figure was clearly a phenomenon. Sylvia's description of her father is somewhat idealised, contrasting with less-kindly assessments. She allows that his platform voice was high pitched, which she admits struck some as 'weird and wonderful', though she says it became deeper as he got older. Apparently the Labour politician Philip Snowden recalled that his voice caused him sometimes to be mistaken for a woman![1] Sylvia states that he 'charmed and challenged', and Helen Moyes, suffragist and journalist, partly agreed:

> In the pursuit of what he deemed the public good he was indifferent to considerations of personal interest. Uncompromising in his opinions, he never entertained ill-will towards his opponents. Indeed his disposition was always kindly and genial … Men I knew who knew Doctor Pankhurst and knew all about him said he was a 'difficult person' and 'rather arrogant' and 'dogmatic' and he was rather likely to 'antagonize than win people'.[2]

Many who knew him seem to have perceived that, in Sylvia's vivid description of him at the Manchester Brasenose Club, he was always 'at the centre of animated argument, easily coping with a score of opponents, flinging about him bright sparkles of wit and eloquence'. When giving a speech he 'poured forth his ardent thoughts in impromptu periods, glowing with an enthusiasm which cast its enchanting spell upon all around him.' His strong principles were in Sylvia's view paramount. She relates how he resigned his membership of some 'old club' when it 'deserted plain living and high thinking' and the final straw occurred when it blackballed an applicant to membership because he was the son of a small-scale butcher.[3]

Her view of his oratorical powers is supported in many accounts by contemporaries, and his entry in *Manchester Faces and Places* is testimony to his prominence during his own lifetime. It concludes:

> As a speaker, Dr. Pankhurst is always thoughtful, thorough, and convincing, and possesses the power of being able to say exactly what he means. If on the platform he is bitter and unsparing in his denunciations of what is unjust or anomalous, it is because he feels strongly, for in private life he is at once the most agreeable and even-tempered of men.[4]

One membership that Sylvia missed, or at least omitted to mention, was her father's allegiance to a body that has a rather mixed reputation as a secret and sometimes rather sinister influence within the British establishment, the Masons. He was initiated as a 26-year-old solicitor into the Lodge of Affability, no. 399, on 6 December 1860.[5] Then in 1867 he was a founder member of the St George's Masonic Lodge no. 1170, which was for the City Derby District of Manchester.[6] He resigned his membership of the Lodge of Affability on 7 January 1869, presumably finding it costly in terms of money and time to keep up two memberships.

The Masons have traditionally been influential in commercial life and would have given an aspiring young lawyer like Richard some useful connections. On the other hand, the secrecy of their ceremonies and membership caused the society to be suspect in the eyes of many. Moreover, despite an avoidance of politics by the English Grand Lodge, the Masons were associated in the public mind with the French Revolution and with further upheavals across Europe in 1848, including the establishment of a French republic.[7] This rendered them alarming to many in Britain. But their radical reputation, along with their connections to 'liberty, equality, fraternity', may have made them attractive to an idealist like Richard, and could even have influenced his outlook on monarchy.

He would have found a comfortable home among them in several other ways. Much of the ideology of the organisation was modelled on the family, engendering loyalty and duty, mutual support in times of hardship, bonds of affection and patriarchal authority in the form of the lodge master. This may have had a particular appeal due to the circumstances of his early life and the privations and insecurity of his father's bankruptcy. Other aspects of the fraternity also chimed with his ideals. In line with the development in Richard's thinking, it was international and ensured 'that a Mason, destitute and worthy, may find in every clime a brother, and in every land a home'.[8] Then too, the fraternity was based on a basic equality between all members, esteeming 'every man the peer of his fellow in nature and rights ... All preferment among Masons is grounded upon real worth and personal merit only ...'[9] The main prerequisite for joining was to acknowledge the brotherhood of man and the fatherhood of God, or at least of a being described as 'the Great Architect of the Universe'.[10] This too would reflect Pankhurst's personal faith in the 1860s, and that the Masons were open to membership in principle from any faith would have also made them accessible to a non-conformist. In particular, the Lodge of Affability owned four copies of the Bible, most notably a Geneva Bible dated 1607 – presumably a text with which Richard would have been familiar.[11]

Their secretive rituals established and reinforced these principles. There was an emphasis on the 'inviolable adherence ... never improperly to reveal any of those Masonic secrets which have now been ... entrusted to your keeping'.[12] Brothers passed through three main stages, and it is interesting to note that to enter into the 'Apprentice Degree' a partially naked Richard would have been blindfolded and constricted by a rope around his neck to learn about the central 'landmarks' of the fraternity, when it would have been clear that he was entering a new set of relationships that demanded a lifelong commitment. It is not known how far he climbed in the hierarchy, but if, as seems likely in view of the longevity of his membership, he entered the next degree of Fellow Craft he would have learnt about the secret meanings of geometry and the Great Architect of the Universe. The third Degree was entered in the ritual of the Master Mason, which included a re-enactment of the murder of Hiram Abiff, the master builder of Solomon's Temple, who sacrificed his life to protect the secret knowledge of his craft brotherhood.[13] Richard remained a paid-up member of the St George's Lodge until his resignation in September 1876; he had been a mason for sixteen years.

Perhaps less controversially, Pankhurst relished his membership at the Brasenose Club, where from 1869 he shared the convivial facilities for forty-five minutes at lunchtimes with a membership dominated by well-known scions of the Arts. Sylvia asserts that he saw lunch there as 'a sacrament of fellowship and good will'.[14] He was one of 100 original members, and by the twenty-first anniversary dinner in 1890 he had clearly made a strong impression. Alderman Bailey, making a toast, referred to the 'superb oratory', of

> that splendid good fellow Dr Pankhurst – a lover of wit, a sparkling good fellow, a learned and distinguished lawyer, and above all we love him for the very robust, liberal and free way in which he will guide public opinion. (Cheers) The doctor is afraid of neither man nor beast –

(Laughter) – and can look sin in the face with utter fearlessness. He does not care at all whether the pill is popular. Although we cannot agree with his opinion – (Laughter) – we can believe in the heroic times of the past, and when we see such eloquence and such courage connected with such genius, we are bound to admire the pluck whatever we think of the argument – (Laughter).[15]

The company was treated to a sample of Richard's oratory when, called on to speak, he praised the club's ethos as 'a call … to plain living and high thinking …a retreat and resource in the stir and din and struggle of this busy commercial community … Here we ask one question. Not what is a man worth, but what is the worth of the man?' However, it must be admitted that the living was not so plain that evening: the menu included three soups, turbot with lobster sauce and other fish, veal, beef, mutton, pheasant, with several vegetables, followed by mince pies, duchess pudding and other sweets, then dessert! Reflecting the thoughts of the alderman, Richard referred to a certain freedom of speech in the club: 'We come here and dare speak and say the things we think and feel.' The result was, he claimed, that he had there formed his 'strongest and warmest friendships'.

In the Brasenose Richard would have basked in the warmth of the dialect poet Edwin Waugh's approval; according to Sylvia, the latter observed his brilliant repartee and commented: 'The doctor's gradely agate this evening: he is, by gum!' There was also advantage to be had in the outside world. Alderman Bailey mentioned in 1890 that 'any man in Manchester who can say he is a member of the Brasenose will … be estimated as a man worthy of some note and observation'. Richard's legal training added to his worth to other members of the club; when the Manchester Literary and Dramatic Reading Society resolved to perform Shakespeare's *Merchant of Venice* in the Athenaeum on the anniversary of the bard's birthday, it was Richard who applied for a licence.[16]

The Fledgling Lawyer

Having completed his professional education with flying colours, Richard was apparently ready to embark on a successful legal career. According to Sylvia, he was even at this early stage prepared to ignore convention, as his pointed, French-style beard contravened the meticulously observed custom of the legal clean shave, and occasionally there were 'other small departures from the then conventional dress of the profession'.[17] He also early adopted an unconventional role model in a radical lawyer of the previous generation, Ernest Jones, and both the style and content of his campaigning echoed Jones's.

Pankhurst's espousal of democratic ideals and later on socialism were influenced by Jones, who had been a leading Chartist agitator for universal male suffrage and who had met Friedrich Engels and Karl Marx in England. Their impact on Jones's thinking was clear in May 1851 when he wrote in his new journal, *Notes to the People,* a seminal article which posited that society had to pass through a series of stages, from kingship to feudalism to plutocracy, then to democracy.[18] A believer in co-operation, Jones advocated many ideals associated with socialism, notably the nationalisation of the land and the right to work. He congratulated the French in 1848 on their revolution – an event regarded with horror by the English establishment as an attack on monarchical rule.

Like Richard Pankhurst, he was a rousing and vivid speaker. When in the 1850s the Chartist movement was in disarray he began the work of rebuilding it, editing newspapers, such as *The People's Paper* and *Notes to the People,* stressing the principle of 'the Charter and something more', which by the later 1850s implied land reform. His commitment and doggedness went so far that he ended up in prison for two years; this was avoided by Pankhurst but probably only because by his time the establishment hoped to neutralise such ideas by allowing more latitude to those who preached them.

In Jones's professional life too there were similarities with Pankhurst in that both men did not reach their earning potential. Finding himself short of money, from 1859 Jones began to work steadily at his legal practice, but as well as bread-and-butter cases he specialised in briefs from trade unions and poor people for which he would not have been paid the full fee. This was very much the pattern adopted by Richard later on. Moving to Manchester in 1861, Jones joined the Northern Circuit where later Richard Pankhurst was to forge a career. In the later 1860s, Jones famously defended with great aplomb one of the Irish Fenian terrorists after they had killed a Manchester policeman in the process of releasing their fellows from a prison van. It is remarkable that, having found the defendants guilty, Mr Justice Lush publicly thanked Jones for the able way he had conducted the defence.[19] After his death *The Times* recorded:

Some of those in court during the Old Bailey trials of the Fenian prisoners recognized in the rich tones of the stout, fair-haired, red-faced gentleman in wig and gown the voice which had so often roused excited public meetings into tumultuous enthusiasm; but few remembered the depth and breadth of the trials and vicissitudes the middle-aged prosperous barrister had undergone for what he believed to be his country's cause.[20]

Apart from the notable difference in their physical appearance and vocal performance, the description could equally be applied to Richard Pankhurst.

In the last ten years of his life, Jones espoused internationalism and campaigned in support of the north in the American Civil War. In Manchester he was working with the grain because the city had a tradition of hostility to the slavery defended by the southern states, voiced clearly by Pankhurst and many others. Having attempted and failed to enter parliament on four occasions between 1847 and 1868, initially as a Chartist candidate, and latterly as an 'advanced radical', Jones died in 1869 at the age of 50. The repeated failure to win a seat was a disappointment later shared by Pankhurst.[21]

In February 1877 Richard delivered a lecture on the life and achievements of Ernest Jones in which he associated him primarily with the onward march of democracy:

> They were there to commemorate a noble English democrat. It was the word democracy which it had been sought to cover with opprobrium, but which they hoped ere long would be one of the proudest words to the English heart. That noble and heroic leader of the progress of the people, Ernest Jones, suffered in his day and time the hardest and bitterest things in the name and for the sake of democracy.[22]

Going on to praise the Cromwell era of the seventeenth century as 'the militant period for the democracy of England', he argued that it would now be succeeded by 'the period of democracy triumphant'. For him, this summed up the underlying theme of Jones's career and achievement, and Pankhurst took that torch and ran with it.

Then as now, the law was considered an honourable profession and Richard's career was no doubt a source of pride to his doting parents. Yet his day-to-day experience of the courts was almost certainly not as impressive as might be imagined. The writings of Charles Dickens, though perhaps coloured by the need to make a good story, help modern readers to understand the conditions under which Victorian lawyers plied their craft. Two reports on the English Courts of Law from 1842 and 1845 confirm Dickens' descriptions of courtrooms:

> ... although honest attempts are now being made to erect courts of justice such as they ought to be, there is scarcely a court in the width and breadth of the land that is not a disgrace to the country ... simply from a servile love of precedent and disregard of utility ...

> Very few of our courts are built on any sound principles of acoustics.
> Some of the old courts are better adapted for hearing than the new ones.
> The worst we know in this respect are the new courts at St George's
> Hall, Liverpool.

As for the lawyers themselves:

> … these gentlemen, proud in their calling, are humble in their necessities,
> and wherever duty calls them, gently submit to be thrust with a dozen
> others into a back closet, termed 'the robing room,' and share with
> them, in preparation for the court, one towel, the one bit of glass, the
> one comb, and the three pints of water.

The court, disorganised and disorderly, showed no respect for clients, witnesses, members of the jury or of course the accused; there was a great deal of bullying.[23]

It was not as if the barristers had pleasant chambers to which to retire; the office of the lawyer Jaggers in *Great Expectations* is not unrepresentative:

> Mr. Jaggers' own high-backed chair was of deadly black horsehair, with
> rows of brass nails around it, like a coffin … The room was but small,
> and the clients seemed to have had a habit of backing up against the
> wall; the wall, especially opposite Mr. Jaggers' chair, being greasy with
> shoulders.

It is to be hoped that Richard's Manchester chambers at number 3 St James's Square, which he occupied from 1876 to 1884, moving thereafter for the rest of his career to number 10, afforded him a little more cheer and comfort than the gloomy and depressing environment in which Mr Jaggers held his interviews.

He began his career with minor cases such as that of Joseph Atkinson of the working class Ancoats area of Manchester. Atkinson was accused of gaining money under false pretences from the New United Friendly Burial Society when he claimed his deceased wife had paid in without intermission for over thirty years; the trustees argued she had missed payments for two years. Pankhurst appeared for the defendant, and successfully showed that the society was wrong and blamed its own mismanagement, arguing that under the rules there was no security for members actually getting their benefit. It was on cases like this that he was to build his reputation for probity and outspokenness.[24]

That he was not always on the side of the accused was shown later the same month, when he was the prosecuting counsel in a case of burglary. A Joseph Speakman was indicted and pleaded guilty at the Salford hundred sessions to stealing during the night from houses at West Houghton. Pankhurst outlined the case only, as there was a desire to deal with it in the minor court and not send it to the overworked assizes, and the sentence imposed was twelve months' imprisonment.[25]

The work was nothing if not eclectic, and not always successful; shortly before Christmas Pankhurst represented to the magistrates an application for a dramatic licence for a circus proprietor who he argued was a 'man of great experience and excellent character'. The licence was needed because it was proposed to add dialogue to an equestrian act about the highwayman, Dick Turpin. There was much concern about whether there was a danger of unruly behaviour and drunkenness. The case failed because the magistrate felt he could not decide the matter without a full bench of justices.[26]

One case that may have caused awkwardness between Richard and his father was that of Pankhurst v Brownhill, reported in May 1868. It concerned a complex intestacy, and whilst Henry Francis was the administrator of the estate, Richard was one of four lawyers for the defence. On the other hand, it could be argued that the Pankhursts were making as much as they could out of the affair by supporting both sides; in the event the case was decided in favour of the plaintiff, Henry Francis.[27]

Richard defended freedom of speech in a case heard in the Salford hundred quarter sessions in July 1868, when he and Mr Kydd appealed against the decision of the Rochdale magistrates to order the destruction of some books that had been judged 'obscene', dealing as they did with 'The depravity of the priesthood and the immorality of the confessional' and including 'several filthy passages'. On this occasion too, he did not succeed, due to the danger of the books' 'effect upon boys and others who read such publications'.[28]

A third failure may be cited in 1869 in a case at Salford, when he acted with Mr Leresche for the plaintiff, John Law, who claimed he had been assaulted during the general election at Ashton-under-Lyne by the two defendants. Although witnesses were called to support the allegations, the jury deliberated 'for a considerable time' and in the end expressed a doubt 'and wished to give the defendants the benefit of it'. It was often difficult to persuade a local jury to convict, and this could have been as much due to fear of reprisals, or sympathy for a neighbour, as to concerns about the reliability of the evidence.[29]

At the County Police Court in August 1869, Richard's doomed defence of a father who had illegally refused to have his baby vaccinated against smallpox might be seen by many today as the work of a crank. However, at that time the germ theory was a novel development, and his reasoning was logical, if wrong. He fully recognised that the matter was important, referring as it did to national health. But he questioned on behalf of his client the effectiveness and safety of the procedure; the latter believed improvements in sanitation were the cause of a decline in smallpox, and that inoculation would in fact introduce other diseases into the child, including tuberculosis and scrofula. The basis of Richard's argument was that the law had established, under penal consequences, one medical theory that was not proven. After a lengthy exposition of his client's viewpoint, one of the magistrates said that Richard should be in the House of Commons! Then they inflicted the full penalty on his client.[30] Interestingly, much later, when standing for parliament in 1883, he referred back to this case, and admitted that in fact he thought vaccination was a good idea, and indeed had had his own daughters, Christabel and Sylvia, vaccinated. He had taken his brief seriously and defended his client's right not to vaccinate his child. The fact that the presiding magistrate in the case, John Maclure, had ever since thought he was an anti-vaccinator, he took as 'a great compliment to him as a counsel'.[31]

In April 1870, his star began to rise in defending an institution in which he also believed. As a keen proponent of the co-operative movement, he was engaged to defend the Manchester and Salford Industrial Co-operative Society in an 'important' case where the society was accused of cheating a man who had lent them money. The judge decided for the plaintiff, nevertheless for the defence Richard resolved against the judge's wishes to take the case to a higher court.[32] Indeed, he was becoming familiar with those higher courts; in January he had appeared in the Court of Exchequer for a defendant, assisting Mr Manisty QC in a case about the performance of contracts in the cotton trade. In serving this kind of apprenticeship, he seemed clearly destined for greater things and at this stage may well have expected eventually to take silk and thereafter to enter the judiciary himself.

A great believer in the principle of arbitration at all levels, from the international down to local trade disputes, Pankhurst was engaged in June 1873 to present the case for the Manchester tailors who were agitating for a pay rise of a halfpenny per hour. He successfully achieved not only the increase in pay, but its backdating to the previous April, which amounted to a rise of 20 per cent.[33] In view of such success, Richard was appointed in 1875 to represent over 3,000 carpenters and joiners of Manchester and Salford, winning for them a reduction in hours to fifty-two per week in ten months of the year and an increase in wages by a halfpenny per hour.[34] In 1877, he further established his pro-worker credentials when he appeared in the city Police Court to defend them when they were accused of obstructing passengers at London Road Station to intimidate other joiners who had been brought in as strike-breakers.[35]

At this time too, he began to appear as lawyer for the Manchester Corporation. In the first instance, in November 1870, he joined Mr W.F. Robinson to defend that body in the Chancery Court of Lancashire in a relatively minor case over a corporation bond. This was the start of a very successful alliance between Pankhurst and the corporation which it was hoped would in the future prove extremely lucrative for the up-and-coming lawyer.[36]

Richard's interest in education extended to a willingness to pass on his legal expertise to a new generation of lawyers, and he often featured in the classified advertisements of the local press giving of his knowledge to the Law Students Society. On 17 November 1874, for instance, he spoke to them on 'Certain Difficulties in the Study of the Law' – a suitably vague title that gave him latitude to discuss topics of current interest. It turned out to be, as usual with his speeches, 'an elaborate and interesting address'.[37] At the self-congratulatory annual meeting in October 1877 he gave an 'exhaustive' review of 'Government and Legislation'.[38] Even after his marriage he did not neglect his training duties, for instance delivering a talk on 'The law and practice of bankruptcy' on 3 November 1880.[39] When he addressed the law students on 7 November 1882 he delivered an interpretation of novel legislation, bringing his audience up to date on conveyancing law, land law, and very close to his heart, the new Married Women's Property Act of 1882, which he himself had drafted. He described it as 'the greatest change in the law ever effected by a single measure'. He ended with a plea for a 'consolidation and digestion' of all English law.[40]

We gain a glimpse of the long and deep thinking that went into his practise of the law and his theoretical pronouncements and writings by studying his brief and fragmentary notes, preserved in his daughter Sylvia's archive in Amsterdam. He devotes three pages to Aryan or Teutonic laws on homicide, and a similar section on the laws relating to women under Teutonic and Roman Law systems. He covers a further two pages with notes on medieval fiefs, which may have later fed into his radical belief in the reform of the laws of land ownership.

His publications included several articles including 'Judicature Acts', in which Gladstone's 1873 reform of the higher law courts was analysed, and the referral of appeals to the House of Lords was criticised; 'Pax Hominis under the Reign of Law', where the establishment of an international tribunal was advocated; and 'Bankruptcy Reform' and 'International Law'. In addition, he worked to effect reforms in patent law and labour law.[41]

Chamber of Commerce

Early in his career Pankhurst began to appear in meetings of the prestigious Manchester Chamber of Commerce, becoming a member in 1862, sponsored by Malcolm Ross, a future president.[42] He may have been recruited so that the chamber could benefit from his knowledge of the bankruptcy laws, which had been reformed the previous year.[43] In the later 1850s the National Association for the Promotion of Social Science (NAPSS) had taken an interest in the matter and drafted a Bill to reform the system.[44] It seems probable that Richard, as a then young law student with a personal interest, followed these developments closely.

Richard's interest in commercial law made him a valued member of the Chamber. In 1866 he joined a committee looking into patent law amendment and contributed to the deliberations of the Patent Law Reform Association. He was personally thanked for his advice on bankruptcy in the Chamber on 28 April 1869.[45] It may have been as a member of the Chamber that he joined the Association of Trade Protection Societies, which specialised in debt collection, and was noted as its treasurer at its Westminster meeting in 1870, as well as a member of the executive committee of the Manchester Guardian Society for the Protection of Trade.[46]

He took it upon himself to suggest improvements to the legal system with regard to debtors. In June 1872 he presented a memorial to the Lord Chancellor that the sitting times of the County Court judges in Manchester should be extended because there were far too many cases of debt that were not heard, or 'plaintiffs were … obliged either to remain in court many hours at a great loss to themselves, or they must take the risk of judgement going against them by reason of their absence'. The Lord Chancellor was sympathetic, but offered little help, beyond suggesting that the summonses should be arranged in alphabetical order, or that they could be put in batches and a specific hour be fixed for each group. The pressure on an overworked court system is nothing new![47]

The reported discussions of the chamber illustrated Sylvia's later opinion that they

> heartily welcomed Dr Pankhurst's efforts to simplify the course of justice, to remove its delays and inadequacies, and reduce its costs, in commercial matters of interest to themselves; but many of them entertained quite opposite feelings when they saw him applying the same drastic logic towards Parliamentary and economic institutions, on behalf of the labouring people they employed.[48]

As Sylvia implies, his interest in the activities of the Chamber of Commerce was much wider than they might initially have anticipated. At first this was probably welcomed. In April 1866 they convened with representatives of the Manchester Council in the mayor's parlour of the Town Hall to discuss how Manchester businesses could be encouraged and enabled to participate in the forthcoming Paris exhibition, and how any space offered to the city should be apportioned. Although 600 had been invited, in fact Richard was one of a very select twenty-three who attended.[49]

As he grew in experience and confidence, it appears that Richard's contributions were less well-received in some quarters. He was prominent in the chamber's discussions on the slump in trade in February 1879, and keen that they should recognise and criticise the role of the Conservative government in creating this situation. He put it that their policies, notably their 'belligerent foreign policies' in India and China, had a direct bearing on the problems of both capital and labour. He urged the chamber to lobby for a parliamentary committee to look into the causes of the slump, believing that it would find the government had put obstacles in the way of prosperity. The members were divided over this and eventually put off voting on his resolution.[50]

Later that month, at a general meeting that was well attended, Richard had to counter views that enquiring into commerce and manufacture was not the business of parliament by citing examples from the past to show there were precedents, thus bringing his encyclopaedic knowledge of history into play. While acknowledging that 'capitalists were in a state ... of considerable distress', his main motivation for insisting on this resolution was that the working classes were descending into misery, with increased hours of work and diminishing remuneration. He had trade statistics at his fingertips, and listed the causes of the problem – high food imports, the operation of commercial treaties, Indian tariffs, and wars that reduced the purchasing power of Britain's trading partners and cost the country a lot of money. He suggested arms reduction talks with other countries, and better management of the land to increase food production – which would mean releasing it from its 'antiquated fetters' of ownership and law.

As may be perceived, this was a long, complex and wide-ranging discourse and the meeting began to get restless. The president objected that it was longer than necessary to support the resolution, a Mr Fogg found it patronising as they were already 'acquainted with these matters', but another member defended Richard: 'he was enjoying Dr. Pankhurst's speech very much ... It was the ablest speech delivered in that Chamber for a long time.' With the danger of not reaching a vote again, Richard was constrained to wrap up his remarks quickly by concluding that all these issues could be sorted out, and that this was therefore a matter of politics and the proper business of parliament. He could not resist a high-minded final salvo:

In opposition to the existing tendency towards imperialism, ... the future ... belonged to the people and to peace. Empire was now created and maintained by liberty and labour, and if we recognised the fact that neither commerce nor civilisation could now live except in so far as it was bound up with liberty, the people, and peace, we should give that direction to inquiry in this matter, which would not only emancipate us from the present distress, but put ourselves, and ... all the nations of the world upon a career of prosperous and continually increasing development.[51]

The meeting soon descended into disorder. There was protracted argument and insulting language about the government and its policies, referring to foreign policy in particular. The members finally reached the end of their tether and demanded a vote and no more talking – squashing attempts by Richard and others to add more to their points. In the end the more conservative elements prevailed and the resolution was lost 34 votes to 26.[52]

Even after this, Richard continued to be an active member, in 1880 for example participating on a committee to draw up rules for a proposed scheme of arbitration in business disputes.[53] His interest in commercial law was unabating; in 1882 he introduced a course of lectures on the topic in the Manchester Athenaeum with a discourse on the need for legal codification, amendment of the laws of partnership, limited liability and bills of sale, and the complete abolition of the Statute of Frauds Act.[54] Around the same time, supporting the interests of commerce, and significantly for the future, he put his name to a meeting to approve the building of a Manchester Ship Canal to enable the establishment of a port of Manchester.[55] It is a mark of the value he put on his membership of the Chamber of Commerce that right up to the year of his death he continued to pay his guinea subscription, despite the fact that he could by that stage ill afford it.[56]

CHAPTER 3

A Social Conscience

Richard Pankhurst did not limit himself to the rarified circles of the affluent establishment. There were other vital aspects to his endeavours that entailed close connection with the poor and those who were engaged in the work of enabling the lower classes and empowering them through political reform. In addition, his social conscience extended to frequent attempts to convince those with power and influence of the value of reforming and of improving international relations so that his optimistic vision for the whole of humanity could reach fulfilment.

A very worthy body with which he was early associated and where he began to hone his speaking skills was the Union Chapel Essay and Discussion Society, at which members of the Baptist chapel on Oxford Road in Manchester and their friends presented essays for debate. His involvement shows that at this stage he was a keen chapel-goer, and this is confirmed by a later claim in a court case that in 1866 he was so committed as to be baptised by the minister, the famous and revered Dr McLaren.[1] By 1858 Pankhurst was a committee member of the Essay and Discussion Society, and delivered in January 1859 a paper on trades unions. Other topics presented by his fellows, which he no doubt would have heard, included the Roman invasion of Britain, legendary lore, 'the Comprehensiveness of Creation', the factory system, liquor laws and the loaded question: 'Have political causes or the nature of the Irish people been most powerful in retarding the prosperity of Ireland?' The club's ethos was also social, offering three tea meetings a year and a summer picnic, where earnest young men could share their idealistic aspirations.[2]

Educator of the Poor

The inspirational Dr McLaren may well have had a profound influence on the young Pankhurst, as he did on many others in his large congregation. Urged on by his religious beliefs, Richard early on became engaged in the education of the poor. Sylvia relates that her father 'as a youth' taught not only the night classes at Owens College, but also the poor in Baptist Sunday schools. He shared a common belief that it was through education that the working classes could improve themselves and be elevated for the betterment of society. That there was a clear religious dimension to his involvement is illustrated by his talk on 'The Dignity of Sunday School Labour'; he was fulsome in his assessment of the significance of the teacher:

> He ... pointed out that the work of the teacher was first of all to endeavour to arouse in the plastic minds of the children religious emotions, then an obedient will, and thirdly religious habits. Dr. Pankhurst concluded with some eloquent remarks upon the joy and delight which was experienced by the Christian in seeking after the Divine Ideal.[3]

Richard was active in the Manchester Sunday School Union, as can be seen at the annual meeting on 29 February 1864 when he issued a warning that the schools must move with the times, though what exactly was required is not reported. He may have had in mind a proposal made at the Sunday School Conference in Wigan, when he backed a suggestion to improve discipline and rules and adopt a more systematic approach to teaching.[4]

Like many who had seen the need for education at first hand, he was an active member of the National Education League, formed in 1869 to campaign for free, compulsory and non-sectarian education for all children. It is not clear exactly when he joined the organisation but he was prominent at their meeting in Manchester Town Hall on 29 November 1871, when their national chairman, Joseph Chamberlain, later MP for Birmingham, addressed them.[5]

Pankhurst's support of training for the Arts was evident when he attended the Manchester School of Art prizegiving in the Royal Manchester Institution (now the Art Gallery) a week before Christmas 1872.[6] His daughter, Sylvia, also attests to his fascination with science in an age of remarkable scientific advances, and relates how his voracious reading 'in buses and trains and wherever he might be' extended his knowledge, and stirred his enthusiasm to

> open the minds of the people to the expanding treasury of knowledge, and to wed scientific training to the manual experience of the worker

and the craftsman, in order that men and women might no longer be as mere automata in the industrial process, but intelligent and interested participators.[7]

Accordingly, from 1863 to 1876 he was honorary secretary of the Lancashire and Cheshire Union of Mechanics Institutes, set up to enhance the technical education and effectiveness of factory operatives. It was apparently a successful initiative in terms of provision, though perhaps less so in that the institutes tended to attract the lower middle classes rather than workers.[8] Of a piece with this was Richard's appearance on 18 October 1867 in support of the Accrington Mechanics Institution. He joined an illustrious company headed by Lord Hartington and MP Colonel Wilson-Patten in delivering a speech at their prize-giving. His belief in the efficacy of the institutes was profound and far-ranging:

> Between the speculation of the philosopher and the work of the artisan there is a permanent connection. The thought of the philosopher passes down through successive stages until it arms the man at the loom, or the man at the bench, with that knowledge ... He who begins his education at the beginning in the first rudiments should be able ... to rise, stage by stage, higher and higher, until he reaches those seats of learning, the universities, whose highest end and purpose is not to train men for callings and professions, but to keep alive speculation and thought; and he who takes advantage of these may go up from the beginning to the sublime ...[9]

This was followed up at a similar occasion at the Manchester Mechanics Institution on 18 November.[10] His whole philosophy of education, though couched in Victorian modes of expression, had a remarkably modern ring to it. He argued that teachers should understand the way the minds of their pupils developed, tendering knowledge 'as a sort of mental food ... either for information, or as gymnastics – to strengthen the faculties and power of the mind ... so that they may enter into the pursuit of truth'. To sum up, 'the man who is capable of sustaining protracted thought is, in the intellectual world, the monarch of men ... he who has learned how to learn can soon learn anything'.[11]

The union was not just a 'talking shop'. They lobbied the government to effect changes in aspects of the system which were under their control, notably in 1869 when Richard and others spoke to the Lord President of the Committee of Council on Education requesting that the government give the same help to discrete night schools as it gave to day and night schools.[12] In August 1872 their requests for more 'rudimentary' level science and art examinations, and for the extension of capitation grants for science schools, were turned down. Some of their initiatives were more successful, such as a widening of the group to whom payment on results was granted, by the raising of the qualifying income limit from £100 up to £200 a year. The *Manchester Guardian* believed that this latter concession would 'prove of very great service to an important section of the middle class, and … give to science teachers throughout the kingdom an additional and much-needed stimulus'.[13]

The institutes were at best half-hearted in encouraging provision for women. Sylvia relates how a Fanny Hertz in 1859 pleaded at the National Association for the Promotion of Social Science (NAPSS) for this cause, and claims that Richard and others invested effort in trying to attract female students, but progress was at a snail's pace. In 1878 he successfully championed the inclusion in the list of a woman, Miss Willis, who wished to stand for the post of Director of the Union; disappointingly she received fewer of the votes than any of the men.[14]

Looking beyond the Institutes, Richard was always keen to support the provision of higher education for the working classes. In the same month in the Mechanics Institution he chaired a committee set up to hold an industrial exhibition and sale to raise money for his *alma mater*, Owens College, 'thereby extending its usefulness among the working classes'. One obstacle seems to have been that these beneficiaries do not appear to have been suitably enthused, as discussion focused on 'the difficulty which appeared to exist in reaching the working classes'.[15] Perhaps in an attempt to mitigate this apathy, by 1877 the Manchester Mechanics Institution boasted a 'Pankhurst Exhibition' worth £10 per annum and tenable for three years to fund evening classes at Owens College.[16] Pankhurst was present at the first convocation on 4 June 1880 of the new Victoria University, which incorporated Owens College, and at these gatherings was vocal in proposing resolutions, including one of congratulation on behalf of the Associates of Owens.[17] He characteristically expressed a hope that the university would be 'a school of free enquiry' producing people who possessed 'the old fire of devotion to city, to country and to mankind'.

In the wake of the establishment of school boards under the 1870 Education Act, which Richard dubbed 'the Magna Charta [sic] of Elementary Education', he put himself forward as an 'independent' candidate for the second Manchester Board, elected in 1873. In this same year he had moved into the limelight by establishing a Republican Society in the city, and probably as a result of this his candidature for the school board was not sponsored by the Liberals and he was forced to stand as an independent.[18] Not closely aligned with either the 'church' party or the 'unsectarians', he nevertheless opposed religion in schools. Indeed, the *Manchester Guardian* reported that his friends 'recommended [him] as the only thorough-going secular candidate'. The Manchester School board, like all such bodies, relied quite heavily on church schools, owing to the requirement that the board only provide schools where the existing provision was insufficient. Richard attacked the church schools because they seemed to put religious instruction before quality of education. He made it his business to collect statistics to prove that the vast bulk of the cost for such schools was borne by the government and the boards, and so argued that religion was being propped up by them. His public statement, characteristically long-winded, was a blistering attack on the vested interest of religion. In it he argued that education should not only be compulsory and free of religion, but that the whole church school system should be repealed as part of an imminent disestablishment of the Church of England.[19]

At a riotous meeting in support of his candidature he reasoned that the pre-existing religious system of education was 'a political engine and sectarian instrument, and the welfare of the child was wholly sacrificed to these two things'. And therefore he contended that there should be a purely secular, publicly administered system of education. This appears to have been the first time that his extreme views occasioned serious attacks; religion was a highly sensitive area, and he was accused of the dread moral crime of atheism.[20]

The Conservative *Manchester Courier* was dismissive: 'There were two independent candidates, Mr. Charles Darrah ... and Dr. Pankhurst, whose special qualification was not quite clear, except that probably he claimed to be the representative of the Republicans and Secularists.'[21] Sylvia, perhaps with a degree of hyperbole, records that he was 'vilified as an Atheist and a Communist'. The condemnations were effective and he was not elected, gaining only 10,585 votes, as the twentieth of twenty-one candidates.[22]

The National Association for the Promotion of Social Science, and Other Talking Shops

Richard Pankhurst was a life member, and for several years a dedicated participant in the activities, of the NAPSS. His contributions to debate reflected his involvement in the Chamber of Commerce, but also his wider interests in the knotty legal issues of the day.[23] The NAPSS, founded in August 1857 by legal and social reformers and women's rights campaigners, focused on remedying defects in legislation. Originated by women as well as men, it was unusual in welcoming women to attend and even to speak at its conferences. The women, most notably Elizabeth Wolstenholme and Barbara Leigh Smith Bodichon, called for the organisation to sponsor a change in the law pertaining to the property of married women. The issue had been taken up by the Law Amendment Society (LAS), of which Richard was a member; it was a ginger group of lawyers eager to bring the ancient and cumbersome practices of the law into the nineteenth century. It qualified for their attention as an area requiring rationalisation and modernisation; the society had proposed a Bill in May 1857 that was only dropped because a concurrent divorce Bill partly superseded it and was passed.

The NAPSS was modelled on the established and dominant institution of British intellectual life, the British Association for the Advancement of Science. Accordingly its conferences were divided into sections reflecting key issues: in this case, law amendment, education, crime, public health and social economy. Prestigious names in public life supported the new body, such as William Farr, Florence Nightingale, Lord John Russell, Lord Stanley the future Earl of Derby and Lord Brougham. The week-long conference was usually held in a major conurbation in the autumn, beginning with an ecumenical service and the president's address. The evening entertainment included dinners, conversaziones and soirées. The food was good, described to Stanley Jevons by his uncle as a 'Feast'. There were organised visits to country seats, natural wonders, mills and other local sites of interest.

The aim was to provide a sort of alternative parliament that would point the legislature proper in new directions, providing expert guidance and specialised knowledge for social reform. It also acted as a lobbying organisation, and even drafted legislation. It was therefore not so surprising that its leading proponents were Liberals, who were traditionally the party of moderate reform, and that its governing council of 250 was over 75 per cent Liberal. Most of its members were middle class, and the association responded to their interests. It also boasted a large number of MPs.

Besides these it hosted members of the 'labour aristocracy', the skilled and unionised workmen, who enjoyed debates on trade unions and benefited from the arbitration and conciliation procedures the association pioneered. Each conference from the 1858 meeting in Liverpool onwards held a working men's meeting, attracting thousands of artisans. At Manchester in 1866, for instance, the Earl of Shaftesbury chaired a gathering of 7,000 working men.

The association was a victim of its own success. It sponsored changes to commercial law, public health, penal reform and women's property rights. Gladstone's first ministry (1868–74) enacted many of the reforms it had called for, to a greater or lesser extent; politics was adapting to the demands of a new age. It faded quickly in the 1880s and was wound up in 1886. But it had established social policy as an integral part of government.

Richard Pankhurst played his part in this achievement. He was a dedicated member of the NAPSS, to the extent of paying his annual guinea, joining its council, and acting as secretary in the economy and trade section, as well as taking his place on standing or executive committees for international or municipal law, and attending most conferences. He was a frequent speaker either on the platform or in discussion. His pronouncements in the NAPSS also reflected an enjoyment of the cut and thrust of academic debate which challenged his strong intellect. His attendance, like that of many others, faded after the mid-1870s. This may have been due to his increasing radicalism but was probably even more a result of the fact that the association was becoming obsolescent in the new political climate.[24]

The views that Richard expressed over the years in NAPSS conferences apparently remained his consistent beliefs throughout the rest of his life. They also demonstrate his high-minded idealism and a typically Victorian Liberal belief in progress.[25] He was mostly concerned in this forum with matters relating to the Law, though he made occasional forays into education. Perhaps surprisingly in view of his other campaigns, he did not stray into women's rights or the plight of workers and the poor. This may have been expedient; during the years when the NAPSS was active, he was busy establishing his credentials and career as a prominent lawyer.

In these public utterances Pankhurst demonstrated that he was strongly influenced by the contemporary ideal of a shared public morality, which was based on individual strength of character, altruism and duty. One of the most prominent exponents of this philosophy was John Stuart Mill, whom Sylvia notes was a great hero of her father.[26] The high-minded oratorical content and style of the two men was not dissimilar. Both believed that the peculiar strength of character and moral vigour of the English fitted the country for representative government, and this boded especially well for the future. They claimed a superior reputation for England as 'incomparably the most conscientious of all nations', which meant that she also was bound to lead the way in standards of international morality. Mill's idea that history provided evidence of a general progress towards equality, and that relics of the past that were incompatible with that progress must disappear, is found frequently in the pronouncements of Richard Pankhurst on all manner of issues.[27] Both were sons of non-conformist fathers, and they both gravitated towards religious agnosticism. They hoped to refine society's moral sensibilities and encourage their influence in public issues. It has even been argued that the second edition of Mill's *Principles of Political Economy* became a basic text for British socialism, of which Pankhurst was later in life a committed disciple.[28] Mill saw himself as a lone crusader fighting a righteous cause, and that is certainly how Sylvia portrays her heroic father. And Richard's speeches reflected Mill's written tone, as described by Stefan Collini; Mill conducted the reader 'through the logical deficiencies of arguments like a severe, slightly sarcastic, and not altogether patient tutor dissecting a pupil's essay'.[29]

Pankhurst's speaking career in the NAPSS began in 1862 in London with a disquisition on the temperance lobby's Permissive Bill, aimed at allowing each locality to decide for itself on whether public houses would be allowed in their area. His opinions were in the classic liberal mould, attacking the Bill on the grounds of the liberty of the individual. The following year in Edinburgh, he joined a discussion on land law, expressed the view that capital punishment was ineffective as a deterrent, and read a paper on the Union of Lancashire and Cheshire Institutes, explaining its basic principles, organisation, and aim to achieve improved teaching and standards of attainment. His final and overarching remarks betrayed his unquenchable optimism and belief in progress; the institutes were helping 'to diffuse through the whole system a higher order of life and purpose'.[30]

At Manchester in 1866, his paper demonstrated his commitment to the modernising aims of the LAS. He explained at length and in detail why a codification of English law on scientific principles was expedient and practicable. Readers of the novels of Dickens, such as *Bleak House* and its case of Jarndyce and Jarndyce, will appreciate why such a reform was called for. The aim was to create a legal system that would be precise, clear and consistent, thus benefiting both the law profession and the public. It was arguments like Richard's that led the Gladstone government to pass the 1873 Judicature Act, rationalising the system of higher courts. In 1876 at Liverpool, Richard discussed the effects of this and subsequent Acts on commercial cases and again advocated the codification of the law to create 'an organic whole'.

In 1867 at Belfast, now a qualified barrister, Richard really got into his stride and was extremely active both in delivering papers and entering into discussion about several aspects of law. His speech about the need for justice to be local was typical of his erudite approach in that he delved into the historical origins of the system and explored the judicial systems in other European countries by comparison with those in England. The theme of local justice was similarly examined by him at Newcastle in 1870. He focused especially on the role of stipendiary magistrates within the system of local justice and supported the establishment of a court of appeal. In 1882 at Nottingham he cited the Chancery Court of the County Palatine of Lancaster, where he appeared as a barrister, as an exemplar of good practice. He appealed for a system, based on the County Courts, with important cases being removed to a judge of the High Court on circuit in the local district.

Another significant interest both in 1867 and again in 1870 was international arbitration, which he defended against suggestions (which still find echoes today) that such a system presupposed the surrender of national political independence. In a presaging of bodies such as the League of Nations, the United Nations and the International Court of Justice, he argued in favour of a stronger, codified system of moral Christianity-based international law, which would be administered by a tribunal. It would be employed as a mechanism to defuse international conflicts in the optimistic hope that they would 'disappear, like a cloud before the sun'. He believed, perhaps naively, that no compulsion would be needed to enforce settlements, because it was in all nations' interests to comply.[31] Other international questions arose in 1868 at Manchester. His main paper was on the laws governing nationality and his dense arguments about their origins and functioning were enough to deter all but the most dedicated of legal scholars from remaining awake, let alone alert. No one could doubt Richard's profound scholarship. He ended his speech with high-flown rhetoric, which gives us some inkling of the aspirational inner man:

> As we have the motion of our Earth upon its axis to represent national interests, so we have its motion round the sun to typify the larger range of international interests; while in the magnificent sweep forward of earth and sun, and all the system towards some central point in the entire cosmos, we have presented to us the sublime conception of the unity of the race, in the character of a mighty organism of which the different members co-operate in a common course of constant and harmonious progress and development.[32]

Other aspects of commercial law continued to be a main focus of his contributions, and were linked strongly to his position in the Manchester Chamber of Commerce. In 1866 he engaged in the preparation of a report on the patent laws, with a view to their amendment.[33] In 1868 in Manchester and 1876 in Liverpool he discussed the Law of Bankruptcy and advocated the adoption of the principles of the Scottish bankruptcy system, which he opined was much clearer than the English.

It is interesting to note that there were several years when he was far less in evidence, although still a member of the council of the NAPSS; from 1862 to 1870 he was active in attendance, and often held an administrative position as well; between 1871 and 1875 he delivered no papers; in 1876 he reverted to his earlier prominence, though he thereafter appeared only once, in 1882. The reasons for these hiatuses are unclear. As he remained on the council throughout, it seems likely that he may have been in attendance but did not speak, or at least not sufficiently to merit a mention in the record. It may well be that some years he was too busy with his legal practice and his social and political campaigns, and in later years with a growing family, to produce a major speech. And perhaps in any case he felt that he had already made his key points in earlier conferences.

However, he did join two other organisations that bolstered and furthered his beliefs concerning social issues and international relations. The Manchester Statistical Society, founded in 1833, the same time as the Royal Statistical Society in London, aimed from the start to influence government policy. In its early years, it was more about ideas than about figures, as the science of statistics as applied to society and the economy was in its infancy. Members read papers to each other based on their particular fields of specialism. He became a member of both the London and the Manchester societies.[34] In 1865 Richard put before the Manchester society his ideas on local courts and tribunals of commerce; he followed this up in 1868 with a paper on rights over private property at sea during wartime. Clearly his law training and his role in the Chamber of Commerce underpinned his approach. In the former, he was forwarding his view that justice should be local, and indeed prefaced his talk with the words, 'To bring justice home to men's doors … constitutes one great end of the English constitution'. And the aim, after long, convoluted, historical (back to the Romans) and detailed exposition, was that 'the earliest and best distinction of the Englishman will be his last and highest – that he is a member of one free nation, with one equal law impartially, uniformly, and locally administered'.[35] In the speech on private property at sea he discussed the concept of a blockade, and advocated tighter rules for its use, to the end that wars would be less damaging.

The development of his interests can be traced in his later speeches; in 1883 he addressed the Statistical Society on the land and the nation, basically advocating a return to an idealised pre-feudal era by returning ownership of the land to local communities. In the case of urban areas, the great cities should own their own land. The interests to be considered were the state, the farmer and the community. This did not leave much room for the current major possessors of the land – the monarchy, the aristocracy and the Church of England – and as such it was a very radical departure.[36]

Four years later his topic was international arbitration. Richard had long been a leading light in the Lancashire and Cheshire International Arbitration Society. In March 1873, for example, he chaired a soirée for the Reverend J.B. Miles of Boston, the secretary of the American Peace Society, and other gentlemen who were interested in the topic. The Alabama Arbitration of 1871 was cited as the basis of permanent peace between the USA and Britain.[37] This had been carried out after the American Civil War to settle a dispute between Britain and the United States. During the war the Southern Confederacy had purchased a British-built ship, the *Alabama*, which was used in attacks on Union shipping. The settlement, agreed internationally but on the watch of a Liberal government, favoured the United States. Although it was very unpopular among Conservatives, more radical souls like Richard Pankhurst were inspired to see in this approach an alternative to warfare of all kinds. His 1887 speech begins with remarkable optimism:

> In the evolution of civilisation Mankind has come into a situation on the great scale of collective existence where further progress demands one supreme object – the establishment of perpetual peace between nation and nation.[38]

After the usual exhaustive tour through the legal history, there is a remarkable collection of appendices with lists of statistics to back up the arguments for international arbitration. And the experience of the Alabama Arbitration was the basis for current hope because 'the two peoples who have historic primacy in the cause of peace have now the opportunity of laying on sure foundation the edifice of permanent, perpetual peace for all divisions of the great family of man'.

Pankhurst's enthusiasm occasioned his adherence to an international body founded in the 1870s; the international Association for the Reform and Codification of the Law of Nations. Its ideals presaged bodies established in the twentieth century, in particular the League of Nations and the United Nations. In the wake of the Alabama Arbitration, in response to a call originating in the United States, it aimed to establish an international congress as 'a permanent guarantee against the peril and even the possibility of war' by substituting 'the arbitrament of reason and justice for the arbitrament of the sword'. Accordingly the first meeting of delegates from the USA and Europe was held in Brussels in October 1873. Richard Pankhurst became a committed member of this organisation, now known as the International Law Association. He was to propagate its tenets enthusiastically and consistently in the NAPSS and the Manchester Statistical Society.[39] One example of his participation was his speech on international arbitration at the annual conference in Liverpool in August 1882. The society agreed to establish a body to investigate the concept, and Richard spread the word further in December with a talk in Manchester in the Friends Institute.[40]

The Liberal

Sylvia makes much of her father's role in the Manchester Liberal Association, noting that he drafted its constitution and was a founder member in 1867. He also served on its council. Even before this he had joined with other Liberal Mancunians to support the North in the American Civil War, despite the damage it caused in the Lancashire cotton industry and the resulting dreadful privation of its workers. Manchester was strongly anti-slavery and hostile to the position of the southern, cotton-producing states.[41]

Yet Sylvia declares that he was 'never a Party man', in that his principles were 'always paramount', irrespective of party policies. She cites his sterling support of the emancipation of slaves, and his denunciation of a Liberal Admiralty circular in 1871 which declared that slave owners could claim their slaves if found on British warships, and a similar directive issued by the Tories in 1876.[42] And it is true that he did not restrict his campaigning to policies pursued by mainstream Liberalism; he was committed to a wide variety of causes.

The following year he joined a very select group at a meeting that unanimously agreed to commemorate the 'advanced radical' lawyer, the late Ernest Jones, a man who would not have met with universal approval among Manchester's Liberals. They resolved to publish the deceased activist's works in a popular edition, and planned a conference near Jones's birthday that would 'make a general review of democratic movements and their progress'.[43] Similarly, in October 1877 Pankhurst attended as part of a Liberal delegation the unveiling of a memorial in Middleton to Peterloo veteran Samuel Bamford.[44]

Nevertheless, behind the scenes he was supportive to the association, attending meetings such as that at Tabley Park near Knutsford, Cheshire, on 26 August 1871 when between 4,000 and 5,000 Manchester Liberals were taken by special trains to hear speeches calling for reform of the House of Lords, who had proved obstructive to measures introduced by the Gladstone government. They singled out in particular the Lords' rejection of the Ballot Bill, which later succeeded in bringing in the secret ballot.[45] Further, on 6 October 1873 in the New Cross Ward of Manchester, Richard was a supporting speaker to Manchester Liberal MP Sir Thomas Bazley, and the meeting passed a resolution approving of the reforming Gladstone government.[46]

According to Sylvia, he strongly supported the reforms of Gladstone's first ministry between 1868 and 1874, including the groundbreaking Education Act, disestablishment of the Irish church and Irish land reform Acts, the abolition of the university tests that had hitherto excluded non-conformists (including, of course, Richard himself), the [secret] Ballot Act and the partial opening up of the civil service and army commissions.[47] For the present, he overlooked the great Gladstone's opposition to women's suffrage, and continued to entertain high hopes for the progress of democracy.

In the fight to gain re-election for Manchester's Liberal candidate, Jacob Bright, who had lost his Commons seat in 1874, Pankhurst attended his appearances to lend his support and joined his extensive Executive Committee.[48] Moreover, like many mainstream Liberals, from as early as 1866 he was a vice-president of the National Reform Union (NRU), which advocated electoral reform, notably the extension of the county franchise to rural labourers and seat redistribution to achieve equal constituencies, and participated in meetings such as that held in Manchester's Free Trade Hall on 15 December 1875.[49]

Then in summer 1877 the Manchester Liberals took an excursion to Hawarden Castle, the seat of their *de facto* leader William Gladstone (though he had at this time stepped down from the official position). Three trainloads of Liberals, numbering about 2,000, rambled around the grounds and danced to bands on the lawns. They had a look at the wooded slopes where Gladstone famously enjoyed chopping down trees with a simple axe, and visited the local church where the Reverend Stephen Gladstone was rector. Gladstone's family eventually appeared on the terrace of the house and Mrs Gladstone chatted with the visitors. Then, after the warm-up act, the great man himself emerged:

> Promptly at four o'clock Mr. Gladstone appeared, walking from his house to the front of the terrace, and his appearance was the signal for enthusiastic cheering ... Mr Gladstone ... came forward, accompanied by several members of his family.[50]

And among the group he greeted was Dr Pankhurst. The 'Grand Old Man' pronounced a speech to rally the party faithful and encourage them to adopt a watching brief on Disraeli's Conservative government, obliquely referring to events in the Balkans.

The Eastern Question has been well described elsewhere; the Manchester Liberals were particularly exercised by a desire to stop Disraeli from shoring up the corrupt and tottering regime of the Ottoman Empire, which had been severely oppressing Christian subjects in the Balkans, to the extent of massacres in Bulgaria. They were equally concerned that the government's policy would bring Britain into collision with Russia, who was keen to take advantage of Ottoman weakness and gain land access to the Black Sea and a warm water port. A war was the last thing the men of commerce, not to mention supporters of the principle of peace like Richard Pankhurst, wanted. But in other quarters war fever was being whipped up among the populace, resulting in music hall songs in support of a fight with the Russians. Richard was lampooned in the press as 'Pankurski' and he and his supporters were the 'Anglo-Russians'.[51]

On 3 January 1878 the Liberal Association met at their club on King Street to discuss the situation. Richard supported a resolution, passed unanimously, to maintain strict neutrality in the situation in the Balkans. He spoke about the dangers facing the country, in particular those presented by a use of secret diplomacy, which meant that the government could act without popular sanction, and by the ability of the government to declare war without recourse to parliament.[52] He desired that this power should be brought under the control of the legislature. To him, Lord Beaconsfield (Disraeli) had a general policy of raising the executive above the control of the people and parliament, which was 'the most dangerous thing that had been done in England since the Great Revolution [of 1688]'. The Crown was being made 'an instrument of party'. He ended on a resounding note:

> Cobden said that Governments were belligerents, but the people were peaceful; let them take their stand on that great political and humane maxim, and ... let them have the question of peace or war no longer in the hands of the Executive Government – let it no longer be used for dynastic ends and purposes of privilege – but place it in the hands of the Legislature, which, being produced by the people, would represent the people's interests and wishes, and so ensure the fulfilment of the national desires.[53]

By the end of the same month, the government was asking parliament for war finance to the tune of a vast £6 million, and had already dispatched the British fleet to the Dardanelles in order to support the Turks, by then under Russian attack. The Liberal club of Manchester's largest and poorest ward, St Michael's, addressed the situation at their annual meeting. The first resolution was proposed successfully by Richard Pankhurst. It supported the anti-war Foreign Secretary Lord Carnarvon, opposed the voting of money for a war, and again contended that all decisions to go to war should be made by parliament and not the executive alone. He stressed the significance of events, and in the idiom of the era that today might be regarded as racist, and certainly as stereotyping, he compared Disraeli's government to an eastern tyranny. 'At the head of affairs we [have] a Cabinet, English in name, but Asiatic in fact – Asiatic in mystery, Asiatic in profligacy of extravagance, and, above all, Asiatic in principles to govern it.'

Referring to the accession of the Queen to the title of Empress of India in 1876, he opined that the Tories 'had taken the rose of England from off the forehead of royalty, and had set in its place the blister of Imperialism ... [which was] a great historic infamy, baptised in the blood of liberty at home and abroad'. He had heard that the Queen had telegraphed the Russian emperor, and thus been dragged into Conservative policy. And he also referred to the hounding out of the Cabinet of the Colonial Secretary, Lord Carnarvon, due to his opposition to war. The government was not trusted at home or in Europe and had propagated the current war between Russia and Turkey by bellicose speeches in support of the latter.[54]

Richard repeated his attack on Disraeli's government the following day at the Manchester Liberal Association. Adding the charge that the government had deceived parliament when they claimed they were only defending British interests, he ended with a rousing call to arms (ironically) for the 'men of Manchester':

Therefore, in the presence of a foe who was both sinister and open, dangerous in policy, procedure, and intention, they ought to look upon that meeting as a kind of council of war, where they gravely settled the preliminary plans, and they would ere long go forth into the open, and the matter would be settled according to the law and the grand old Constitution of England. – (Loud applause.)[55]

The threat of war seems to have occasioned an unusual departure for Richard Pankhurst, in that for the first recorded time he addressed an outdoor meeting of the working classes on the topic in February 1878. Led by their redoubtable radical ex-mayor, Abel Heywood, the Manchester Liberals held a mass meeting in Stevenson Square, the usual place of agitation for the lower classes. With Heywood and other speakers, Pankhurst addressed the 'immense' crowd, one of the largest ever in the square, from the back of three 'lurries' organised as an improvised platform. There was a considerable danger that the meeting might be attacked by roughs sent by the Conservatives, who were holding a pro-war meeting at the same time in Pomona Gardens. However, when the roughs arrived they were so intimidated by the size of the meeting that they made no attempt to disturb it.

While Richard may not have spoken much to the lower classes in the open air, he was certainly known to them as 'there were loud calls' for him. He denounced the government and its evil intentions, suggesting they were dishonourable and untruthful, and opposed to the liberty of the people. They were, he claimed in the now-offensive language of his time, 'worse than a band of Red Indians' as even they, in their council, 'buried the bloody hatchet of war and smoked the pipe of peace'. Once the government were replaced, despotism and tyranny could be driven back in Europe by 'peace, honour, justice and truthfulness'. This would be commensurate with the wishes of 'the masculine and noble humanity and good sense of the English working man … true lovers of justice and desirous of peace'. He was rewarded with cheering throughout, and the meeting ended with unanimity and 'prolonged cheering' for Mr Gladstone, leading opponent of the government, and Mr Bright, the Liberal MP for the city.[56]

Richard's path was not always smooth. A week later, having been invited to chair a lecture by Archibald Forbes, war correspondent of the *Daily News*, who was to speak about his experiences in the Russo-Turkish War, Pankhurst was obliged to stand down at the last minute. The matter was explained in a letter of apology from the adventurous Forbes, published the next day in the *Manchester Guardian*. Not having been aware of the partisan stance of Pankhurst, or indeed of who he was, he only learnt about him an hour before the lecture was due to start. Being unwilling to allow any political colour to enter into his meeting, the speaker had to explain to Richard in the retiring room just beforehand that he would not accept him as chairman. Richard was clearly, and understandably, annoyed at this departure; this kind of thing did not happen to him often.[57]

At the National Reform Union he successfully put forward a resolution to condemn the government, prescribe a neutral stance for Britain, and further to advocate an international congress 'to settle the Eastern Question'. And there Britain should adopt a policy aimed at securing 'the freedom and autonomy of the oppressed nationalities in South-eastern Europe'.[58] In other words, in line with Gladstone's own pronouncements, he advocated the right of self-determination for the Balkan peoples of the Turkish Empire.

At this point, Gladstone was still officially in retirement. However, a movement was afoot amongst the peace party in the Liberal camp to persuade him to return to his role as leader. His pamphlet on *The Bulgarian Horrors and the Question of the East*, which detailed atrocities carried out by Turkish troops on their Christian Balkan subjects, had marked Gladstone out as the advocate of justice and self-determination for the subject peoples. Richard campaigned hard within the party to restore him to the leadership, and on 30 April 1878 at a meeting of 1,500 north of England delegates in Manchester's Free Trade Hall a resolution calling on the Grand Old Man to return was passed in a 'storm of enthusiasm'. Among the speakers

> Dr. Pankhurst ... was warmly greeted. The audience expected strong meat, and it was not disappointed, for Dr. Pankhurst served up strong meat, well peppered, hot enough for the most exacting palate. His appearance is as youthful as his voice is searching, and his words incisive. He declared that they were met in the midst of a grave and terrible crisis to oppose a guilty government bent upon war. There was a stir in the assembly, and men pressed close together as the winged words of the intrepid speaker were sent hissing through the hall ...[59]

He insisted that only William Gladstone could preserve European peace, and proposed that an address be sent to him with a delegation of over 100 Liberal representatives from the north; he himself was to represent Manchester.[60]

By this time the government was calling up forces from the Empire, and in July they signed an Anglo-Turkish treaty, by which they would support the Turkish Empire in its Asian possessions, Egypt and the Suez Canal being of particular concern. All of this was carried out under the royal prerogative and without the sanction of parliament; further opposition was voiced by a vote in the National Reform Union.[61] Pankhurst made a major speech to the General Council of the Manchester Liberal Federation on 23 July 1878 in which can be seen his deepest fears for the outcome of Disraeli's imperial ambitions, dishonesty and chicanery in his dealings with the Turks and the Russians:

> We have no conception of what all this really involves, but we know that it can, and will, be made the excuse for an enormous increase in military and naval armaments. For the last thirty years the privileged classes have been manufacturing excuses for that increase. They know that if they can rouse in the people the war passion, they will be able to contract millions of obligations, and send up their bloated armaments to a position still more portentous. An excuse will also be furnished for an enormous increase of civil establishments, whose limit and purpose cannot be defined ... The people of this island, toiling for life, are to be taxed, their property is to be confiscated, they are to be disturbed in their interests and future, in order that an arrangement so criminal, so base, so fraudulent, shall take effect, to their ruin and degradation.[62]

In the end, the threat of British engagement in war receded and the settlement of the Eastern Question reached at Berlin on 13 July 1878 removed the Balkan issue onto a back burner; it did not threaten peace again until thirty years later, with the outbreak of the First World War. The Liberals were not yet willing to move on. In August 1878 at a demonstration in Sandbach, Richard Pankhurst addressed the Cheshire Liberals. Their resolution congratulating Gladstone for his efforts on behalf of freedom and justice, which they saw as having been carried out in the Treaty of Berlin, also included a condemnation of the government. Richard was critical of the methods of the prime minister. He spoke in similar vein to his previous pronouncements, but his language was aggressive:

> They were there to declare that it was a Government which had practised duplicity upon Europe and fraud upon our own country, and involved us in dishonour and expense, and they ought no longer to submit to such a Government, but endeavour by all legitimate means to overthrow it, for if they did not do so the Government would destroy the country.[63]

No sooner was the Balkan situation dealt with than Afghanistan became a focus of attention when the second Afghan war erupted in November 1878. The basic issue with this territory was that it was a buffer between British India and the encroaching Russian Empire; British control was essential to imperial security so, when it was threatened by the refusal of the Emir to accept a British government resident, it had to be asserted. There was also a fear that Disraeli, who had a most romantic love of the Indian Empire, was at heart an imperialist who wished to keep extending the borders and control of the British Empire at any cost. Liberals again opposed the aggressive stance of the Conservative government, and its willingness to declare war on the Emir of Afghanistan without consultation with parliament.

The result in Manchester was an extremely riotous meeting attended by both critics and supporters of the government, enlivened by 'vigorous specimens of the residuum – a number of roughs, who most successfully carried out their mission to disturb the proceedings', creating a 'continual uproar' that meant no speeches were heard. Nevertheless, the meeting managed to pass the resolution put by the Liberals against the government. Though he did not apparently speak, Richard Pankhurst was prominent on the platform, and at a more orderly meeting of the Liberal Association on 12 December he proposed a resolution, which was unanimously adopted, condemning 'the unconstitutional and despotic action of the Government in committing the nation to war without consulting Parliament'. It continued by expressing the view that the policy was in any case 'indefensible both politically and morally', calculated 'to inflict great injury upon India, and to lower the character as well as imperil the liberties of this country'.[64]

The Manchester Liberal Association committee minutes are representative of his dominance in their discussions in 1879. In the face of the policy of aggressive imperialism adopted by Disraeli's Conservative government with regard to the Balkans, Afghanistan and then South Africa he pushed for the impeachment of the prime minister and demanded again that the power of peace and war be transferred from the executive to parliament. This was supported by the National Reform Union and other Liberal bodies.[65] As the ministry of the Conservatives drew towards its end, Pankhurst favoured William Gladstone's adoption for Manchester as the peace candidate in the forthcoming parliamentary election.[66] Failing that, he proposed radical alderman Abel Heywood instead. But in the end the moderate John Slagg was chosen and Gladstone set off on his famous and ground-breaking Midlothian campaign.[67]

CHAPTER 4

The Ultra-Radical Emerges

That Richard acted more upon principle than party considerations had put him at odds with the more moderate Liberals on more than one occasion, and eventually it resulted in his resignation from the association in August 1883.[1] The movement away had really begun a decade earlier as his conscience pushed him increasingly into ultra-radicalism. In his late thirties he joined the small, vociferous band of anti-monarchists and espoused republicanism. He advocated the nationalisation of land for the people. His personal religious beliefs moved from non-conformist to agnostic, perhaps even atheist. By 1883, the women's votes campaigner Lydia Becker was describing him as a 'firebrand'.[2] He still called himself a Liberal, in the absence of any alternative political party that might fit his stance better, but the Manchester Liberals began to look askance on his extreme views.

The Orator

At the BAAS conference of 1861, held in Manchester, Pankhurst attended a debate on the then very radical idea of progressive taxation, though what he said was not felt worthy of record, perhaps because he had not yet at that date made his mark as a speaker.[3] In these early years, his forays into public speaking were not a success, according to the satirical *City Jackdaw* in 1876. The journal referred back to his very first address, made at the National Reform Union: 'the truth must be told that his first notable attempt was, even in the opinion of his friends, a sorry failure'.

The meeting was held in an upper room of the Clarence Hotel, and Mr. George Wilson, the revered president of the Union, as he had also been chairman of the still more famous League [the Anti-Corn Law League], conducted the proceedings. The scarred veteran, whose only figures of speech were hard facts, encouraged the boy orator [Richard Pankhurst], whose ambitious flights of eloquence ill accorded with his painful self-consciousness, his stammering tongue, and floundering periods.[4]

But the writer goes on to explain how the hesitant and nervous young man had since developed into a speaker of some brilliance:

Since then many years have passed away – more than any one possessing only a slight knowledge of the gay, volatile, missish young bachelor, who is still the favourite of every circle, and scatters pithy epigram with his pertinent homethrusts, leaving rippling laughter as well as food for reflection with every group he joins – could readily believe, and the readily-flustered young student has acquired ready coolness in public address or in debate that has stood him in good stead in many a stormy scene. No public man in Manchester has more distinctly the courage of his opinions; his sturdy independence refuses to budge an inch for the persuasions of a friend or the defiance of foes.

The article continues to develop its theme:

His perfect frankness and transparency, and unfailing good humour, are such that, notwithstanding all his strange metamorphoses and the apostolic ardour with which he has in turn prosecuted each new fad by which he has become possessed, Dr. Pankhurst has never lost the regard of a single acquaintance he has made, and he has no enemy who knows him.

Nevertheless, it is admitted that

his shrill screaming voice makes it impossible that he should ever be a successful platform speaker. This we regard as a wise and merciful dispensation of Providence, since, had he been able to tackle a Free-trade Hall audience with ease, he would have been a constant spouter.

The conclusion is that the best places for him to speak were smaller venues such as the Mayor's Parlour. Or that his topic should be 'some purely educational question, when his political vis has not seduced him from the sublime heights of philosophy in which he specially delights to soar, to the level of practical hard-hitting'.

The article pokes fun at Richard's style of argument:

... being assigned the pleasing duty of moving the resolution, he proceeds to give a neat and concise history of the world from the time of the Flood down to the period when this society was inaugurated, followed by an explanation of the origin and scope of Roman Law. From the premises thus somehow obtained, he derives three root-principles, which he forthwith proceeds to build up by endless ramifications to a giddy altitude, and tops with a cloud of green and flowery verbiage. Much of his speech is Greek to the ordinary ladies who listen to his learning with open-eyed wonder; and his phraseology is sometimes not entirely understanded [sic] of the reporters, who have to wait with patience till he touches earth with some practical conclusion.[5]

On occasion his colourful metaphors gave offence to those who did not know him; his allusion to the Church of England as 'that grotesque monster' was a case in point. To him, according to *City Jackdaw*, it merely seemed 'an ancient institution covered by modern growths and excrescences' and therefore something out of the common order of nature. This expression caused a storm and nearly lost him the position of honorary secretary of the Union of Lancashire and Cheshire Mechanics Institutes.[6]

The article does admit that, although widely liked, one group who 'intensely hated' him were the 'violent section of the Tory party ... [on whom he had] pretty much the same effect as a red rag has in exciting a mad bull to greater fury'. It cites for instance John Ashton, backed up by the Dean of Manchester. Ominously, though, 'even among more respectable circles, Dr. Pankhurst is looked upon with some degree of distaste, if not aversion'. Bishop Fraser of Manchester had shared a platform with Richard to extol the virtues of public spirit, which was felt at that time to be flagging and under threat in political circles, due to the unprincipled nature of Disraeli's Conservative government. The bishop had paid him a compliment on his 'frank and upright public conduct'. Hearing this, respectable audience members 'visibly shuddered'.[7] One of the main reasons for this aversion was that Pankhurst had publicly taken up the cause of republicanism.

The Manchester Republican Club

Having been at the radical cutting edge of challenges to the establishment in the first half of the century, Manchester was uncharacteristically slow to set up a Republican Society. By the later 1860s other cities were beginning to take the lead in challenging the greatest bastions of power, the monarchy and the aristocracy. In January 1871 a Republican Club was established in Birmingham. The movement was inspired by events in France and perpetuated by discontent about the cost of the monarchy in Britain, at a time when the Queen was still in prolonged mourning for Prince Albert and was not performing any official functions. Republicanism grew in strength in the following two years, and clubs appeared in many other towns and cities.[8] At the end of 1872 at a Sheffield conference, the National Republican Brotherhood was set up, and at a further meeting in Birmingham in May 1873 the National Republican League was also established. It was only now that Manchester acquired a Republican Club.

The energy was not sustained, and republicanism never became nationally organised, was weakly represented in parliament, and remained a purely popular movement. With a growth in sympathy for the monarchy, due to the illness of the Prince of Wales at the end of 1871 and an attempt on the life of Queen Victoria in February 1872, it began to decline and had faded away as an organised movement by 1880.

It is perhaps Richard Pankhurst's role in the origins and as president of the Manchester Republican Club that most clearly demonstrates him as a radical, even among radicals.[9] It was founded at the same time as the 1873 Birmingham conference, and Richard was following the lead of that notorious radical MP, Charles Bradlaugh, who had become the figurehead of English republicanism. Pankhurst's opening address to the new body, intended 'To promote by moral and legal means the Establishment of a purely Elective and Representative Government' on 13 May 1873, was delivered to a small, invited audience of sympathisers, with some representatives of the press. He attacked hereditary power with fervour: 'The hereditary element keeps alive and perpetuates class-interests, class-legislation, and class-government.' He believed that such a system rested, not on merit, but on 'accidents and things external'. Having explained the excesses of the French Revolution as a response to the attacks of royalists and foreign invaders, he stated that it 'initiated for Europe and the world the great principles of political and social freedom upon which modern progress is based'. This was anathema to most Englishmen, who regarded the upheavals in France as the worst kind of assault on civilised society. Yet Pankhurst's aim was to achieve a peaceful 'transformation' in Britain, not a revolution, arguing that 'the tendency towards democratic government is an irresistible law in human affairs, which neither kings nor aristocracies ... can control, hinder, or overthrow ...' He went on to say that Britain was best prepared for a republic because of its 'national intelligence and political virtue'.

Republicanism was very much at odds with mainstream thinking, even among the Liberals, and Jacob Bright, MP for Manchester, was highly critical of this attack on monarchy. A letter by 'G.H.P.' in the *Manchester Guardian* also set out the case that the monarchy reflected the celestial hierarchy, and sarcastically hoped that if ever a republican government should obtain power, '"President Pankhurst" will be gentle to the monarchists'.[10] Sylvia summarises the impact of her father's actions as raising 'a veritable hornet's nest of indignation and prejudice about his head'. An enraged Reverend Hains, who heard him speak in Tyldesley, wrote to the press declaring him a 'Red Republican, a Communist, and a reviler of all religion'.[11]

Little is known about the activities of the Republican Club, but it is notable in the career of Richard Pankhurst because it was the first known obstacle that seriously threatened his success in respectable circles in Manchester. While the perhaps slightly more unconventional, even Bohemian, atmosphere of the Brasenose Club seems to have embraced their firebrand member and to have rather revelled in his eccentricity and extreme views, the Liberal party establishment was a different matter.

At the start of 1874 there was discussion among the radical wing of the party in Manchester about putting Richard forward as a Liberal candidate in the coming general election. At their meeting on 27 January they agreed that they were happy with the candidature of Jacob Bright, already a Manchester MP, but were reluctant to support that of Sir Thomas Bazley due to his 'defections from the cause of the working classes'. They listened to a report by Mr Freeman, who had attended the Reform Club where the official selection meeting had been held. He described a tumultuous meeting where people were speaking over each other. When it was suggested that Pankhurst be put up in place of Bazley the reaction was 'like a hurricane', with calls both for and against. In the end fears that the Liberal party would be split, allowing the Conservative Romaine Callender in, led the party to agree on Bright and Bazley. However, Bazley and the Conservative Callender were elected, reflecting a general swing across the country to the Conservatives, and the return of a Conservative government under Benjamin Disraeli.[12]

A further threat to Pankhurst's standing was staged at the annual assembly of the Union of Lancashire and Cheshire Institutes in October 1874, which began innocuously enough with the usual report and self-congratulation on the success of the body. However, when the time came to elect the new committee, an attack was launched on the position as honorary secretary of Richard Pankhurst.[13] Everyone was full of praise for the way he had worked 'bravely' for the union, but his 'prominent position in connection with a certain political association' was a bad influence on the subscribers. He was urged by Dr Kerr to withdraw from secretaryship and to work just as an ordinary member of the council, 'rather than expose the Union to any damage in the public eye'. In his defence,

Mr Robertson of Crewe said that if everyone with strong beliefs were removed, 'he did not know where they were to get efficient men to serve them'.

Richard came back fighting, describing Dr Kerr's attack as 'a sad and humiliating office to perform'. He wanted to see the proof that his views had exercised a bad influence. Admitting that three subscribers had withdrawn due to his public opinions, he was angry that 'they had gone to such a mean and dastardly length, and that their love for popular education was restricted by such considerations'. Yet at a council meeting other members had by implication, rather than direct confrontation, pressed him to retire. Disappointingly for Richard, they included Dr John Watts, chair of the present meeting, and well-known radical. 'They had been friends for many years. He had stood by Dr Watts because he knew he had suffered for his opinions and he believed they had been dear to each other.' Harry Rawson too had taken the same line, and he too avowed himself 'one among his [Pankhurst's] oldest, his closest and most personal friends'. This was clearly a deep and serious wound. However, Richard broadened his point by arguing that the aim of education was 'Independence of character and capability to judge without heat, temper, or passion, according to the evidence and the very right of the case. They would corrupt the whole sources of education if they were to institute a policy as that suggested by Dr Kerr.'

The upshot was that he resolved to stand his ground, and clearly there were those who supported this in the meeting as his speech was greeted with 'Hear, hear' and applause. Richard continued in his post for a further two years.[14] But this was an omen for the future, as his activities and pronouncements became increasingly beyond the pale. His calling the Church of England a 'grotesque monster' in 1876 seems to have elicited a similar storm, and it was in this year that his tenure as secretary was ended. After 1894, when he joined the avowedly socialist Independent Labour Party, respectable society decisively turned its back on him, resulting in a detrimental effect on his standing and commissions as a barrister.

For now though, in 1874, it was business as usual, and two days later at a meeting for the promotion of technical education for operatives in the Mayor's Parlour of Manchester Town Hall he expressed a general opinion that workmen with such knowledge would be better than those without, though he did not at this stage join his colleagues in offering money to fund exhibitions for the students to attend the Grammar School or Owens College.[15] His standing does not seem to have been questioned in 1875 when he was chosen to chair a prestigious lecture at the Athenaeum by Frederic Harrison on 'The Use of Books – Home Reading'. The speaker focused on the training of the faculties and recommended suitable literature for a good education.[16]

Commensurate with his republican principles, Richard and his allies organised meetings in 1876 to oppose the Disraeli government's policy of creating a new title for the Queen, namely Empress of India. He set out his views to the Regent Ward Liberal Club in Eccles in March, arguing that England was an aristocratic commonwealth rather than a monarchy because sovereignty lay with parliament, to which the Crown was subject. He agitated for the removal of the Crown as an institution because it was 'the shelter of privilege, the centre of vested and sinister interests'. Its removal would promote the public good, as it stood in the way of a democratic commonwealth.

Here Richard also clarified what he hoped to see in place of all this; a new representative assembly, elected by a fully enfranchised people, which would nominate the executive to serve the assembly and the people. For India too he did not want an imperial government, but a government that would prepare her to become a self-governing country. Moreover, he feared that the imperial title 'would associate in the minds of the people the notion that England is governed by Imperial sway'.[17]

On 16 March the Manchester Republican Club met with Richard in the chair. He spelled out his fears – that the Royal Titles Bill showed that the government was 'at its wits end for a new excitement', and that the imperial title meant in fact a despotism wielded by one person. He may have unleashed forces that were not welcome; when a resolution advocating the condemnation of the Bill was proposed, Mr J. Bullicliffe seconded it by saying that 'the Republic had been fought for in France, and it would yet be fought for in England if it were necessary', to which the peace-loving Pankhurst exclaimed 'Oh, no!'[18]

The Conservative *Manchester Courier* was predictably snide about the aspirations of the republicans:

The Manchester Republican Club still survives. At no time has it exhibited much vitality, and it has never displayed any quality at all attractive or commendable ... As a class English Republicans have an unsavoury odour. They are composed of what Mr [John] Bright calls 'the residuum' of the population ... There is in the Manchester centre only one representative of anything like peculiar intellectual capacity [Richard Pankhurst]. He ... is remarkable more on account of his eccentricities than his influence. His political vagaries excite more amusement than alarm.[19]

Feelings ran very high on the issue of the royal title, and the public gathering organised by Pankhurst and other republicans on 1 April 1876 in the

Manchester Co-operative Hall was the scene of a wild meeting that included respectable working men and a group of 'hired roughs'. A Mr Maltby, the Conservative agent and hostile to the organisers, muscled his way onto the platform and began speaking when 'a short, thick-set man walked deliberately from the floor of the hall and pitched the Conservative agent off the platform'. He was helped back up, and fights broke out. When order was restored, the speakers could not get a hearing and there were further fisticuffs 'in which chairs were freely used'. There was cheering for 'the Queen' and 'the Empress', and a spokesman, Mr Blatherwick, got on the platform 'and was holding forth there in the most theatrical of attitudes, throwing his arms about and shouting to the top of his voice'. Four policemen arrived and removed some of the disturbers; Mr Blatherwick with two or three others 'was thrown down the back stairs'. The tumult was still drowning out the speeches, but a resolution was proposed condemning the addition to the royal title as 'inconsistent with the traditions of the English people and hostile to the principles and spirit of their free government'. Richard Pankhurst seconded this and began to speak. Mr Blatherwick and his friends got back on the platform, but not for long as 'violent hands would have been laid upon them'. The resolution was carried very noisily by a large majority.[20]

By 7 April, the Republican Club was meeting to discuss the polarisation of the issue. Richard, by now being distinguished in the satirical *City Jackdaw* as 'our Chief Republican', opined that England was entering into the final phase of the long struggle between the prerogative of the Crown and privilege, and the principle of popular government and equality of right.[21] In the present pass this took the form of imperialism, which would put the monarch above the law, versus republicanism. The resolutions included one congratulating the French on peacefully establishing a democratic republic. For monarchists this was extreme and frightening, recalling as it did for them the darkest days of the Terror.[22] In the end the government prevailed and Victoria got her coveted title of Empress of India, and Conservative PM Disraeli consolidated his assurance of royal favour.

The attack on the monarchy extended beyond it to the privileged classes, led by the House of Lords. In January 1876 Richard's rhetoric was fairly moderate, and in keeping with mainstream radical Liberal thinking:

The House of Lords existed for nothing but obstruction and reaction. The fact was that for nearly 200 years every measure which had been framed for the benefit of the people had suffered either death or mutilation at the hands of the House of Lords ...[23]

It was not long before he was condemning the House in intemperate terms as 'The most significant piece of medieval mummery ... without doubt the most preposterous institution in Europe.'[24] In an age of corrupt empires, that was saying something! He elaborated:

> How silently the great Lords slumber on the body of the English nation, rolling in such infinite content, and ever wondering that everybody is not satisfied, since they themselves are! ... A public abattoir where the liberties and interests of the people have been butchered like cattle of the field, for the profit of the privileged few ... no more a legislative assembly than was Procrustes with his den of blood and his mutilation.[25]

Of course, a substantial element in the Lords consisted of the episcopate of the Church of England. He declared that, 'Privilege is a creature that goes on two stilts; one of which is property, the other the Church of England.' He had no time for the temporal role of the Church:

> Let them be ... sent about their spiritual business, and keep them there until the day of disestablishment and disendowment ... Let them be followers of the meek and lowly Jesus, and leave the gilded Chamber of the State.

And the clergy in general were a 'portentous beadledum'. Manchester Cathedral was 'an obsolete medieval residuum'. This hostility towards the Anglican Church surely originated in Richard's non-conformist background, but was perhaps sharpened when he began to fall away from religion of whatever stripe, during the 1870s.

His antipathy to the Lords continued unabated. In September 1884 he returned to his theme at an open-air meeting of over 1,000 people in Salford; the peers had rejected Gladstone's Bill to give agricultural workers a vote on the same terms as town dwellers. He pointed out that the Lords were attempting to usurp the power of the Crown, and if they succeeded it would mean the end of English liberties. Although not all in that crowd agreed with him, in the end a large majority supported the resolution that 'the House of Lords was useless and dangerous, and ought, therefore, to be abolished'.[26] Moreover, he had by now given detailed thought to what should replace it, and advocated one representative chamber that could not be dissolved by the executive, but would sit continuously. It would be renewed by the annual election of 25 per cent of its members. 'Such a legislature would possess the great qualities of stability, of organisation, continuity of policy,

perpetual adjustment to the ever-varying action and movement of public opinion.'
By 9 February 1885 Pankhurst was vice-president of the People's League for the
Abolition of the Hereditary Legislative Chamber.[27]

The abolition of the Lords continued to be Richard's aim for the rest of his
life; as late as 1894, in the context of a Hyde Park demonstration on the issue,
he was writing to the newspapers: 'Anything short of abolition is as difficult as
abolition, and will prove both dangerous and useless. The nation must face this
decisive alternative – either abolition or nothing.'[28]

Land Reform and Co-operation

In the light of all this, it may not be so surprising that Pankhurst also argued
for the reform of the land system in England.[29] He looked back to Anglo-Saxon
times and argued that collective ownership was the original system, individual
ownership being a 'modern innovation' inaugurated by the Normans to defend
their possession of the conquered kingdom. He explained how the growth of the
economy of modern cities such as Liverpool had resulted in immense wealth for
the owners of their land: 'In respect of the land upon which the Liverpool docks
were built, formerly mere foreshore of the Mersey, Lord Derby receives £40,000
a year.' This was in the context of the transformation of green countryside into
'blighted wastes' and squalid and overcrowded living conditions for the workers
in the new docks and factories. And those still working in agriculture were also
objects of his sympathy: 'What is the most forlorn object in the world? The
dependent, degraded agricultural labourer of England.'

The answer was to nationalise the land and put it under the control of local,
elected councils. This would enable its improvement by 'chemical skill and
scientific appliances' led by 'public-spirited men' under a flexible, experimental
and competitive system of long and short leases, peasant farming, large farming
and co-operatives.

Such challenging ideas were not limited to the land; in words that today
we associate with Marxist ideology, Richard proposed that mines might be
similarly organised:

The great natural agents of the land, such as coal, iron, and minerals,
should no longer be the property of a class, to the detriment of the
community, but should be brought under the control of the whole people
in its corporate capacity … Then the whole nation, in the individual and
in the mass, being sustained by the justice of the laws, and the equity of
the social system, and being animated and impelled by a strong sense

of the commonweal, would steadily move forward in a constant course of prosperity and development.[30]

Richard broadened the principle as an answer to all disputes between capital and labour, which were a loss to the community: 'Co-operation and self-government rest on the same foundation … The strong sense and love of commonweal …' He had long recognised the attractions of the co-operative movement. As early as July 1868 he and Lydia Becker of the Manchester women's suffrage campaign had attempted to set up a co-operative clothing warehouse; the following year they wanted to establish a women's rights journal produced on co-operative lines by women only.[31] Now in 1876 he saw the co-operative as 'a self-governed community'. While trade unions were a stepping stone in an era of conflict between capital and labour, co-operation embodied the higher principle of conciliation between the two, because they were united in the same person and would give 'to each a fair and full share of the products of joint exertion'. This would result in 'a constant course of prosperity and development' for the whole nation.[32] Like many of Richard's tenets, it was a noble ideal, but its fulfilment looked a long way off to all except other idealists.

Personal Belief and Religion

Although his upbringing was non-conformist, at some point at the end of his thirties Richard disengaged from Christian beliefs.[33] In the 1880s he publicly admitted to agnosticism, but it was claimed by others who wished to attack him that he was in fact an atheist. At that time, this was not a respectable position and it may be that he denied this attribution more because it would harm him in his attempts to gain election to parliament than because it was untrue.

In 1858, aged 34, he was on the committee of the Oxford Road Union Chapel's Essay and Discussion Society in Manchester. Since the rules stated that 'the society must be composed of the members of the Church and Congregation and their friends' this suggests that Richard was still a believer. The society's rules had been amended in Richard's own hand, proving that he was strongly engaged with its activities at this time. Furthermore, it was later stated in court that he was baptised into the Baptist church by the distinguished minister, Dr McLaren, around 1866.[34]

There is evidence of his continued commitment to Christianity as late as 1871, when in April he attended the conference of Sunday School teachers in Ashton-under-Lyne, described in the *City Jackdaw* as a 'Good Friday saturnalia of tea and toast and mild and genial bigotry'. He proposed a resolution 'that this Conference, whilst bowing with submission to the divine will, expresses its regret at the loss sustained during the year through the removal by death of Mr. E.S. Rogers, the late secretary of the Lancashire, Cheshire and Derbyshire Association of Sunday School Unions ...'[35]

It was not to last. By the time of the elections to the Manchester School Board in November 1873 Richard had resolved to stand, not as a 'church man', but affiliated to, though not one of, the 'unsectarian' interest opposed to any religious education in board schools. The *City Jackdaw* had some fun with his religious change of heart and its impact on his Christian erstwhile fellows: 'While his enfranchised spirit has gradually but surely soared from beyond their ken, they have watched him as a Whitsunday [ie religious holiday] crowd at Belle Vue [Manchester pleasure gardens] might gaze upon an ascending balloon ... at last disappearing altogether from their view ...'[36]

A practical symptom of this change of heart can be seen in Richard's championing of Sunday activities in the face of Sabbatarian opposition. He argued that Manchester's botanical gardens should be opened on Sundays, when working people were able to visit them, because those who claimed it would breach Sunday observance were trying to impose their own views on others. In the same vein, when discussion broke out over the Sunday opening of libraries and museums, he joined a long list of signatories in support. Whereas most who spoke in favour of such measures would have agreed with Alderman Abel Heywood that they were conducive to the edification and elevation of the lower classes, providing 'rational recreation' as an alternative to the more frivolous delights of pleasure gardens and public houses, Richard saw the issue of Sunday opening in a different light. The attempt by Sabbatarians to prevent others from choosing how they should behave on a Sunday amounted in his view to a form of 'persecution'. The fact that he used such a strong word indicates the passion with which he defended his position, and he rammed the point home: 'It is an outrage upon morality, upon justice, and upon order, and upon good sense.'[37]

Pankhurst soon turned his forensic skills to exposing the fallacies of the Established Church, and was clearly a confirmed disestablishmentarian in 1877 at the annual meeting of the Manchester and Salford Auxiliary to the Liberation Society, held in the Memorial Hall of the Unitarians on Albert Square. As early as 1874 he had given a speech, indicating the direction of his beliefs, at the opening of a Liberal Club in Tyldesley:

During the evening the Rev. Philip Hains and Mr. Gouldthorpe, barrister, who were to speak after him, left the meeting in consequence of a violent speech on disestablishment and the land question by Dr. Pankhurst of Manchester, a very advanced politician.[38]

The Liberation Society was a body that represented the non-conformist sects across the country; in the meeting, they discussed a resolution that 'the State Church system is in opposition to the scientific spirit of the age and has become an intolerable burden on the spiritual energies of the earnest' and the meeting was 'greatly encouraged by numerous indications that disestablishment is felt to be a national necessity and that it must form a prominent item in the programme of the next Liberal Government'.

Seconding the resolution, Pankhurst argued that the Church of England was a purely civil and secular institution ruled by the law, and bishops were public officials maintained by public money. He cited the situation in Manchester, where the Church of England was proving an aggressive and divisive force in local society. The Dean, he noted, had preached a sermon condemning the 'false preachers' of the non-conformist churches, and had thus poured 'sacerdotal petroleum' on the community. To reinforce his argument, Pankhurst also pointed out the divisions within the Anglicans themselves – between ritualists and evangelicals. He concluded by arguing that the disestablishment of the Church of England would bring to the nation 'unity, peace and concord' and bestow on the government 'a new power of freedom, economy and progress'. The resolution was passed, but the church remained established.[39]

At some unspecified date, Richard wrote a detailed exposition of his thoughts on religion, entitled 'Religio Laici'.[40] This may have been a response to Dryden's 1682 poem of the same name, translated as 'A Layman's Faith', which had aimed to assert the validity of the Anglican church in the face of Catholic criticism. Richard's writings have the tone of lecture notes and of personal musings. As usual they show his erudition and knowledge of history. They reflect his consistent view about the relationship between the past and the present; that conditions in the past gave rise to laws and institutions which supported them, but that with progress those conditions had disappeared and the laws and institutions were therefore now obsolete and required revision and reform. Along the way, he refers to the thinking of Paley, Newman, Carlyle, Bacon and Voltaire, Huxley and Mill, and later also Rousseau, Diderot, Locke and the great early church father, Chrysostom, and even the most eminent pagan philosopher, Aristotle.

The depth of thought he put into his analysis of general religious belief in this document is perhaps an indication of the personal spiritual journey that he made from non-conformist believer to agnostic, perhaps even atheist, and it may be that these writings were created in his later thirties and early forties when he was experiencing a reassessment of his religious beliefs. In general, he does not openly state his own view, though there are occasional glimpses, such as his brief disquisition on observance of the Sabbath: 'Will any philosopher say that it is a natural and native instinct to observe the Sabbath and to feel virtuous indignation against those who neglect it?'

As the document goes on, his own views begin to emerge, though still somewhat obliquely:

> Christian antiquity will have to be discredited as a source of moral or religious knowledge just as Pagan antiquity has been as a source of scientific and philosophic knowledge. The notion that St Paul or St John or the Fathers at Nicea were in a position to know more about the Maker of the world and his dealings with mankind than we are is as … [illegible] and unwarranted an affirmation as the affirmation that Aristotle knew more about the elements than modern chemists do.

In the section 'Christianity – an Enemy of Culture', Pankhurst analyses the difficult relationship at various points in history between religious belief and cultural and scientific developments. His reading extended beyond Christian thinkers, and he saw the opinion of the Muslim scholar, the Caliph Omar, an influential contemporary of the Prophet, as summing up the approach of all religion: 'If then books agree with the Koran they are superfluous. If they disagree with it they are pernicious.' He goes on to discuss the dilemma presented by modern times of whether to choose belief or intellect.

His conclusion in 'Symptoms of the decline of Monetheism' is that: 'The blinding light which the mere name and thought of God once flashed before men's eyes is waning, is dim. The intellect finds it difficult nay impossible, the heart fails to draw refreshment as of old.' Although this is expressed in general terms as the experience of 'men', it is clearly something that Richard was encountering in himself. The corollary is that: 'Mankind is beginning to find it must be its own providence. We are orphans then … Perhaps for the first time we may realise how important it is to love one another …' So it may be understood that, whereas the young Pankhurst was motivated by a love of God in his actions, the mature man based his life's work on a nascent humanism.

But that he is still debating within himself also seems clear, as the following section deals with 'The Consolations of Religion'. He cites the fear of Hell and 'the ceaseless lure of an eternal hereafter'. He writes about the Catholic ascetic, Mother Margaret, and of the mystic books of the 'Romanists' he says: 'Nowhere else do I find such a wellspring of beautiful pure emotion.' It was clearly very attractive to him, as to many of his contemporaries who found their home in the Catholic church, most notably among them Cardinal Newman, with whose writings Richard was clearly familiar. 'But it is hard to believe that all this spiritual beauty is destined to fall away with the system which first gave it birth.

There must be and there is a positive translation of all this tender effusion which will not be confined to the little rills of religious ... [illegible] but flow into the broad river of humanity.'[41] Later in the papers is his apparent summary of Kantian thinking that: 'The mind of man does and can know the finite and phenomenal. The mind of man does not and cannot know the infinite and noumenal.' He also notes that religion originates with a sense of dependence in man and 'the awe of the heart before the unknown'. Although it is not clear at what stage in his life these notes were made, they demonstrate that his was an ongoing philosophical journey.

Women's Suffrage to 1880

The promising young lawyer and man about town did not publicly exhibit radical inclinations until his early thirties, but then in the 1860s he found a cause in which to express aspirations for social and political change that was to have huge implications in the future. When a small group of liberal-minded people met in Manchester at the home of Dr Burchardt on 11 January 1867, they were building on discussions that had occurred as early as 1865 as to the viability of forming a committee to agitate for women's suffrage. Richard Pankhurst had been one of this embryonic organisation. It is probably no coincidence that in London the Kensington Society was established in the same year. This was initially focused on providing training and employment for middle-class women who had no means of support, but had also begun to discuss the idea of women's votes. In 1866 one of their leading lights, Barbara Leigh Smith Bodichon, spoke in Manchester at the NAPSS conference. This was the occasion when Lydia Becker was inspired to join the movement, and it may also have been the spur that led the Manchester suffragists to reconvene their committee at the start of the next year, on 11 January 1867.[1]

This revived body included Richard Pankhurst, along with Jacob Bright (from 1868 MP for Manchester), Unitarian minister Reverend Samuel Steinthal, Max Kyllmann, Mrs Gloyne, Elizabeth Wolstenholme and Dr Burchardt himself.[2] Richard's motivation is a matter of speculation. He relished as a lawyer the machinations, tactics, strategies and arguments that the espousal of such a cause demanded of him. As a deep admirer of John Stuart Mill he was also following his hero's lead. In 1867 Mill had unsuccessfully presented to the Commons a petition in favour of a women's vote amendment to a Liberal reform Bill that was eventually voted down.[3]

The papers of Richard Pankhurst preserved by Sylvia contain notes and ideas about the right of women to vote.[4] These would appear to have an early date, being headed 'Woman Suffrage', which was the first title for the campaign, dropped by August 1867 when the Manchester National Society for Women's Suffrage was formally constituted. The jottings afford a fascinating insight into the thought processes of the young lawyer. He became a central force in the committee as its legal adviser, drafter of Bills and committed lieutenant to the redoubtable honorary secretary, Lydia Becker. His lifelong style of argument, which analysed the historical origins of the exclusion of women from political power in order to show how such a situation had come to pass by the nineteenth century, was deployed in this campaign.

He attributes prevailing laws and beliefs to the influence of Teutonic Feudal law, which, whilst not denying the full right of women, exempted them from the armed assembly. Strikingly, he claims that: 'The idea of women as "men of the female sex" has always been present to the Teutonic mind.' He later opines that the chivalric ideal has been subverted by an Anti-Chivalry that wages war for men, to deny women the help and strength of political power, civil right and full citizenship. The impact of this was to diminish both sexes. 'The age of chivalry is indeed passed. The manhood of men is fast passing too.' Later on he deals with the rights women possessed under Roman Law, citing their execution of public functions. One woman was even an advocate in court until a law was passed preventing it. He attributes some of the limitations of the role of women in early times to the influence of the Church.

The thoughts in these notes culminate in a list of 'Objects' for women's suffrage. The first was adopted as the overarching aim of the Manchester committee and eventually the national movement: 'To obtain for women the grant of the suffrage on the same terms as it is or may be granted to men.' At this point Richard's notes go further, presaging an extra aim to end 'coverture' for married women by adding 'and otherwise to secure for women political and legal equality'. This was later adopted by some, but not all, suffragists; the seeds of division were present in the suffrage movement from the start. His second object was 'To improve the educational and industrial position of women'. The very last note dates from 1894, recording details about the enfranchisement of women in New Zealand, which he may have used to boost his arguments for the emancipation of British women. He notes (seemingly quoting a published report) that in the first election in Auckland: 'There was no confusion, no cries or jeers or interference of any kind with the voters and very little more excitement than at an ordinary election. During the whole day not a drunken man was to be seen anywhere, and the women passed to and from the polling place without any annoyance ...'

The Manchester National Society for Women's Suffrage

It is not clear what exactly was decided at the Manchester meeting on 11 January 1867. It certainly provided for a further encounter the following month, and on 13 February the committee was joined by the remarkable woman who was to become effectively the leader of the British women's suffrage movement for twenty years, Lydia Ernestine Becker. According to the list provided by Helen Blackburn, Pankhurst was not present at this meeting, but this was probably not significant; Jacob and Ursula Bright are also not listed, and they were stalwarts of the new committee.[5]

These activists were to become Richard's colleagues and allies in the women's suffrage fight, and he and Lydia Becker in particular worked closely together to establish Manchester as the leading city of the campaign. Becker proved the mover and shaker who put into motion the legal measures suggested to her by Pankhurst. While we do not have any personal documents that might reveal how Richard regarded the body of which he had become such a crucial part, the letter book of Lydia Becker spanning most of 1868 affords a remarkable insight into her attitudes and relationships, not least towards Richard Pankhurst himself. Richard's own papers include letters from Becker, many of which are quoted in Sylvia's *The Suffragette Movement*.

Richard spoke at the first ever public meeting for women's suffrage in the Free Trade Hall on 14 April 1868.[6] This was also the first meeting at which women appeared on the platform and proposed the resolutions, though supported by the chairman, Henry Pochin, mayor of Salford, and other men. That Richard's public support for this movement was principled is demonstrated by a story retold by his daughters, Christabel and Sylvia. At Rhyl in 1878, Richard got a chance to attract the interest of William Gladstone, leader of the Liberal party and destined to become prime minister for a second time in 1880. In the words of Christabel:

> His [Pankhurst's] championship of votes for women was the first handicap he put upon himself. He was a Liberal in politics, and Mr. Gladstone was then Liberal leader and dispenser of favour to brilliant young men. The Liberal Party was always on the look-out for such as Richard Marsden Pankhurst – the happy possessor of a brilliant mind and the magnetic appeal that wins the masses and makes the leader of men. The great Gladstone saw and heard this gifted young man and Dr. Pankhurst got his chance. He used it to plead in the presence of the Liberal leader for the political enfranchisement of women – a measure to which Mr. Gladstone was most bitterly opposed and which

he had forbidden his Front Bench colleagues to support. Gone were Pankhurst's prospects of political fame ...[7]

According to Sylvia, he kept digging and went on to advocate the democratic reorganisation of the Liberal Party itself, which is unlikely to have endeared him to its authoritarian and hugely controlling leader. Certainly, both daughters, probably basing their views on Richard's own analysis, believed that this event was the initial reason why he was not awarded a safe Liberal seat in parliament, thereafter putatively moving on to a Cabinet post and a title. He was too honest and principled for his own good.[8] On the other hand, Martin Pugh has plausibly argued that Pankhurst's predilection for women's votes need not have precluded a political career under Gladstone. Indeed, men like Sir Charles Dilke, Henry Fawcett and James Stansfeld managed to espouse the cause and rise to Liberal ministries, and even to keep their posts when defying the agreed Cabinet line.[9] Clearly there were other factors in his failure to achieve what at the time was considered his potential.

Relationship with Becker

Lydia Becker's admiration for Richard Pankhurst's forensic skills and knowledge of the law grew with acquaintance, and she was full of praise for his achievements in arguing on behalf of women's rights, as well as his written works on matters such as international law.[10] It seems that the admiration was mutual, since according to Lydia he had suggested she would make a very good lawyer.[11] He apparently valued her intellectual abilities, and had promised to find out whether a woman could legally qualify as a solicitor, so highly did he regard her potential.[12]

Perhaps there was more. Lydia was seven years his senior, but in *The Suffragette Movement* his daughter, Sylvia, records that there was talk of a romantic attachment. And this was certainly rumoured locally; when Richard stood for parliament in 1883, a speaker asked the rhetorical question 'Who is Richard Pankhurst?', to which a heckler responded 'Miss Becker's sweetheart'.[13] By this time, of course, Richard was married to his young and beautiful wife, Emmeline.

Becker's letters around this time demonstrate a strong desire to write about him to her friends and colleagues in the movement. To Jessie Boucherett, campaigner for women in London, she wrote: 'He is clever and original – and will do our cause good service' but: 'He has some odd notions, and to hear him talk you would think he despised our sex utterly.' She continued this theme to Josephine Butler. 'The oddest part of the matter is that he pretends to despise women, and says they are men's natural enemies!!' June Purvis has suggested that Lydia's accounts of their conversations by letter have a flirtatious tone.

When they had disagreed about some disparaging remark he had made about 'women's reason' she wrote archly: 'We shall not think more about the expression … you will never feel tempted, I am sure, to use it again …'[14] Lydia's claims that Richard betrayed a disparaging attitude towards women are intriguing; there does not seem to be any other source that describes this tendency. Certainly, his public pronouncements do not reflect it. It is certainly possible that this was flirtatious teasing on both their parts.

Although not generally disposed to write in philosophical terms, the letter she sent to Richard on 24 May 1868 certainly reveals a depth of feeling about the joint venture on which they were engaged. He had demonstrated that their aim was

> the full recognition of the principle that every human soul is an independent kingdom – nay, a universe over which the individual soul is sovereign – The notion that anyone owes subjection or subordination to another is fatal to the higher life of both ruler and subject. Freedom and equality not only do not prevent self-devotion to the welfare of others but seem essential to it – essential also to that enlightened and voluntary obedience which is the only safeguard against anarchy, the only guarantee for the maintenance of peace and order in the commonwealth.[15]

She spent much time talking with him on 5 June, and seems to have been unable to tear herself away, writing to her non-suffragist friend Sarah Jackson:

> He is a very clever little man – with some most extraordinary sentiments about life in general and women in particular – and so much to say on them that it is really dangerous to venture into his den. I called at his chambers on Friday [5 June] to give him a paper and intended to stay five minutes, and found it impossible to escape under two hours! I wonder what you would make of him![16]

So perhaps there was indeed some romantic attachment. If we are to judge by his attitude towards his wife Emmeline later on, it looks as if Richard would have made an ideal husband for Lydia, who wrote on more than one occasion that she would only marry a man who would treat her as an equal. Sylvia reported that she once said to Emmeline: 'Married women have all the plums of life!' And later in life there was some bitterness in Lydia's attitude to Richard, which may, at least in part, have been due to disappointment that he had looked elsewhere for a spouse. Frustratingly, there are no extant documents that afford even an inkling of Richard's own view and feelings about his personal relationship with Lydia Becker.

The whole thing was clearly undesirable to Richard's parents, who must have feared for his legal career when he embarked on such a radical course as to support women's votes. It is a healthy reminder that we cannot always accept Sylvia's opinions and judgements at face value; whereas Sylvia claims that there was never 'a jar' between Richard and his parents, Lydia Becker's letter to Josephine Butler of July 1868 indicates otherwise:

> He has a good deal of home pressure to withstand in following up his own convictions. His father, whom I accidentally encountered, told me he had no sympathy with our cause – said he wished his son had nothing to do with us, and said his mother is quite wild about him. But there is no half-heartedness about the son – he has gone into the work heart and soul – and borne himself bravely ...[17]

Her concerns may have been heightened because she worried that he was over-burdened; in an earlier letter she had said: 'I am sadly afraid that we are taking too much from him ... He seems to be my mainstay on the committee now ...' His relations with his parents may have been soured even more deeply than we know. While in August 1865 his father was writing to him from a holiday in the Isle of Man in the most friendly terms, addressing him as 'my dear Dick', in the will he made in 1871, after Richard had embarked on the women's suffrage agitation and was drafting Bills to be presented in parliament to effect this reform, Henry Francis made no mention whatsoever of his lawyer son. His wife, Margaret, Richard's mother, was his sole executrix and everything (effects worth under £800) was left to her. It seems perhaps odd that Richard was not mentioned, in view of his legal expertise, and the fact that he had advised his mother earlier in her dispute with her family.[18]

Lydia confided in Richard that she too sometimes struggled, when she explained that she was subject to low moods: 'I never do believe that anything that will make me very happy will really come to pass.'[19] Her eagerness the following November to ensure that he attend in good time a committee meeting at which a bitter dispute in the committee with the Kyllmann sisters was to be resolved was based on her belief that, as her ally, he would help defend her from their attacks and attempts to reduce her power and autonomy in the campaign. She furnished him with a full, blow-by-blow account of the sisters' visit to her home when they launched a verbal assault on her. At the very least, in the early years of the suffrage campaign, Pankhurst was a trusted friend and confidant.

The Persons Campaign

It may be that the committee's decision to launch a major campaign based on the Second Reform Act of 1867 was inspired by an unusual event in the Manchester by-election of November the same year; a woman by the name of Lilly Maxwell found her name on the voters' register, and was persuaded to exercise her vote by Lydia Becker. It is unknown how her name came to be included in the first place, but what is certain is that this event proved the precursor to a much wider campaign in the general election of 1868, when the *Daily News* estimated that up to 1,000 women all over the country voted.

Two young lawyers were responsible in that year for the legal basis of the women's claims to a vote, put forward initially by Manchester and later by the other major committees, and known as the Persons Campaign. Thomas Chisholm Anstey showed that before the 1832 Great Reform Act, which stated that votes were limited to 'male persons', some women had been entitled to vote and indeed had exercised that right. He cited in particular the case of Anne Clifford, Countess of Dorset (d. 1676). He also argued that Lord Brougham's Act of 1850 had declared that wherever the term 'man' was used in laws on the constitution, it applied by default also to women, unless they were explicitly excluded. He and Richard Pankhurst therefore put the case that if the ratepayer clauses in the 1867 Reform Act applying to 'men' also applied to women, which was agreed by all, then the clauses in the same Act which referred to 'men' voting also applied to women.

This implied that the efforts of the highly revered John Stuart Mill to pass an amendment to the Act that would allow women to vote on the same terms as men by changing the word 'man' to 'person' was based on a false premise, and that the 1867 Reform Act did not require any modification to allow women to vote. Indeed, Lydia Becker reported that Pankhurst had referred to the proposal of the amendment as 'a fatal blunder'.[20]

Pankhurst published an article in the *Fortnightly Review*, the leading organ of advanced opinion, explaining the arguments. His basic point was that every man and woman was equal before the law and was entitled to all the rights of a citizen, including the franchise. To be human and sane were the only essential conditions to entitlement to the franchise, supplemented (at the time) with property qualifications. He put it dramatically that

> to hold that women are incompetent to vote in the election of members
> of Parliament is to hold them to be the subjects of absolute and incurable
> mental defect, and, as it were, to sign against the duly qualified women
> of England a certificate of perpetual lunacy.[21]

The problem was that high-flown idealism and logic like this was to come up against a different value system, which based its arguments on practice, prejudice and tradition.

Gaining acceptance for women to vote in the forthcoming general election in 1868 was going to be a challenge. It would require local authorities to agree to women with the correct property qualifications registering to vote. A registration could also be challenged once recorded, and the question would then go to a barristers' court for a decision, so sympathetic barristers were needed. And of course, there was also the matter of persuading qualified women themselves to go through the daunting process of registering and actually going to the poll and voting publicly – there was no secret ballot until 1872 – exposing themselves to possible hostility and ridicule in a sometimes riotous atmosphere.

It was decided late in 1867 to begin by visiting the overseers of the registers to persuade them that women should be permitted to register, but the real work was kick-started by the public meeting in Manchester's Free Trade Hall assembly room on 14 April 1868. It was emulated by other major cities, notably Birmingham, on the urging of Becker. Richard Pankhurst and other male radicals appeared on the platform, supporting the women who were breaking new ground in speaking up and proposing resolutions. The first was that women should be given the vote 'on the same condition as it is or may be [given] to men', the second expressed support for friends of emancipation in parliament, foremost among whom at this time was John Stuart Mill, and the third urged all women with the necessary qualifications to put their names on the voting registers.

To prepare the ground for the election, Becker organised meetings in person with the overseers of the registers, relying on a prominent local radical and Unitarian minister, Reverend Samuel Steinthal, who was intended to lead the explanations to the Manchester officials about the legal loophole the lawyers had uncovered. In the event, Steinthal was detained in London and Lydia was extremely alarmed that only she, Alice Wilson and Richard Pankhurst, who at this stage was an unknown quantity, were able to attend the interview. She need not have worried as Steinthal's role was ably assumed by Pankhurst. Lydia was soon enlightened as to his oratorical skills and penned many letters at this time praising his cogency and persuasiveness. The overseers were polite and amazed at the evidence, and the chairman said they had 'opened his eyes'.[22] Sylvia quotes her father's high-minded words, though they may reflect Richard's recollections much later as much as what he actually said to convince the overseers:

We have no true conception of what political liberty means; we have no true idea of its real power in the world until we see that every sane human being ... shall be enfranchised by the law of the land in which we live … There is one way in which the liberty we have won shall never pass away from us, and it is this: Liberty will be everlasting when liberty is universal: then and then only. The granting of the present application will be a great step to the realization of that postulate.[23]

He apparently went on to dazzle with his erudition, citing St Augustine and the plays of ancient Roman Terence to argue that in Roman Law, *homo* meant not only 'man' but also 'human being'. Further in *Magna Carta*, revered as the foundation of English liberties, the term 'free man' applied to women as well as to men. He went on to argue the same from case law dating from the Middle Ages onwards, and from actual usage of women who voted before 1832. He also explained that the only ground given for denying women a vote was 'mental imbecility', a state that proved harder to refute than the campaigners expected.

Lydia Becker wrote to him on 29 June praising his eloquence:

I have had it on my mind to endeavour to express to you my sense of gratitude and obligation to you for consenting to act for us, and admiration of the great powers of reasoning and of oratory you have displayed. It has been a hard, uphill fight – against hopeless odds, but if any man could have won – you are he! … It is no light thing that you have done and you must not think that we estimate lightly the cost at which you have done it.[24]

Not everyone was convinced. When the overseers of Chorlton-on-Medlock denied women the electoral right, Becker cited Pankhurst's arguments from his article in the *Fortnightly Review* of September 1868.[25] She deduced from the article that the overseers were acting as though women were in a perpetual state of infancy and mental imbecility. It must have been even more disappointing when the Manchester overseers apparently changed their minds and also refused to put women on the register.

As expected, many of the women who did manage to register found their applications challenged and were subject to a barrister's arbitration. Becker was advised by Anstey that the women should have legal representation, and she asked Richard to put this to the committee and later to help find a suitable lawyer; a technicality in registration law meant that he could not represent the claimants himself. In the end they settled on Mr Cobbett.[26] When the barristers' court finally met, Pankhurst was in evidence, much to the admiration of Becker, though he had warned her that the women would likely be 'smiled out of court' by the barristers. On the day, as expected, the unsympathetic Mr Hosack rejected the women's claims to vote, despite the forceful presence of Richard Pankhurst, who in the words of Becker was 'filing his nails in the court – and I know that if he only had the chance he would have sprung on the Barrister like a tiger and "had his blood" as he says. Did not I long to see him at it!!'[27]

Although Becker fought hard and successfully in the court for the women's right to appeal against the decision, in the aftermath she was hesitant due to the prohibitive cost of such an action. Sylvia, who sees her father as the real brains behind the Manchester committee, quotes his words on the matter:

> For myself, I cannot help feeling that the stopping of proceedings at this point wounds the honour of the movement, and seems a breach of good faith with the public, to whose justice and sense of right we have appealed … we must remember that if the judges decide that women have no part or place in the constitution, public opinion can create for them that position which judicial decision appears to deny.[28]

Lydia was grateful to Pankhurst for taking the matter into his own hands and persuading the committee to support an appeal; generally, Lydia liked to be in control, but she made an exception for Richard Pankhurst, a measure of her high opinion of his abilities and judgement.

The high court case of *Chorlton v Lings*, which used a test case to rule on the issue of the women's rejected votes, was fought on behalf of the Manchester committee by Sir John Coleridge QC, ably assisted by Richard Pankhurst, who had prepared the detailed and convoluted case. It was heard by Lord Chief Justice Bovill and Justices Willes (the Master of the Rolls), Keating and Byles.[29] However, all the cogent and logical arguments proposed were overruled on the grounds that women had not actually voted for centuries, and in any case should not be subject to the roughness of the poll, and that decorum should prevail. Pankhurst attempted somewhat to retrieve the situation by pressing the judges to hear a second case of *Chorlton v Kessler*, but he was overruled on the grounds that the first case also decided the second. His plea that: 'It is so great a subject; there is so much to urge. It involves so vast a mass of material …' was met with laughter, according to *The Times*. The court had heard enough.

Despite this setback Lydia estimated, based on the report of the contemporary *Daily News*, that up to 1,000 women across the UK voted in the general election of December 1868. This was in no small measure due to the assiduity of the Manchester committee, not least the formidable Lydia Becker, and credit is also due to the abilities and commitment of Richard Pankhurst.[30]

Women's Electoral Disabilities Bills

The loophole that allowed women to vote in the 1868 general election was effectively closed for all future elections by the High Court decision of November 1868. It was decided within the Manchester committee to pursue a new course. Armed with more petitions that would be gathered across the country, and with the knowledge that many women had voted and even more had wanted to vote but had been prevented, they made a decision to introduce a private members Bill into the Commons that would give women the vote 'on the same conditions as it is, or may be, granted to men'. This was the stated aim in the constitution of the Manchester National Society for Women's Suffrage (MNSWS), written in 1868, quite probably by the society's unpaid legal advisor, Richard Pankhurst. He was at the forefront of the attempt at legislation, having drafted their proposed 'Bill for the Removal of the Electoral Disabilities of Women'. At the MNSWS AGM late in 1869 he moved that the Bill be introduced in the succeeding session; it was to be presented to the House in May 1870 by MPs Jacob Bright and Sir Charles Dilke. It would make law the principle that

> wherever words occur which import the masculine gender, the same shall be held to include females for all purposes connected with and having reference to the right to be registered as voters, and to vote in such election ...[31]

Some of the campaigners, unaware of the intractability of a large number of parliamentarians, were over-optimistic in their belief that they were close to achieving their goal. Becker herself was of the opinion that they simply had to present logical and cogent arguments, and the day would be won. Bright, now with over a year's experience in the Commons, was much more realistic in his assessment of their prospects and tried to warn her that any such change to the system would take a long time.

One reason for the suffragists' hope was that in 1869 a local government Act had in fact granted the council vote to women on the same terms as men in major cities. The original 1835 Corporations Act had ended the ancient right of women property holders to vote in local elections in the major cities that adopted municipal corporation status, by bestowing the franchise only on 'male persons'. When a Municipal Corporations Bill under the charge of Mr Hibbert, the MP for Oldham, proposed to give the municipal franchise to every male occupier who had resided in the borough for a year, an amendment was moved in committee to leave out the word 'male'. The originator of the idea of removing the word 'male' is not entirely clear; Lydia Becker claimed to have suggested it to Jacob

Bright, having seen in a morning paper that a woman named Jessie Goodwin had illicitly voted in a Manchester council election in December 1867.[32] On the other hand, Sylvia credibly claimed the credit for her father, Richard, as the drafter of the amendment.

It was introduced in the early hours of the morning, perhaps in an attempt to keep it 'under the radar' and the women who supported it kept deliberately silent to avoid provoking an opposition that was as yet unfocused. Becker wrote on 3 May 1869 to Jessie Boucherett 'we must be very quiet until notice is actually given of the amendment, and then we must work for it, as hard as we can'.[33] The government allowed it to stand, and it was passed in the Commons without opposition. Richard told his daughter, Sylvia:

> There were high men in Parliament who would have scouted the notion of giving the Parliamentary franchise to women, but they did not take much part in Municipal affairs themselves, and, therefore, they decided that it would not perhaps be too much to give the Municipal franchise to women.[34]

It might have been anticipated that the Lords could prove more of an obstacle, but the urban nature of the legislation may well have also reduced their interest in the matter, and Becker worked hard to persuade the influential arch-Conservative Marquess of Salisbury by appealing to his sense of tradition and the rights of property owners, be they men or women.[35] The Lords also passed the Bill, much to the delight of the campaigners.

While many of the legislators may have regarded this as a side issue with little bearing on the bigger matter of women's suffrage in national elections, for the suffragists this was a first step on the road, and a pilot for further emancipation. Becker wrote to the Home Secretary on 12 April 1870 explaining how committed to voting the women in municipal corporations had been in their recent elections, and described the removal of the disabilities with regard to the parliamentary vote as 'the natural sequence of the removal of municipal disabilities'.[36] At the MNSWS AGM in December 1870 Richard pointed out that: 'A Parliament that grants the municipal franchise to women can with no consistency whatever refuse to concede the parliamentary suffrage.'[37]

In view of the ease with which the women's vote had been achieved in municipal corporations, hopes were high when the suffragists introduced Richard Pankhurst's private member's Bill, supported by petitions, in May 1870. The measure would have given the vote to only single and widowed women who had property on the same terms as men; married women at that time could not own property because, under the laws of coverture, on marriage all they owned or earned became the possession of their husband. Yet the terms of the Bill were framed to allow for future, hoped-for changes in the status of women by specifying that the vote would be granted on the same terms as to men, whatever those terms might be.

The potential opposition had not at this stage been mobilised, and the turnout in the Commons for the vote was not high; out of 658 MPs, only 216 voted. The Home Secretary stated that the government did not have time to decide on the question and declined to guide the House, let alone back the Bill. However, those present voted in the second reading to pass it by 125 to 91. It looked as if the cause might succeed. Unfortunately, no account had been taken of the views of the hugely dominant leader of the ruling Liberal party, William Gladstone, and he was firmly opposed to women having any role in politics. As the Bill entered the committee stage, he pronounced his view:

> I think I may say, for most of my colleagues as well as for myself, that we felt something more than surprise – that we felt disappointment – at the result arrived at on Wednesday last. We do not attempt to limit the freedom of any one on such a subject, either within the official body or elsewhere; but undoubtedly it is an opinion prevailing among us – and one which I for one strongly entertain, in common with all those now sitting near me – that it would be a very great mistake to carry this Bill into law.[38]

Gladstone did not need to 'limit the freedom' of his MPs; such was his clout within his party that they voted as he wished, many of them changing their decision, and the Bill was defeated on its third reading by 220 to 94.

At the MNSWS AGM in December of that year Richard explained his rationale as a supporter of women's suffrage. His statement reflected very much his stance as a dispassionate lawyer, tracing the origin of the current establishment to an early human society ruled by force. This was bolstered by laws, and thereafter by opinions based on those laws. In the mid-nineteenth century the first two conditions had disappeared, but the opinions remained, now without any foundation or reason. He pointed out that all new ideas have historically encountered prejudice, citing belief in the earth moving around the sun, the abandonment of the divine right of kings, the freeing of slaves, and free trade. Richard's hopes for their movement betray his idealism most clearly:

> We have these things to gain; first of all, we are putting a great human relation on the basis of truth; secondly, we are increasing the material good of the world in the opening up [of] careers of activity and energy;

and we increase the quantity of moral good in the world by giving to all human beings a larger view of destiny and duty in giving them a free development of their nature. And I say, further, that we shall immensely add to the sum of human happiness in the removal of those repressive influences which keep down character, and prevent it being developed and formed into noble, excellent and useful types and adaptations. Taken as a whole, then, this is a movement in the direction of human progress and liberty. That is a sublime conception which presents the totality of mankind under the idea of one grand colossal personality – always living, always growing, always learning.[39]

In 1871 the theme was developed at the next AGM when he explained that the constitutional inequality that still prevailed meant women lacked rights and protection. It also prevented women from participating in the 'duties of the empire'. He could not resist high-flown rhetoric when he continued that it was

clear that if there was to be a great union of humanity on the basis of common rights, it must be by putting the legislation of every country, upon this high human basis ... And in contributing thus to the welfare of our own country, we put ourselves in living sympathy with all the great progressive peoples of the world. Then would become possible those great universal reforms which were peculiar to no nation or people, but were universal to mankind and common to humanity.

One of the arguments against a women's vote, especially for married women, was that it would destroy domestic harmony. Richard, however, put it that home life would be improved by sharing in the wider interests outside. His classical education came in useful here for an analogy:

if the home were like some Greek temple, open to the sky of public duty and public spirit of patriotism, philanthropy and universal charities, not to feel the influence of which was to be a practically uneducated person, they would see go out of that home life a much nobler and grander generation than ever they had been able to get out of it in the history of the world before.[40]

At the 1872 AGM Pankhurst was fulsome in his praise of the movement, its leaders Becker and Bright, its members and their generosity in commitment and financial giving. He attributed this to 'no accidental or superficial causes ... but to the fact that it was a part of the great movement which had transformed modern Europe from mediaeval conditions to the conditions of progress in which we now lived'. This view, very much of its time, reflected the prevailing liberal philosophy that progress was inevitable. And indeed, politically this seemed obvious: 'Class after class that was put under political and social subjection had conquered its way into the constitution of the country and had been incorporated into the national life. No class in our country, except the class of woman, now remained outside the constitution.'[41]

He proposed that men alone could no longer bear the burden of public duty, and it must be apparent to 'every thoughtful man' that: 'An infinite supply of genius, ability, and enthusiasm … was waiting to be admitted into the constitution, and waiting to serve the country. Why should they not apply to women the grand and stirring maxim of an open career for talent?' And, he continued, this implied full admission for women to education, citing lines by Pope that summed up male defensiveness:

> In beauty or wit
> No mortal as yet
> To question your empire has dared –
> But men of discerning
> Have thought that in learning
> To yield to a lady was hard.

It seems that, having thus got off his chest his reasoning for women's votes, he thereafter began to run out of steam at the AGMs. In January 1874, at the sixth, he contented himself with the usual congratulations on the hard work of the leadership and the success of the campaign, citing evidence that the latest Commons vote on the women's suffrage Bill was the most favourable yet and that candidates in elections were not openly declaring themselves against.

Richard's original draft of the Bill for women's votes was presented from 1870 to 1873, but the opponents of women's suffrage were beginning to marshal their forces and became increasingly effective in blocking it. What was needed was government backing. However, under Gladstone there was no way that could be achieved. And matters did not improve when anti-suffragist Gladstone was defeated in the 1874 general election, and the pro-suffrage Conservative Disraeli succeeded him as prime minister; the bulk of the new party in power was at this stage overwhelmingly hostile to women's votes.

Letters are extant that give us some insight into the reaction of the women towards these events, but the lack of similar sources on the role and attitude of Richard Pankhurst hides him from the view of history. His commitment as the drafter of the legislation indicates that he would have shared the highs and lows of Lydia Becker and the other committee members. He may also have shared their naive view of MPs, namely that logic and moral right would overcome the power of party politics and personal ambition.[42]

His feelings about the modification of his draft Bill in 1874 are easier to ascertain. In 1870 he had drawn up another important piece of women's rights legislation aiming to give married women property rights; the upshot was that married women, in theory at least, gained control of their own earnings.[43] This could have meant that, were the suffrage Bill to pass, some married women might qualify to vote, though the law of coverture could be construed to prevent them in any case. Married women were a particularly thorny issue. There was an argument that if a married woman voted differently from her husband, this could cause marital breakdown. On the other hand, not giving married women the vote would leave those who were regarded as failed women with it – single women, widows, even prostitutes.

In 1874 Jacob Bright lost his seat in the Commons and the campaign, on the suggestion of the more conservative London committee, invited Conservative MP for Marylebone, William Forsyth, to take on his mantle as its parliamentary leader. But Forsyth would only agree to do so if married women were specifically excluded from the franchise. While Becker very reluctantly agreed to this condition, Pankhurst and others on the Manchester committee, notably the Jacob Brights and Elizabeth Wolstenholme Elmy, were hostile. There appears to have been deep disagreement within the group. This was the start of a rift in the women's suffrage movement. At first it was not too profound. Those against accepting Forsyth's modification continued to subscribe to the MNSWS, though with decreasing enthusiasm. The change proved to be intermittent; in 1876 Jacob Bright recovered his seat, and the offending clause was removed for a time. Year after year Pankhurst's draft Bill was put before the Commons, but to no avail.

In 1879 a major change in Richard Pankhurst's status surprised everyone, but did not at first affect his commitment to the women's vote. Indeed, it may have strengthened it. By the later 1870s, the public had Pankhurst down as a confirmed bachelor who was so dedicated to his forensic and political roles that he would never have time for a wife and family. So his marriage at the age of 45, after a speedy courtship, to 21-year-old Emmeline Goulden must have been unexpected to many, and was perhaps an unpleasant development for Lydia Becker.

The young bride was inducted onto the MNSWS and the Married Women's Property (MWP) committees and participated in both with her doting husband.[44] Richard and Emmeline made generous annual donations to the

Manchester suffrage society of a guinea each in the early 1880s.[45] However, as time went on, he increasingly remained in the background, leaving the limelight to Lydia. There were other calls on Richard's time and talents in both his public and his private life, and common to both, the issue particularly of property rights. The Pankhursts' donations to the MNSWS ceased after 1885; in 1886 they moved to London.

CHAPTER 6

Married Women's Property

While it is widely known that women were normally unable to vote in general elections in the nineteenth century, common knowledge does not extend so clearly to the other 'disabilities' under which women suffered.[1] Perhaps most critical was their economic subjection, particularly notable as a legal issue in the case of married women. A woman who entered matrimony came under the common law status of coverture; she and her husband became one legal entity, one person, and that person was the husband. Accordingly, a married woman's property and income, and also her debts, became those of her husband. In many cases, this did not cause an issue. While Elizabeth Gaskell, the renowned Manchester novelist, recorded that her husband, William, locked up all her business letters when he went away, and pocketed for banking her cheques from writings, she actually enjoyed remarkable freedom in their marriage, financing frequent trips, including abroad, without any check on where or for how long.

On the other hand, in the case of an abusive husband there was no legal redress for the wife if he absconded with all her worldly goods and left her destitute. Many such cases were cited in the debate about this issue. Caroline Cornwallis's article in 1856 roused public sympathy by detailing the example of a famous actress, Mrs Glover, whose husband abandoned her to live with another woman. She pursued her acting career to support herself and their children, but a court decided (reluctantly) that her salary should be paid to the husband.[2]

Some wealthy women avoided the worst effects of coverture by means of an expensive settlement under the law of equity, whereby male trustees were in control of their property and money; such arrangements were usually put in place by the woman's father. However, the courts of Equity and Chancery had become cumbersome and slow.[3] And the 90 per cent of women without this sort of protection, poor women who worked and heiresses alike, were entirely at the mercy of the man they married.

By the mid-nineteenth century there was growing concern about husbands who abused their power in this matter, and petitions were gathered that described marriage as a form of slavery. The Law Amendment Society (LAS) featured prominently in a public meeting on the issue, and as a result they referred the matter to their committee on Personal Laws for a full investigation. This resulted in a report and a Bill to be presented to the House of Lords by Lord Brougham early in February 1857, and then to the Commons in May by Sir Thomas Erskine Perry. According to *Punch* magazine it was greeted with hilarity, and personal abuse was directed at the women who openly supported it. The Bill passed its second reading, but stalled when the government promised to bring forward their own Bill and then failed to do so.

The passage of a Divorce Act in the same year, which included provision for deserted wives to have some protection of their income through a court order, 'took the wind out of our sails' according to Erskine Perry. In this way, parliament sidestepped the issue; many men in power regarded the idea that a woman should have access to her own earnings as 'an affront against nature', because they feared that women would become independent and thereby social and political institutions would be undermined. Negotiating her own business in the world might even lead a married woman into 'immorality'.[4]

Opponents were well aware of the concurrent women's suffrage campaign, and behind the spoken objections there lurked a fear of a parliament 'in petticoats', though supporters of property reform, such as Lydia Becker, pointed out that it would weaken those arguments for enfranchising women that were based on prevention of the abuse of power by husbands.[5]

In 1864 the LAS affiliated with the NAPSS and in this forum many areas of women's lives came under scrutiny, including women's education, job opportunities, rights over children, local public service and voting in local elections. The particular battle for married women's property rights and the end of all the limitations of coverture was one in which Richard Pankhurst was a leading figure behind the scenes. Although very closely engaged on the Married Women's Property (MWP) Committee, Pankhurst left it to others, especially Elizabeth Wolstenholme, to speak up for that issue in the NAPSS. But he was present in support when they did so.

The question arises as to why a young and successful unmarried lawyer should interest himself in the knotty issues of women's rights. It may well be that his interest was sparked by his personal experiences. His own mother had suffered a bitter battle with her family over property she believed had been left in trust to her by her father, which was apparently withheld from her by her brother and his widow.[6] Moreover, arguments that poor women would benefit from a change in the law probably helped to convince him; it was pointed out that 24 per cent of married women earned an income outside the home, and this did not include those who worked in their husband's business. This was reinforced by discussions in the LAS and the NAPSS.

According to Lawrence Goldman, it was the NAPSS that came closest to representing women in public as an organisation. Many of the ideas and proposals of the LAS were broadcast to a wider public and parliament through the conferences of the NAPSS, and this was clearly an important part of the process that led to proposals to reform the law. The NAPSS is credited with contributing to legislative reform in the women's cause, particularly in the guise of the Married Women's Property Act of 1870, and further, more effective, legislation on the issue in 1882. Its conferences allowed women a platform to present their case to a mixed audience, not all of whom were sympathetic. Elizabeth Wolstenholme, leader of the MWP Committee, reminded her group that they 'could never have succeeded in the manner they had done had it not been for the Social Science Association [the short name for the NAPSS], who had done by far the larger portion of the work'.[7]

The Married Women's Property Committee and the Acts of 1870 and 1882

During the passage of the 1867 Reform Act, which extended the right of voting to an extra million men, the most prominent advocate of the embryonic women's suffrage movement at that time, John Stuart Mill, had cited the economic suppression of married women as a key reason for giving women the vote. In the same year, at the NAPSS congress held in Belfast, one of the leading lights as secretary of the association, George Woodyatt Hastings, presented a paper proposing that England should emulate reforms adopted in New York State that granted married women the same property rights as unmarried women.[8]

The baton was taken up in Manchester, where a very effective MWP Committee was established under the leadership of its secretary, Elizabeth Wolstenholme. She was notable as a local headmistress who was unusually radical in co-habiting unmarried with Ben Elmy, a minor poet, though they were persuaded to marry in 1874 when Elizabeth became pregnant. The personnel of this committee to a large degree duplicated that of the MNSWS; it included Lydia Becker; Josephine Butler of Liverpool, who was active in defending the rights of working women and prostitutes; Jessie Boucherett of the Society for Promoting the Employment of Women and editor of the *Englishwoman's Review*; and Richard Pankhurst, who gave legal advice. Wolstenholme, Butler and Boucherett prepared a memorial to put before the executive of the NAPSS, proposing that the association should take up the cause of MWP law. This had the potential to be very effective in achieving change.

The first Married Women's Property Act of 1870 was drafted by NAPSS member Richard Pankhurst. The Bill, completed in February 1868 and introduced in parliament in April, was similar to the one that had been introduced in 1857; Pankhurst did not reinvent the wheel. It allowed equity settlements to continue, but in all other cases married women were to hold all their property without any control by their husbands, with the same powers as an unmarried woman to acquire and alienate property, and to dispose of it in their wills. If they died intestate, the same rules as would apply to a husband would apply to the wife's property, except that the husband would still be entitled to a life interest in their realty. Married women could enter into contracts and sue and be sued, and would be responsible for their own debts.

To whip up popular support for a Bill, a general MWP Committee was formed in Manchester, emulated by other cities, with an impressive executive led by Elizabeth Wolstenholme and Josephine Butler as joint secretaries and Lydia Becker as treasurer.[9] They were also joined on the committee by Manchester Liberal MP Jacob Bright and his formidable spouse, Ursula. Two nieces of Jacob's sister, the Edinburgh suffragist leader Priscilla McLaren, Lilias and Sophia Ashworth, also joined. Other MPs represented on the executive were Russell Gurney, the Conservative MP for Southampton, and suffragist Liberal Leonard Courtney, MP for Liskeard. Millicent Fawcett, the future leader of the women's suffragists, also participated. Famously she recounted that when she had appeared in court to testify against a thief who had stolen her purse, she was astonished to hear him charged with stealing the property of her husband. The aristocracy was represented by the beautiful and unconventional Lady Kate Amberley, whom Queen Victoria considered ought to 'have a good whipping' for her speech on women's rights in 1870. Other prominent members included Frances Power Cobbe, Emilie Venturi and Isabella Tod of Belfast. All these committee members were involved in several other aspects of women's rights campaigning, which gave them the widespread influence they proceeded to bring to bear on the MPs and Lords debating the Bill in parliament.

The committee solicited support through letters to MPs and publicised the issue through gathering signatures on petitions to be sent into parliament. This was a slow and laborious task, but Richard Pankhurst was very keen that it should be done properly. In May 1868 he intervened to stop two paid canvassers from their work because he was unhappy about how they had acquired signatures and 'marks' (from the illiterate). This had discomfited Elizabeth Wolstenholme Elmy, and caused her friend and colleague Lydia Becker to write to her in slightly proprietorial tones about Pankhurst: 'Don't be vexed with Dr. Pankhurst. He has done no harm, but a great deal of good, in stopping Mrs Young and Mrs Poole's canvas which not only did no good, but a great deal of mischief.' She was slightly contradictory in then encouraging Elmy to stick to her opinions and resist being overwhelmed by Pankhurst's. 'I do not quite understand your sudden collapse and readiness to give in to Dr. Pankhurst.' To Richard himself she wrote: 'You did a very good turn in stopping one of the canvassers, in them I have no confidence at all.'[10]

Despite such difficulties, in total they presented an impressive twenty-nine petitions with 33,000 signatures in 1868, and in 1869 113 petitions with over 42,000 signatures. The NAPSS continued its support as the Bill made its way through the Commons and into the Lords. Papers were presented at its conferences in Birmingham in 1868 and Bristol in 1869. Books were published, most notably JS Mill's *Subjection of Women* in 1869. Articles appeared in newspapers and journals, some of which were reprinted in the form of pamphlets by the MWP Committee.

The case of Susannah Palmer in particular struck a chord with the public. As a poor working woman, she was convicted of stabbing her husband and sentenced to imprisonment. The circumstances illustrated the need for reform for the married women's property laws:

> Her husband had treated her brutally for many years, beating her, turning her and their children out of the house into the streets at night and bringing in other women, and at last showing an incestuous interest in his own daughter. Susannah Palmer had finally left her husband in order to establish a new home and support herself and her children by her own efforts. But then her husband appeared and seized all her possessions, as he had every legal right to do, and at last she struck back. The facts of the case, detailed in court and publicized by Frances Power Cobbe in The Echo and by other writers, aroused such interest that a public subscription was raised to provide for Susannah Palmer and her children. Fortunately she had only wounded and not killed her husband, and when she was released from prison after a few months a post was found for her where she would be safe from him. But, a final irony, the money and articles of furniture collected for her could not be given to her legally, for then they would have been her husband's property, so that everything had to be put into the name of the sheriffs of London as the legal owners.[11]

The Bill was introduced in April 1868 by George Shaw-Lefevre, MP for Reading, at that time a promising young man tipped as a future prime minister.

Encouragingly there was no high-profile opposition in the Commons; this was one of the first debates there on the rights of women and potential opponents were caught off guard. Voting in the Commons was tied on the second reading, but it was passed when the Speaker used his casting vote in favour. In the committee stage the chair was held by Shaw-Lefevre, and the committee included sympathisers Russell Gurney, Jacob Bright and Robert Lowe. After protracted consideration, the Bill was returned to the Commons unaltered in all essential points; it was passed by 131 to 33. Although it went to the Lords, there was insufficient time left in the parliamentary term, and it was left in abeyance until the next session.

The Lords therefore had time to rally and when it reached them it was a different story. Despite individual petitions from the MWP Committee, the Bill met with universal disapproval from a body that was overwhelmingly Conservative. Their select committee would take no evidence from the MWP Committee and proceeded to modify the Bill as they saw fit. It was, in the words of Holcombe, 'torn to shreds'.[12] Fourteen of its seventeen provisions were removed and replaced, and three were amended. They did concede that poor women needed more protection. The only property to which women were now entitled was their earnings and some forms of investment. In this way, the wages of poor women were protected, but not the property of other women. The 'parliamentary mountain had brought forth a mouse'.[13]

Well aware of the limitations of the Bill, the MWP Committee decided nevertheless to accept and support it; there was insufficient time left to debate amendments in the Commons, and it was seen as a first instalment. The Act came into operation on 9 August 1870. Described by MWP supporters as 'that legislative abortion' and 'a feeble compromise', one lawyer declared it to be 'full of blots and itself a blot on our statute book, and the most absurd Act he had ever read'.[14] Elizabeth Wolstenholme, in her speech to the NAPSS later in 1870, pointed out that it still did not protect any savings a married woman had made before the Act was passed, unless invested in specific ways. And banks and stockbrokers refused in any case to receive deposits or honour cheques from a married woman, requiring her husband's signature. For women without the financial resources to get legal advice, the legislation was impossibly convoluted. Yet what the vestiges of Richard Pankhurst's Bill had achieved by passing into law was that from 1870 the principle was established that, in some circumstances, married women could own and control their property.

Between 1870 and 1882 the committee continued to battle on, with some change in its personnel. Pankhurst remained committed throughout. At their annual meeting in Manchester Town Hall he supported a resolution to continue the fight, and summarised the problem:

He said the House of Lords had amended the House of Commons bill by substituting another which rested on no principle, and was therefore vexatious, complicated, and obscure in detail. The new measure had left the old and bad principle in existence, only cutting off certain of its most barbarous and atrocious consequences, so that where the partial limitations of the bill did not operate the old state of things injuriously continued. (Hear, hear). The present state of the law involved flagrant injustice, and many glaring anomalies; indeed we had in regard to husbands and wives one of the most cruel laws that existed. It was surely time that we should follow the example of other nations in securing justice by means of equality in this respect. (Applause).[15]

The campaign continued with tactics such as speaking at the NAPSS, petitioning and distributing pamphlets. It is impossible to say how involved Richard was in these efforts, but it does seem highly probable that he engaged in the political and legal work that scrutinised legislation which might have a bearing on married women's property rights. This included Bills relating to taxation and the criminal law.[16] He almost certainly helped in giving legal advice about the workings of the 1870 Act, found in the pages of Lydia Becker's *Women's Suffrage Journal.*

The committee always remained alert to the possibility of introducing a further Bill, and in 1873 the moment seemed right. John Hinde Palmer, Liberal MP for Lincoln, brought in a measure of thoroughgoing reform. Based on the original Bill of 1870, it had been drawn up for the MWP Committee by Pankhurst. It aimed to repeal eleven of the seventeen clauses of the 1870 Act, and secured to married women all property on the same terms as that held by unmarried women. In a Commons dominated by Liberals, it passed on its second reading by 124 to 103. However, delays and postponements killed the Bill. By the end of the year Disraeli, the Conservative opposition leader, was describing the governing Liberal front bench as 'a range of exhausted volcanoes', and the following year he triumphed in the general election and led a Conservative government into power. Over eighty sympathisers lost their seats, including Jacob Bright and Hinde Palmer. Apart from a couple of 'tidying-up' measures, the new government was not interested in married women's property rights.

Some attempts were made by the MWP Committee to introduce new Bills in 1877 and 1878, but there was clearly no hope of success while the Conservatives were in power. The return of the Liberals under Gladstone in 1880 gave fresh heart to the MWP Committee, especially as it was estimated that they had 300 friends in the Commons, and fewer than 100 opponents.[17] The first attempts at a Bill in 1880 and again in 1881 were stopped by pressure of parliamentary business and the dominance of Irish issues. The committee needed government support if their Bill was to succeed.

Help came from an unlikely quarter in the person of Lord Chancellor Selborne, who had opposed the Bill of 1870 but had apparently experienced a change of heart. Holcombe attributes this, not to a belief in women's rights, but rather to his view as a jurist that such reform was a logical consequence of broader legal reforms already enacted in the Judicature Act of 1873.[18] In spite of a stroke in the preceding year, in 1882 Selborne introduced the Bill into the Lords in the original form drafted in 1870 by Richard Pankhurst; it was passed by the end of May. In June the government introduced it into the Commons and it speedily passed its second reading. Despite claims by Charles Warton that the Bill would 'make the woman, instead of a kind and loving wife, a domestic tyrant', it was passed in the nick of time on the day that parliament went into recess. A revolution had taken place in the marriage relationship. As Holcombe explains, 'every married woman without a settlement under equity law was to hold all her property as "her separate property, in the same manner as if she were a feme sole [unmarried woman] without the intervention of any trustee".'[19]

Sadly, the dearth of private papers means that there is no window into Richard Pankhurst's mind at this time. Yet there can be no doubt that he must have been delighted that after twelve long years of struggle, the law he had drafted was finally enacted, and a major step forward in women's rights had been achieved. The MWP Committee held its final meeting in London on 8 November 1882. They offered their heartfelt thanks to Lord Chancellor Selborne especially. And accolades were also given to Ursula Bright and Elizabeth Wolstenholme Elmy, still the leading lights of the campaign. *The Times* editorial pronounced: 'Today several Acts of great importance … come into operation. Without denying their significance, we may truly say that all yield in practical consequence to the Married Women's Property Act of 1882, which … in fact revolutionizes the law upon a vital subject [that] concerns every husband and wife …'[20]

PART 2

Marriage and Children 1879–93

CHAPTER 7

An 'Ideal Marriage'[1]

Sylvia Pankhurst's account of her mother's first sight of the man she was to marry is striking:

> The first she saw of the Doctor was his hand, 'a beautiful hand,' opening the door of the cab in which he was arriving at some great meeting. When he appeared, rejoicing in his mission, and irradiating the fervour of his hopeful convictions, greeted with cheers and waving of hats and handkerchiefs by expectant thousands, her thoughts were set on fire.[2]

This has the ring of a family story, polished and embellished by numerous tellings. It is hard to imagine that the 20-year-old Emmeline Goulden was bowled over on such a slim acquaintance by a man of 44, though she was undoubtedly impressed by his renown and the reception he received. Her parents were supportive of the women's suffrage campaign, and she was aware at an early age of Richard's role in drafting the women's suffrage Bill of 1870.[3] She had been primed within her family to admire 'the Doctor', who at the time of their meeting was at the centre of the anti-war agitation of 1878.[4] Her father was a supporter, her mother found him charming and eloquent. It was not difficult for her to fall in love with his idealism and commitment to equality for women.

Much of the information available about the private life of Richard and Emmeline Pankhurst emanates from the pen of Sylvia, their second daughter. A passionate and partisan spirit underlies much of her account, and even in factual evidence she was sometimes inaccurate, despite a serious attempt to approach her subject systematically with supporting archival material. Yet she was also a first-hand witness to much that she describes, and her testimony demonstrates all the strengths as well as the weaknesses of her position.

Essentially, her writings are the main source of what we know about the early life of the young Pankhurst family.

However, there is a little-used corrective to her view in the writings of her younger sister, Adela. Where Sylvia idolises their father and largely blames their mother for the shortcomings in their parenting, Adela aims to move the burden of guilt from Emmeline to Richard. Although she agrees with Sylvia that their parents were so engrossed in their campaigns that they failed to notice distress in their children, she accuses Richard of moulding not only his offspring to his will and ambitions, but also his very young and impressionable wife. Christabel's memoirs in *Unshackled* are perhaps the least partisan. Whilst she reveres both parents and shows less hostility than her sisters, she portrays a rather hapless Richard, influenced by an ambitious Emmeline into a life in politics.

Already set in his ways, everyone seems to agree that when he meet Emmeline, Richard was consciously a 'confirmed bachelor' who was settled living in the family home with his widowed mother.[5] Christabel, who gained possession of her parents' love letters, which it seems were later destroyed, claims that: 'Father had resolved to remain unmarried for the sake of his public work.'[6] It is likely that he was completely inexperienced in dealing with young women; his life in politics, the law and his clubs would have been an extremely male affair.

Much to Emmeline's astonishment and delight, he was completely captivated by the very beautiful, graceful and unusually headstrong young woman. She was flattered that the great man noticed her. He could not resist her. Her violet-blue eyes, jet black hair, golden voice and pretty Parisian clothes, worn without apparent art yet somehow very winningly, were irresistible to his poetic and ardent nature. Christabel relates how circumstances favoured Richard's suit; Emmeline's mother and siblings were holidaying by the sea but she herself was called back home to keep house for her father when the housekeeper fell ill. In the peaceful surroundings of 'the summer garden' she was courted and won, apparently without much difficulty. Her mother chided her for 'throwing herself' at her suitor, failing to demonstrate the proper reserve. Christabel explains how quickly their relationship developed by quoting extracts from her father's letters.[7] On 8 September he wrote:

Dear Miss Goulden,

There is, as you know, now in action an important movement for the higher education of women. As one of the party of progress, you must be interested in this. I have much considered the subject and sought to frame a scheme for making such education as real and efficient as possible ...

By 23 September, just two weeks later, his tone had changed remarkably:

> Dearest Treasure,
>
> I received with greatest joy your charming likeness (sent with too few words). The Carte itself has honestly tried to express you as you are, but of course it could not. The fire and soul of the original can never consent to enter a copy. Still, when the original is absent, the copy consoles and animates.

So far, so predictable. However, with Richard Pankhurst the great ideals were never far away, though his emotions seem to have caused syntax to desert him:

> In all my happiness with you, I feel most deeply the responsibilities that are gathering round us … Every struggling cause shall be ours … So living, we even in the present enter, as it were, by inspiration into the good time yet far away and something of its morning glow touches our foreheads, or ever it is, by the many, even so much as dreamt of.

And he relished the prospect of sharing the work of social improvement together:

> Help me in this in the future, unceasingly. Herein is the strength – with bliss added – of two lives made one by that love which seeks more the other than self. How I long and yearn to have all this shared to the full between us in equal measure!

Sylvia relates that, as part of their courtship, they discussed the legal disabilities of women, and perhaps the unconventional arrangements of radical luminaries such as Mary Wollstonecraft and Percy Bysshe Shelley. She recounts a story that Emmeline impulsively suggested that she and Richard should likewise live together without the legal formalities of a wedding; Richard, she implies, was at least worldly enough to know that this would mean social death for Emmeline, and probably huge damage to his own reputation, not to mention his legal practice. However, Christabel spins this differently, stating quite plainly that: 'Mother was no revolutionary in her views of marriage,' and explains that on the eve of their marriage she asked: 'Are you sure you will always love me and want me forever? Wouldn't you have liked to try first how we should get on?' To which she imagines 'how tenderly he smiled and how completely he satisfied her wish to hear him say, yet once again, all that the morrow's marriage meant and always would mean to him'. In this interpretation the conversation was about reassurance, not a rebellion against social norms. The fact that Sylvia was co-habiting unmarried with the father of her child, and that her mother had irreversibly fallen out with her at least partly on this issue, may explain her interpretation of her parents' discussion.

On 6 December 1879 Richard's mother died. He was devastated, and fearing that he would break down completely, and indeed would not survive until the spring, Emmeline agreed to marry immediately.[8] As Christabel puts it 'the lonely one could not be kept waiting'. This resulted in a ceremony that was disappointingly low key, due to the fact that they were in mourning and there was no time to arrange matters. There were few guests and no bridesmaids, there could be no bridal orange blossom, and the bride wore brown. Her dress was doubly a disappointment because when it arrived at the last minute, having been made for her by Manchester's department store, Messrs Kendal Milne, she cried at the decoration of brass buttons down the front, which she felt made her look 'like a little page-boy'. She was an unprepared bride in terms of sex, and when her mother tried to inform her on the night before the event she refused to hear her. She apparently did not perceive her lack of knowledge as a problem; when the time came to inform her own daughters, it was her husband, Richard, who initiated the 'talk'. This was occasioned by an incident in the Russell Square gardens when some big boys asked an unaccompanied Adela 'strange questions'. The parents were alarmed, and Emmeline began, 'Father says I ought to talk to you.' But the words dried up and Sylvia declares that she never again referred to the subject.[9]

On the eve of their wedding Richard wrote ecstatically to Emmeline: 'It is only a few brief hours that separate us from that oneness of life which ought, which will, hold for us an existence of joyous love.' They were married by licence on 18 December 1879 at the splendid parish church designed by George Gilbert Scott near the Goulden home, St Luke's in Weaste, Salford.[10]

The Gouldens

Sylvia researched her forbears on both sides, and she relates that Emmeline was the eldest daughter in a family of ten siblings. They were well-to-do, living in Seedley Cottage in Salford, a large house surrounded by gardens and fields, near to the calico printing and bleach works owned by her father, Robert Goulden. He was a self-made man, who had started out as an errand boy in a large Manchester manufacturing company.

His father, also Robert, had early fallen prey to the press gang, then later returned to marry and found a family; Emmeline's grandmother, Mary, was a fustian cutter. The family had long held progressive views. In 1819 Emmeline's grandfather had joined the hopeful throng demanding a vote at St Peter's Fields, which had resulted in many injuries and deaths. The events have gone down in history as the Peterloo Massacre. Pursued by soldiers, he had rushed into a cellar dwelling and hidden in someone's bed. In the 1840s both grandparents had joined the Anti-Corn Law League.[11]

By the 1870s, their son Robert Goulden had several textile business enterprises, and an interesting, if then rather risqué, hobby. He had a reputation as an enthusiastic amateur actor, known especially in the Athenaeum Society for 'his portrayal of great Shakespearian characters'. He even ran his own theatre, the Prince of Wales in Salford. His marriage to a Manx woman, (Sophie) Jane Quine or Craine, reputed by some to be the beauty of the island, produced five sons and five daughters. The link with the island was maintained by family holidays in a house in Douglas Bay. At Seedley Cottage Jane grew vegetables and fruit and worked alongside her maids in the manner of a farmer's wife, making butter, jam and pickles, and baking bread and cakes. She was a strong role model for Emmeline in that she was top of the pecking order in the home. Emmeline's third daughter, Adela, recalled that Jane was 'a handsome, imperious woman whose word was law to her husband and her sons. She had her own opinions about everything she understood and expressed them freely.'[12]

Family tradition relates that Emmeline was her father's favourite; he once expostulated that it was a pity she was not a boy, so clever was she. It was said that she was literate at 3 and read his morning paper to her father at breakfast. She took advantage of any book that was available, and Sylvia notes that she was especially impressed by Bunyan's *Pilgrim's Progress* and Carlyle's *French Revolution*. But it was novels that she really relished.

The atmosphere in the family was very political; Robert was a Liberal, like many in Lancashire a keen opponent of slavery, backing the north in the American Civil War in spite of his business's reliance on imported American cotton from the south. After emancipation he campaigned to support impoverished ex-slaves. He was a member of the committee that welcomed Henry Ward Beecher when he lectured in Manchester, and little Emmeline was recruited to take a 'lucky bag' around to collect money for the cause. Jane too supported it and her reading with her children notably included the famous Harriet Beecher Stowe's *Uncle Tom's Cabin*.[13]

Also in the 1860s, Irish liberation became a hot topic when Fenian terrorists killed a policeman in Manchester in their bid to release fellow Fenian prisoners from a police van. The 9-year-old Emmeline recalled the site of the public hanging in 1867 of the three 'Manchester Martyrs', which she and her brother, Walter, passed by each day on their way to school. She shuddered in horror each time. Martin Pugh believes that despite this she learnt from the tactics of the

Irish and put some of them into action during the militant suffrage campaigns of the twentieth century.[14] When in the later 1860s Manchester became the dynamic centre of the newly founded women's suffrage campaign, at 14 Emmeline was taken by her mother to a suffrage meeting. She was already primed because at home she had read the *Women's Suffrage Journal,* produced by Lydia Becker. The young girl was enthused by Becker's speech, which she later claimed turned her into 'a conscious and confirmed suffragist'.[15]

There appears to have been plenty of discussion of current affairs and the arts in the family home. Surprisingly in view of the radical leanings of the parents, in the early years Emmeline seems to have adopted as her hero the unlikely, but romantic, figure of Charles I. By the time that Emmeline met Richard Pankhurst, Robert Goulden had become a firm admirer of 'the Doctor' and supported especially his campaign against war in 1876–78. Indeed, that first meeting of Richard and Emmeline occurred at a speech the former was delivering on the topic in Manchester.[16]

Emmeline's formal education was limited, though she was sent to a local school, which was not necessarily expected for a middle-class girl of that period. She was grounded in the 'three Rs' plus some French, history, geography and grammar. At 14 she was enrolled by her father in the Ecole Normale on the Avenue de Neuilly in Paris, a move that reflects her father's social ambition in that such an education was more commonly found among upper-class girls. It may also reflect Emmeline's precocity; it was a progressive institution that offered academic subjects. Yet she seems to have rendered formal lessons optional, with the excuse that she was too ill and frail to attend. It would not have helped that her French was too poor to participate fully, though by the end of her time in Paris she had become fluent. She remained there for most of her teenage years.

With her fellow student, Noémie, daughter of the aristocratic and heroic communard Henri de Rochefort, she roamed around the city and adopted for the rest of her life Parisian modes of dress, cooking, language and literature. So enamoured was she of the romanticism of revolution that she ever after claimed as her birthday 14 July – the date of the storming of the Bastille in the French Revolution. Perhaps she never saw her birth certificate, which stated it to be the much less interesting 15 July. But she certainly revelled in the auspicious date, and later claimed: 'I have always thought that the fact that I was born on that day had some kind of influence over my life … it was women who gave the signal to spur on the crowd, and led to the final taking of that monument of tyranny, the Bastille, in Paris.'[17] She sympathised with the city, which had until quite recently been occupied by German troops in the Franco-Prussian War, and resented the German annexation of Alsace-Lorraine. Her antipathy towards Germany and desire for revenge on behalf of the French seems to have lasted until at least the First World War. The Paris Commune of 1871, in which Noémie's father had played a dominant role, and after which he was imprisoned, appealed to her sense of heroism and romance.[18] She also read a large number of French novels. All of this lent her an unusual glamour and sophistication when she returned to grimy Manchester.

She brought Paris fashions into the family, developed her singing – her voice was later noted as a rich contralto – and was adept at playing the piano, though she did not practise much. She displayed physical courage, according to Christabel thinking nothing of tearing down window curtains to put out a fire. When in 1878 her younger sister, Mary, was also sent to Paris to be educated she petitioned to be allowed to accompany her and settle her in. Her friend, Noémie, now married to a Swiss artist, Frédéric Dufaux, introduced Emmeline into exalted literary and artistic circles. She was particularly taken with Madame Edmond Adam, who presided over a glittering political circle.

Having hatched a plot with Noémie that they would both marry and live near each other in Paris, each presiding over their own salon of politicos and literati, she naively assumed that her father would pay the dowry demanded by the suitor her friend had organised for her. Sylvia relates that, to his credit, Robert 'flew into a passion and declared that he would not "sell" his daughter to any man'. Christabel adds that he disapproved of her marrying a foreigner and of living abroad.[19] The suitor withdrew, claiming that she had broken his heart and ruined his life. It was almost certainly a fortunate escape; she had not been in love with him, and when Emmeline met him again many years later, he was 'a dreadful creature', middle-aged and corpulent, who was rumoured to abuse his wife.[20]

Sylvia shows some understanding of Emmeline's point of view, however. Bearing in mind that a married middle-class woman could own no property or money effectively until 1882, unless it was tied up in a trust for her, Emmeline told her daughter that she remembered scenes between her parents when her mother presented the household bills. She regarded the dowry as a way of acquiring her own money and independence in the marriage and was angry that her doting father refused her. This was the first known quarrel between them, but it was not to be the last. And according to Sylvia, she long continued to advocate dowries and arranged marriages.

She did not mope for long, since as Christabel points out, she had just wanted 'a wider life … Her ardent nature moved her to desire to do some great thing, and yet little seemed possible in those times for a woman.' Her father's general indulgence and willingness to encourage her intellectual development may well have nurtured this sense of destiny.[21] However, she had failed to take advantage of the education offered in Paris, which might have equipped her for a career in the new areas that were opening up to young women, particularly in offices, shops, nursing and teaching. The usual route out of the parental home, an advantageous marriage, was not attractive to her; she later declared that the young men she met at this time were of no interest to her, and she felt uncomfortable in their company.[22] On the other hand, she was looking for an escape from the domesticity and expectations of Seedley Cottage and marriage seemed her only option.

So it was that when the great 'Doctor' turned his gaze upon her soon afterwards, she seized her opportunity. And when he promised that 'every struggling cause shall be ours' she saw in him the potential to fulfil her dreams. Indeed, Martin Pugh has surmised that to her he was a sort of English Henri Rochefort, prepared to sacrifice himself for his ideals. Through him she would achieve a political role and work on good causes; marriage was not for her 'a one-way ticket into domesticity'.[23] As it turned out, she could not have chosen better. Her vague ambitions were to be crystallized and more than fulfilled in their life together and in the thirty years of her widowhood.

Husband and Wife

At some time after his father's death in 1873, Richard and his mother had moved to 1 Drayton Terrace, Old Trafford, and this is where Richard and Emmeline began their married life six years later.[24] It was a very happy union, by almost all accounts; their children, their friends, and their political associates all seemed to agree. In a letter of 12 September 1957 to her own son, Richard Keir Pankhurst, on the occasion of his marriage, Sylvia wrote: 'To my mother my father was always the greatest man in the world and he was ever devoted in love with her.'[25] Any disagreements or ill-feeling were well concealed. There is just one, very vague reference in a letter in the Billington-Greig collection of 20 July 1956 from an anonymous 'J' who has clearly been asked about Richard Pankhurst:

> I do not think that I ever saw P, and what I remember about him only tributes to his generosity and expansiveness. I do not know whether I am or am not right in sensing a certain lack of harmony between him and Emmeline. Some thought of that kind is vaguely alive in me.[26]

While it is impossible to imagine a nineteen-year union with absolutely no disagreements or aggravations, if this is the strongest available signal of disharmony the balance of the evidence does indicate an unusually harmonious marriage. Sylvia cites as evidence that Richard rarely called his wife by her name, but addressed her with endearments, the most frequent of which appears to have been 'my lady'; perhaps it was a playful tease on her pretensions to make a name for herself as a great political hostess.[27] In 1938 Sylvia expands on this further:

> He was always her lover. I can see him, with the eye of memory, holding her at arm's-length and with a joyous admiration, to view, at her demand, some new or transformed dress – and she was cunning at transformations.[28]

Adela, their third daughter, adds 'My father ... deferred to her continually. He put her forward in everything and never cared to go anywhere without her.' This cut both ways: 'My mother, though she had obstinate prejudices, was of a most dependent disposition. She never learned to stand and act alone. She married young and my father was many years her senior; she adored him and adopted all his views.'[29]

Sylvia relates how Richard's sister, Bess, enjoined on Emmeline that she should keep him away from politics and focus him on his legal career, in which he could aspire to the judiciary.[30] But she misjudged the young woman, who indignantly rejected this idea, and pushed hard for him to stand for parliament. What Emmeline did not seem to appreciate was that, unpaid as they were, many MPs who did not have unearned income from land and investments were obliged to build up their wealth in the pursuit of another career. In many cases, that took the form of the Law.

And indeed, in the year after his marriage Richard's legal career seemed promising. In the spring and summer of 1880 he was engaged as a barrister in an important prosecution of the directors and officials of the Northern Counties of England Insurance Company Limited. He was acting for a director, Samuel Clegg. In the same year, he had the chance to act for Manchester Corporation in its prosecution of Edward Day for refusing to pay the costs of the fire brigade, which had extinguished a fire at his business on Market Street; the court found for the prosecution. It was a small beginning, but it seemed to signify the start of a lucrative career representing the Corporation, which would not go amiss for a growing family.[31]

Emmeline also became aware of her own intellectual shortcomings; it was perhaps disappointing to her that Richard was often engrossed in his books and would gently 'give her his unoccupied hand and proceed unpausing with his work'. In response to her request for help to fill in the gaps in her education, Richard prepared for her a course of serious reading. Her attempt to educate herself was short-lived, however, and she soon abandoned the dry fare on offer. Her husband was by no means put out by this, and instead encouraged her efforts at practical activism, notably on the Manchester Married Women's Property and Manchester National Society for Women's Suffrage committees. In these years, Richard was very much Emmeline's mentor, and he fully supported her activities outside the home. In her autobiography she makes this clear: 'Dr. Pankhurst did not desire that I should turn myself into a household machine. It was his firm belief that society as well as the family stands in need of women's services.'[32] Sylvia explains that in all the radical causes they espoused her father 'took the extreme view', and Emmeline 'with eager enthusiasm adopted him as her guide'.[33]

Sylvia is clear that neither partner envisaged a union set in a conventional home of domestic bliss. They both wanted a liaison that would be active in good causes, would challenge the status quo, and would achieve a better world. On the other hand, Adela's view, which was avowedly to defend her mother from the slurs she perceived in Sylvia's book, hints that Emmeline would have been a more devoted mother had she not been always trying to live up to the demanding ideals of her revered husband, even after his demise.[34]

Verna Coleman, in her biography of Adela, points out that their closeness may not have been an altogether good thing for their children:

> The complete devotion of the parents to one another created a barrier between them and their children. Richard was Emmeline's first concern; theirs was a partnership in all things. Fiercely ambitious for him, Emmeline, not yet a public figure, backed her husband to the hilt in his political ventures ...[35]

Indeed, Adela states: 'My mother, adopting with her naturally whole-hearted nature his views of duty, was ready to sacrifice herself and her children to my father's political career.'[36]

There was no noticeable excitement about the prospect of raising a family, yet nevertheless, whereas many middle-class couples were beginning to experiment with various forms of birth control, they had very little time to get to know each other before their first baby, Christabel, arrived nine months after their marriage, on 22 September 1880.

After the birth of their second child, Estelle Sylvia in 1882, possibly due to financial necessity the young family moved to live a semi-rural life for about three years with Emmeline's parents at Seedley Cottage in Salford, where Frank was born in 1884. Sylvia recalls this period in their lives as very happy, at least for the children; the household was lively and fun, with numerous aunts and uncles delighted to entertain them at Christmas and family occasions. This arrangement was meant to be temporary, but it was the stresses and strains of life with the in-laws that finally put an end to life in an extended family.[37]

CHAPTER 8

Parliamentary Candidate

It was one of Emmeline's fondest wishes that her husband should enter parliament and continue his work for a better world through the great offices of state to which she hoped he would rise. And indeed there were plenty of examples of bright men from non-aristocratic backgrounds who had found success in this endeavour. The Pankhursts were friends and allies of some of them, such as Jacob Bright and Henry Fawcett. It is often implied that it was more his wife's desire than his own that drove Richard to attempt to win the electoral race on three occasions, but there is no evidence that he did not share her vision, though he lacked her aggressive drive to win, clinging always more to principle than to party loyalty.

Sylvia's writings are the first port of call when examining Richard's candidacies, and although she was a small child during the first two, she was an assiduous researcher and among her papers in Amsterdam is a collection of news cuttings which she mined for the detail she was able to include in her account of events. There is a great deal of evidence in the local and national press, ranging from word-for-word accounts of his speeches, through leaders and editors' comments, to letters from the public, and from Richard himself.

A Manchester Seat, 1883

By the early 1880s, Richard Pankhurst was a well-established advocate of all manner of radical opinions. His support for the Congregational minister, Reverend Edwin Paxton Hood, in 1881 was symbolic of his position. Hood was famous in Manchester for his biography of Oliver Cromwell, which extolled the strong protestant, parliamentarian and temperance principles of a man who was considered by royalists of all stripes to be a regicide. But Hood had gone too far for some of his congregation, as well as for some of his fellow ministers, when he had preached sermons attacking the foreign policy of the Disraeli Tory government, in particular their war to establish British hegemony in Afghanistan. The upshot was that he was forced to leave his ministry and emigrate to the United States.

His fans organised a farewell lunch for him in the Memorial Hall on Albert Square in Manchester on 2 September 1881. The president was Abel Heywood, ex-mayor and locally renowned radical, and the chair of the organising committee was Richard Pankhurst. It was he who delivered the key speech, arguing that 'there never was a religion which was not political'.[1]

In a declaration of his beliefs shortly before this, Richard had concluded with a rallying cry:

> We have reached a great crisis in politics. Hitherto to be a member of Parliament has … been the exclusive property of the privileged and the rich. The power of privilege is fast passing away. The illicit and corrupt despotism of mere wealth in politics must be stamped out if public life is to be capable and pure … it is vital to the future of the nation that the career of the public service should be open, and that no organisation, no interest, no influence should be allowed to limit the liberty either of candidature or election.[2]

It was against this background of controversial demonstrations and utterances that Richard Pankhurst made his first attempt to enter parliament in 1883. A by-election was called in Manchester when the death of Conservative MP Hugh Birley left a vacancy in the three-seat constituency. Having in 1878, in the wake of the settlement in the Balkans reached at Berlin, published an address on 'The Future of Liberalism', Pankhurst was disappointed in the direction the party was taking and resigned his membership of the Manchester Liberal Association with the intention of standing as an independent candidate in the next general election.[3]

His programme, first issued shortly before the death of Birley on 7 September 1883, was characteristically extreme: the removal from the constitution of all non-representative elements (i.e. the House of Lords and the Monarchy); adult suffrage for both sexes; indemnity for MPs for their time and expenses; disestablishment and disendowment of the Church of England; the end of religious privilege or disability in public institutions and functions; free, compulsory elementary education; land nationalisation; Home Rule for Ireland; transfer of the power to declare war and make peace from the executive to the legislature; and the establishment of an international tribunal to settle disputes between nations. He foresaw a 'United States of Europe' and ultimately an 'International Commonwealth' of the world. True to the Liberal core belief in cheap government, he proposed an immediate saving of £30 million on expenditure, to be accompanied by tax cuts, by improving the land system and drastically reducing the navy and army.[4]

The By-election and the Liberal Association

The death of Birley and the resulting by-election led the mainstream Liberal committee to deliberate whether to put up a candidate against the Conservatives. Meanwhile Richard, on holiday in the Isle of Man, telegraphed his intention to stand as an independent.[5] It was a typical 'leap of faith' in that he was still building his legal career based in the north, and the question of how he was to support his burgeoning young family when in Westminster does not appear to have presented itself either to him or his wife. MPs were unpaid until 1911; it was partly for this reason that parliament was still dominated by the landed proprietors who could rely on rents to maintain them. Those who entered as lawyers or other professionals usually made sure they had built up their practice and amassed sufficient capital and investments to secure them.[6] Richard lacked either of these resources, but what he had in abundance was idealism and hope.

The *Observer* looked forward to a 'spirited' contest, noting that although his electoral banner bore the 'venerable legend' of Peace, Retrenchment and Reform, the classic watchwords of Gladstonian Liberalism, Pankhurst informed the electors that his interpretation of their meaning was by no means conventional. Reform meant universal suffrage, declaring that 'he who fears the voice of an enfranchised people fears justice and liberty'. Peace indicated putting the power of peace and war in the hands of a democratically elected parliament. The result of reform and peace would be Retrenchment; with national institutions and just laws the country could be run more cheaply for the reduced sum of £50 million. He also, with an eye to principle, but also to the Irish vote, declared support for 'a just measure of local self-government on federal lines' for Ireland. Reference to land law was equally vague, expressing an interest in state ownership, and the rights of those who worked it. He referred to a desire to expand trade, seeing the recently proposed Manchester Ship Canal as a means to that end. The state church and any civil disabilities on religious grounds should be abolished. The empire and foreign policy were not forgotten; he wanted to see India developed by government investment in railways and public works there, and this in the context of a movement towards self-government.[7]

Immediately after the funeral of Hugh Birley on 15 September 1883, the Liberals held a well-attended executive committee meeting at their Albert Square offices to decide how to proceed with the by-election, and it was overwhelmingly recommended not to put up a candidate. When it was proposed to the general committee, only about a dozen out of 600 attendees voted to support the candidacy of Richard Pankhurst.[8] This was partly out of regard for Mr Birley's memory, but more because the electoral system in Manchester that gave each voter two votes for three candidates would mean that, if successful, one Liberal would have to stand down at the upcoming general election in 1885. Due to the decision of the Liberal committee not to put up an official candidate, Richard would have a straight fight with the Tory candidate, William Houldsworth, who could boast a united Conservative party in his support.

Despite a rumour on 17 September that Pankhurst had given up his attempt, his supporters began to rally round and held a meeting at their committee rooms at 98 Albert Square, under the presidency of Abel Heywood junior, son of the alderman of the same name. A series of public meetings, starting with one in the Memorial Hall, got under way within a few days. Clearly rumours abounded at this time. *The Times* picked up one that the radical ex-mayor Abel Heywood senior, whom Richard himself had unsuccessfully put forward as a Liberal candidate in 1880, was about to throw his hat into the ring. Heywood himself scotched this rumour by declaring himself in support of Richard's candidacy.[9]

There was speculation about the Manchester Irish community, and whether they might themselves put up a candidate; as yet, they were not committed to Richard, despite his sympathies for the nationalist cause. Agreement was reached with their leaders, of whom every candidate had to take account, so large were their numbers in Manchester. Richard gained the support of the 'Home Rule party' by promising to back local self-government in Ireland on federal lines (inspired by the USA and Austria-Hungary), which entailed a parliament of native Irish sitting in Dublin. With this support under his belt, Richard could be more confident in his success. And to that was added the backing of prominent trade organisations, notably the Amalgamated Society of Engineers and the Amalgamated Society of Carpenters and Joiners.[10]

The packed meeting in the Memorial Hall in Manchester on 20 September was attended also by Emmeline and her sister, Mary. The chairman, Abel Heywood junior, drew an obvious comparison between Richard's candidature and that of Abel Heywood senior, who had stood in defiance of the Liberal establishment in 1859, particularly in his appeal to the working classes, and in the derision he encountered from the middle classes. The big difference was that now many more of the working classes could vote, as a result of the 1867 Second Reform Act, although reference was made to Houldsworth's encapsulation of the situation as one of David (himself) and Goliath (Pankhurst); it was the 'stripling' David who triumphed over the giant Goliath in the Bible story.

Richard began his speech with a resounding declaration of his support for Gladstone, and in particular his declared aims of 1880 to enfranchise the people and to pacify Ireland without coercion, by which the prime minister had 'won the deep-seated love of the English nation'. That he had not yet achieved these aims was due to 'landlordism', but Pankhurst was sure the Grand Old Man, as Gladstone was fondly nicknamed, would use his mandate to realise them in the end.

He went on to elaborate his other policies, and it is interesting to note that he extended his aim to consult native peoples, within a federal system and short of independence, to the Zulus of southern Africa 'so that Britain might work in conformity with the national heart even in that uncivilised land'. At this time, in a Britain where the Empire was largely an unchallenged given, this was an unconventional view, to say the least. He even criticised the Gladstone government for involving itself in a war to control Egypt, important because of the threat to the Suez Canal that a turbulent Egypt could engender.

He had given a lot of thought to India, Britain's 'jewel in the crown', and its economic development, but again went further than many by supporting the Ilbert Bill, which would have allowed Indian judges to preside over the trials of British colonists and traders in the Raj. In similar vein, during questions, he supported Welsh-speaking judges being appointed for Wales, as 'to send judges into Wales who could not speak Welsh was a piece of petty and vulgar domination'. The speech ended in rousing declarations, cleverly nailed to the very popular mast of Gladstonian tenets. It was this that won over many of the Liberals who voted for him, despite viewing him as an eccentric and excessive radical:

> His candidature was the candidature of the liberation of labour. (Hear, hear.) It was the candidature of principles which gave a fair chance to every Englishman. (Hear, hear.) … he asked them to contemplate the spectacle … of a grand old man – (cheers) – longing in his heart to secure for England liberty and justice, for Ireland peace without coercion. He saw him, toilsome but faithful, dragging up the steep hill of progress a hesitating Cabinet, a reluctant Parliament, a supine and sleeping people. – (Cheers.) By his candidature he called upon the electors of Manchester to stand fast and quit them like men – (cheers) – to stir up the Cabinet, to strengthen Parliament, to rouse the people, that they might again win the beneficent and irresistible victories of the people and peace.[11]

In response to questioning, Pankhurst declared his support for compulsory vaccination and his opposition to the 'local option', a proposal to allow local councils to close or limit pubs if enough of their ratepayers favoured it. He confessed that he had been teetotal for twenty-five years, but not any more, because he no longer thought it was the best thing for him. He wished everyone to have the same latitude of choice, and explained that 'he believed there was a legitimate use of intoxicating drink'. He did not agree with Sunday closing of public houses, advocating that other options might be offered, such as coffee houses, 'houses of innocent entertainment', art galleries and libraries.

The methods Richard adopted to fight the election were high-minded, but not realistic. To begin with, he declared his intention to stand before he had formed any organisation to support his campaign – he thought principles would be enough. The *Manchester Guardian* at first had thought it improbable that he would actually contest the vacancy because he was completely unprepared.[12] Further, he declared that he would observe the terms of the 1883 Corrupt Practices Act, which had not yet come into force. This meant that the amount he could spend was severely curtailed; his rival had no such limitations. While the latter could hire cabs to take voters to the poll, pay canvassers, and give 'treats' to supporters, Richard relied on his own charm and convictions to win over uncommitted voters. As a result, he spent only £541; the Conservative spent over ten times that amount.

His support was even further reduced because the Liberal Association had declared against him, and discouraged their members and Liberal voters in general from supporting him because he had declared his candidacy independently and was thus subverting Liberal discipline. Thomas Ashton, leading Liberal, powerful scion of the local manufacturing classes and High Sheriff of Lancashire, expressed the view of many that any success Richard might enjoy would encourage other Liberals to try their hand in the future. The argument induced Liberal newspapers, the *Manchester Guardian* and the *Manchester Examiner and Times* to attack him, and the *City Lantern* mocked him in a parody of a popular poem, Cowper's *John Gilpin's ride to Ware*:

> He's off! He's off, the renegade!
> Boss Beith [of the Liberal Association] did wildly cry.
> Th' High Sheriff [Ashton] rushed to bar the gate,
> Sly Pankhurst had flown by.[13]

Later after due reflection, the *Manchester Guardian* in its editorial comments adopted a far more cynical view of Richard's tactics, claiming with some apparent justification that he had acted deliberately to challenge the Liberal establishment in Manchester:

> Before the Liberal Association had decided not to contest the seat, before it had even met to consider the matter, Dr. Pankhurst had

announced his candidature and issued his address. The question before the Association was then not whether it should bring forward a Liberal candidate in opposition to the Conservative candidate, but whether it should bring one forward in opposition to the Conservative and Dr. Pankhurst combined … It was Dr. Pankhurst's policy to discourage the Liberal Association from bringing forward a candidate of their own by splitting their ranks. So far is Dr. Pankhurst from having come forward to undertake a task which the Association had abandoned that he himself was the principal obstacle to their undertaking it and had done all that in him lay to ensure that if they did their enterprise should prove a failure.[14]

Martin Pugh identifies a stumbling block hindering his success in the electoral system of Manchester. Since the Second Reform Act of 1867 the city had three MPs, but each voter had only two votes. The usual result was for two Liberals and one Conservative to be returned. The mainstream Liberals saw in Richard's candidacy a danger that, were he to be elected as a third Liberal MP for Manchester, when the next general election occurred the three Liberals would be competing against each other for votes. This could split the Liberal vote and was regarded as potentially very damaging for party unity. The *Spectator* likewise opined that, if Pankhurst were to succeed, this would put paid to the Liberal Caucus arrangement, by which certain powerful 'wire-pullers' controlled the seats.[15] As a result, 'An old radical' wrote in scathing terms of Pankhurst's temerity in standing, calling it treachery and 'a fatal stab at the very heart of all association', and concluding that: 'Every Liberal vote recorded for Dr. Pankhurst … will be a premium paid to disloyalty and desertion.'[16]

On the other hand, Richard did appeal to some notable Liberals. Pugh points out that Richard's programme only predated by two years the radical one of Joseph Chamberlain in Birmingham, which did attract support from other 'advanced Liberals'.[17] His committee, when eventually it was formed, was chaired by Abel Heywood junior, and supported by the latter's father, twice mayor of the city Abel Heywood senior.

It is either a mark of Richard's inexperience in conducting elections, or of his ability to manipulate the system, that it was only on 24 September that he saw fit to reassure Liberal voters that he would not stand against the existing two Liberal MPs when the general election eventually came, but would wait to see if the majority of the Liberal electors called upon him to do so in a representative test ballot. Despite the continuing official refusal of support, several staunch and articulate members of the Liberal party, among them Hugh Mason the MP for Ashton-under-Lyne, wrote to the local press stating that they would vote for Pankhurst as the Gladstonian candidate. Mason sent a generous £100 to his fund and hoped he might win because he had 'brains and pluck'. Richard, addressing the people of Hulme on 24 September, praised Mason as 'a jewel of public spirit'. Mason's vote of confidence was bolstered further by the backing of the poet and local celebrity, Ben Brierley.[18]

Support was sought wherever there was hope it might be forthcoming, sometimes with a disappointing result. The leader of the women's suffrage campaign, Lydia Becker, was approached by Emmeline. Now that they were colleagues on the Manchester committee she hoped that the strong-willed secretary would bring her influence to bear in Richard's support. Much to her fury and frustration, she was rebuffed with the objection that he was a 'firebrand', and the claim that in any case it did not matter who won the election as both candidates were in favour of women's votes.[19] Richard also claimed that the prominent Liberal radical and veteran MP, John Bright, had expressed support for him; this proved illusory when Bright allowed a letter to be read out in which he denied any support for Pankhurst.

The Irish nationalist leader, Michael Davitt, described by Sylvia as 'an old friend', praised him as 'a Radical of the right sort; an Englishman wise and just enough' to wish Ireland governed 'according to Irish ideas'. Even the great Irish national leader Charles Stuart Parnell declared his support and intended to speak for Pankhurst in Manchester, but was deterred by the resolute opposition of the Catholic Church led by local priest Canon Toole, who strongly objected to Richard's advocacy of secular education. Yet there were still hopes that the Irish vote could be won. On 26 September Richard met with a deputation from the Irish National Party in Manchester and promised (and confirmed in writing) that, if elected, he would vote to repeal the Prevention of Crimes and Coercion Acts, which prohibited constitutional agitation in Ireland. The Acts were a response to considerable unrest in the colony, including the high-profile assassination by a Fenian group known as the Invincibles in Dublin's Phoenix Park of Irish Chief Secretary Lord Frederick Cavendish, Prime Minister Gladstone's private secretary, and the Permanent Under Secretary, Thomas Henry Burke. Pankhurst stated, somewhat optimistically perhaps, that he believed Ireland 'in its present position and circumstances' could be governed 'without resort to coercion'.[20] Richard's support of Irish nationalists, indeed of Home Rule, was condemned in *The Times* as an extremely dangerous policy that could 'set Ireland once more in a blaze'.[21]

Discussion extended well beyond Manchester, and Sylvia quotes at length the view expressed in *The Spectator,* at that time a Liberal-leaning journal. It set the tone immediately:

> Dr. Pankhurst is substantially a French red of the humane type, and
> not an English Radical at all … His ideas are his ideas, not those of any
> section of the Liberal Party … We admit that Dr. Pankhurst is honestly
> dreaming; and therefore we prefer, if we are forced to make the choice,
> a sensible Tory to Dr. Pankhurst.[22]

Since it was to support from the relatively new voters of the working class that
the Pankhurst campaign looked, it is instructive to see what he chose to say to
the mainly working-class electors of Chorlton-on-Medlock in their town hall
on 22 September when they were crowded in 'to excess' to hear him, with an
overflow meeting outside. He focused on the theme of peace linked to prosperity,
with a reduction in the standing army and navy leading to cheaper government,
lower taxes and an end to the system by which finances were run to the benefit of
the landlord class. Alongside this would go international peace, so that trade and
industry would flourish. This was very popular with his audience, who accepted
his candidacy by a large majority.[23]

He worked hard to win over the voters, making innumerable speeches and
driving around in a carriage decked with yellow and green. A snapshot of his
speaking programme for evenings in one week in September is provided in the
Manchester Guardian: Tuesday, Miles Platting; Wednesday Cheetham, then
Strangeways; Thursday New Cross; Friday Ardwick then Bradford; Saturday
St Michael's. As usual the local papers recorded his speeches in detail and the
theme was consistent, though expressed in a variety of ways: 'A bad government,
a government of privilege, usurped the interests of the people, and made use of
the people for its own selfish ends.'[24] This would be elucidated by reference to his
programme, focusing especially on universal suffrage, land reform, free trade
and peace leading to lower taxation.

However, it is notable that addressing a meeting of more affluent citizens
in Hightown he focused instead on matters of interest in the Chamber of
Commerce: the proposed Manchester Ship Canal, of which he was in favour;
laws relating to bankruptcy and fraud; local administration of justice to speed
up the system; patent law; and agricultural banks in India. Clearly, he was not
above tailoring his remarks to suit the predilections of his hearers.[25] Some
were of the opinion that Mr Houldsworth, the Conservative candidate, was
making himself so objectionable to those of a liberal disposition that many
who had resolved not to vote were now changing their minds. Richard's
prospects seemed by the day before the nominations to be improving. It did
not do him any harm that Mr Houldsworth resorted to insult, calling him 'a
quack doctor'.[26]

On the eve of nomination day, Richard was very outspoken against the Liberal Association, even though he himself was a founder member and had written its constitution:

> The Association did not, in his opinion, represent true Liberal principles, or good government in any sense ... He expected to be put at the top of the poll by the love of the people ... and every Liberal who did not give him a vote on the polling day was a traitor and a false-hearted craven.[27]

The *Pall Mall Gazette*, quoted in the *Manchester Guardian*, warned ominously that if, by some stroke of luck, Pankhurst was successful this would prove a fatal example to Liberal Associations all over the country, with immense damage to the Liberal Party and its electoral power.[28] On the same day, Richard received deputations from the National Traders' League pressing for tax reductions for local traders, from the Good Templars hoping (in vain) to get him to support the local option of banning alcohol altogether, and from a group of Liberals asking him about his view of the Liberal Association and its operation, which resulted in some bridge building. In the evening he attended an 'uproarious' meeting in Ardwick, where no one got a proper hearing and eventually fights broke out. 'A resolution in favour of his candidature was then moved, seconded and supported by gentlemen, who by straining their voices could just make themselves heard a few yards from the platform.' The meeting was encouraged soon after to disperse by the lowering of the gas lighting, and Richard then moved on to a further meeting in Bradford-cum-Beswick, which was equally rowdy, but less violent, and which voted in his favour by a large majority.[29]

Nomination day dawned, 29 September 1883, and at 11.15 in the morning, an hour after the visit of the Conservative, Richard Pankhurst arrived at the Town Hall with his supporters. His proposers were Abel Heywood junior, chair of his committee, and Frederick William Roe Rycroft, who was appointed his agent a week later. The two candidates were obliged to pay between them £750 for official expenses; a very hefty sum that Pankhurst could probably ill afford.[30] On the same day, an appeal for funds was publicised in the press; the campaign had so far received only another £100 to add to Hugh Mason's donation.

There was also the encouraging news that two key Irish nationalist leaders, Charles Stuart Parnell and Michael Davitt, had pledged their support, and the latter 'recommended the Irishmen of Manchester to vote in favour of Dr Pankhurst' in a letter distributed at mass on 30 September. This seemed to promise the support of a sizeable section of Manchester voters, and an open-air meeting in Angel Meadow where many of Manchester's Irish population resided gave a strong demonstration of their backing.[31] The *Spectator* believed: 'If the body of the Liberals, the more extreme Radicals, and the bulk of the Irish finally declare for Dr. Pankhurst, he will have a heavy vote, and possibly a heavier one than Mr. Houldsworth ...'[32]

It was still a concern that many mainstream Liberals might abstain from voting, so on 2 October Richard's camp put a notice in the press that went further than previously to win them over: 'I undertake, if I should be one of Three or more Candidates at the next General Election, to abide by the Selecting Vote of the Representative Council of the Liberal Association.'[33] Meanwhile, the campaigning continued intensively with at least two meetings every evening. Following a successful one at the Athenaeum, a raucous encounter at the Longsight Mechanics Institution attended by 'a number of young men who had evidently gone with the intention of securing some amusement for themselves' heard that Houldsworth had booked all the cabs in the city and engaged 'a complete army of paid canvassers'. This was contrasted with Richard's methods, which were 'perfectly manly and pure'. But it did not all pass off peacefully. A motion in support of Pankhurst was repeatedly interrupted; disorder escalated until the rowdies were singing 'We won't go home till morning' and 'God Save the Queen'. Nevertheless, in the end the resolution was carried easily in his favour.[34]

That evening the Liberal Association Council was holding a further meeting to decide whether to respond to Richard's olive branch to abide by the selection ballot of the Liberal council in the next election, by withdrawing their objection to their supporters giving him their vote. At the same time the Pankhurst party held an open-air meeting of about 700 electors outside their windows on the steps of the Albert Memorial. Richard attended but did not speak 'owing to the state of his voice', and the peaceful meeting voted in his support. Despite this pressure, the Liberal Association was intransigent and opted 'by a very large majority' to hold to the policy of instructing their supporters to abstain in the election.[35]

It is a measure of his excitement and anticipation that the day before the ballot, Richard attended the Town Hall in person as the officials were sworn in ready for the poll. On election day itself, the voting was slow, and it seemed that many electors were less than enthused by either candidate, and that Liberals on the whole stayed away. Both candidates visited a number of the polling booths; disappointingly, there was no excitement at their appearance. Richard added the slogan 'Government of the nation by the nation for the nation' to his battle cries; for Houldsworth it was 'Our laws, our faith, our Empire, and our Queen'.[36] The largest number of voters to participate was in Manchester's poorest ward, St Michael's in Angel Meadow, where 'a considerable number of Irishmen' voted for Pankhurst, and he also received a lot of support in working-class New Cross, but very little in Cheetham and Bradford. Despite the provision of cabs and omnibuses, the turnout for Houldsworth was similarly disappointing, with cabs standing idle outside committee rooms and public houses, and in fact it was thought that some who availed themselves of his offer in fact voted in the secret ballot for Pankhurst.[37] The count in the Town Hall by thirty officials was attended by both candidates. As the polls closed at 4pm, the result was announced shortly after 7.30pm to a crowd of several thousand in Albert Square.[38]

Defeat

From a voters' list of 52,831 Pankhurst gained only 6,216 votes as against Houldsworth's 18,188. At the previous election in 1880 around 24,000 people had voted Liberal in Manchester; he had been repudiated by three-quarters of the potential Liberal electorate. His lack of paid canvassers and cabs to take voters to the poll probably took its toll on his poor showing.[39] But to judge by the copious volume of letters to the press, in addition to his defiance of the Association he had clearly alienated many by his extremist position. It may well be also that his stance in favour of Irish nationalists served only to annoy his fellow Englishmen, many of whom were hostile to Irish ambitions for self-government, seeing it as the first nail in the coffin of the British Empire.[40] This resounding defeat put an end to any hope that the Manchester Liberal party might adopt him in the next election; in future he would have to look elsewhere.[41]

So it was that in a 'defiant speech' to the faithful in his committee rooms he claimed he had achieved 'a moral and political triumph'. His condemnation of the Liberal Association was fulsome, blaming them for the sending of a Conservative to Westminster. He related how they had failed to support William Gladstone at a time when the leader was struggling to pass a Bill to enfranchise agricultural workers. He explained that he had left the Liberal Association because 'it was impossible for him to work as a free man in that Association'. His solution now was to set up a rival association for Liberals and Radicals, with its own independent newspaper because the 'so-called' Liberal press had been in the pocket of the Liberal Association. He declared himself a perpetual candidate and 'he was proud to know that he united in a policy of wisdom and prudence Irishmen and Mr. Gladstone's government' and added to that his policies on land. He concluded by enjoining on his supporters that they should be 'of good heart' as he was 'not depressed nor cast down ... for he should that night meditate on the candidature which he would commence in the morning, and he would not bring it to an end until the principles they knew and loved were victorious. (Loud cheers)'[42]

There were more blistering attacks on the Liberal Association on 11 October in a meeting of the campaign committee, but those who had voted for him were elevated to a high moral plane as they had 'maintained the political manhood of the city'. He issued a resounding challenge to Mancunians:

> Citizens of Manchester, wake from your supineness, be no longer overawed by irresponsible authority, prefer the agitation of progress to the fatal serenities of reaction, and above all, if you have no longer your old public spirit, at least feel the shame of your present abasement.[43]

Despite keeping his expenses to a minimum, which may have been as much enforced by his limited means as actuated by his principles, Richard found himself embarrassed financially after the election. Within a few days, his election committee was sending out appeals for donations, even to people who had not supported his candidacy.[44] His situation was much exacerbated by a boycott of his professional services by those who were offended and alarmed by his blatant extremism. And when immediately afterwards he won a case against the Manchester Corporation in the Lancaster Chancery Court, which had the effect of preventing the former from levying illegal tolls on small market traders, this may have occasioned further animosity towards him from some of the most powerful men in the corporation.[45]

Within the family too, the election defeat caused ructions. Robert Goulden had been Richard's campaign agent, but his association with the 'firebrand' caused him to lose money. He was forced to retire from business, and bitterly blamed his son-in-law's 'Socialism'. It must have been a very difficult situation, as Emmeline and Richard with their children were still living with her parents at Seedley Cottage. Worse, Emmeline, probably driven by financial necessity, chose this period to raise the question of a dowry, which she claimed her father had promised at the time of her marriage. Whatever the basis of this assertion, Robert had no truck with it now. Early in 1885, the young family left Seedley Cottage and moved to Monford Grove, 66 Carter Street, Greenheys, Old Trafford near Manchester.[46] Emmeline reportedly never spoke to her father again. She even cut off her mother until much later, when they were both widows. The root cause of this dislocation is a matter of debate; Patricia Romero suggests that Jill Craigie, who carried out considerable research into Emmeline's life, believed that they fell out over politics, and not the issue of the dowry.[47]

Richard and Emmeline took her sister, Mary Goulden, who supported their political views, with them to Old Trafford. They were also accompanied by their nursemaid, Susannah Jones, who was increasingly entrusted with spending the weekly household allowance, with which Emmeline was ill-equipped to deal, due to her impracticality and probably also a lack of interest. As Sylvia put it in 1935, 'the maid could stretch it farther than the mistress, who was apt to spend too much on the bonbons and to discover she had nothing left for the muttons'.[48] Both Mary and Susannah became integral to the well-being of the family and provided much-needed stability.

'War declared': the Radical Association

Despite his defeat, Richard was apparently not too downcast. His ideas had gained traction in some quarters and the result was the formation of the Manchester Radical Association, one of many such all over the country. Sylvia sees this as an early preparation for the advent of the Labour Party among the most 'left wing' of the Liberals. Indeed, Martin Pugh is of the opinion that: 'His misfortune was to seek election just in the period when the hey-day of Victorian Liberalism had passed, but slightly before Labour had emerged as a really popular force in the country.'

At a meeting in the John Dalton Street committee rooms on 8 October the process of establishing the new Radical Association was begun by about 100 people. Richard himself declined to sit on the committee that would prepare the rules, perhaps remembering that he had executed that commission for the now-reviled Liberal Association. It was widely feared that the new body was deliberately attempting to split the Liberals in Manchester permanently, especially since Richard had declared that he would stand again in the forthcoming general election.

The *Manchester Guardian* editorial for 9 October 1883 claimed to be at a loss to understand Richard Pankhurst's grievances against the Liberal Association, which were so great that he could not be reconciled. It intimated that he hoped to promote his own importance in the new body, rather than being a smaller fish in the big Liberal Association pond, and the editor warned that his stance set a dangerous precedent for political party organisation in general.[49]

In the event, as letters to the press demonstrated, most Liberals opted to remain in the larger body, working to change it from within, and fearful of splitting the Liberal vote and allowing a Conservative in.[50] This did not deter Richard from embarking on a speaking tour around the country's radical clubs putting forward his policies; he was in Plymouth on 14 November and Southwark on 5 December.[51] Perhaps the strain was telling; he had to excuse himself from attending a celebration of the Manchester Radical Association, which met on 29 December in Hulme to mark the opening of a new branch. He was suffering from 'a severe cold'.[52]

CHAPTER 9

London Adventure

The stress and excitement surrounding the Radical Association was soon superseded by preparations for the general election that would be declared in 1885. Richard's threat to stand in Manchester was not carried out, but he was sought as a Radical Liberal candidate by several constituencies in London. It is not clear how this came about; perhaps he had let it be known that such an offer would be welcome, since Emmeline was extremely ambitious for him to achieve the exalted position in the metropolis that she believed was his due, and indeed Richard was not apparently averse to the proposition, which would allow him to further his ideals in the legislature.[1]

Initially, he was approached by Lambeth as a radical to run alongside the moderate Liberal Sir James Lawrence.[2] He seems to have met with favour from the working men of the area at a meeting held in the Lambeth Baths, expressing his disgust at the way the Cabinet had dealt with the Lords' rejection of the Bill to enfranchise the agricultural workers. The Liberal government had used secret negotiations with the Conservatives, rather than open debate in the Commons, to push the Act through. It was believed that the redistribution of seats that accompanied the electoral change was engineered to compensate the Tories for an expected rise in Liberal votes from the newly enfranchised farm labourers.[3] 'They might as well shut up the House of Commons altogether and give over the Government to a handful of Peers plus the present Cabinet.'[4] The Lambeth offer came to nothing; perhaps Richard did not meet with the approval of the local Liberal Association Council.

As 1885 commenced, he was keeping his options open, being interviewed by various Manchester deputations, with a view to adoption as a candidate. He seemed to favour Hulme, but was beaten to it by Jacob Bright, despite his popularity in some quarters in this respectable working-class suburb. He must surely have been gratified by the compliments paid to him by one of his supporters in that constituency, who described him as

> Learned, clear minded, energetic, eloquent beyond most, and full of sympathy for the suffering millions, he is emphatically one of us, and I for one feel it to be a great disgrace to Manchester that he has been edged and manoeuvred from among us.

Richard was next reported to be considering Newton in north-east Manchester, but that too was a hope that dissipated.[5]

By 20 May he was putting himself forward for South Hackney in London, explaining his usual policies, yet modifying his hostile attitude to the local option on banning alcohol, and coming out against compulsory vaccination; these were minor aspects of his programme that he could afford to change to suit his audience. It was not enough; the general council of the South Hackney Liberal and Radical Association voted 164 to 64 to accept a rival candidate.[6]

The Seat at Rotherhithe

Soon another opportunity to enter parliament presented itself, in the form of a seat at Rotherhithe in the London borough of Southwark. On 10 July Pankhurst was selected out of three candidates to stand for the seat.[7] The news of his adoption as the Radical Liberal candidate for Rotherhithe was greeted with pleasure and congratulations by the societies that shared his opinions; notably the Liberation Society (for Church disestablishment) and the International Arbitration Association.[8] Much as she had done in Manchester two years before, Emmeline began lobbying among the women's movement in her husband's interest; she wrote fulsomely to Caroline Biggs of the London suffrage committee about the long service he had rendered to the women's cause, and of how he could continue to serve it in parliament.[9] Meanwhile, the great round of speeches and meetings began again, this time in London. A crowded public meeting in the Bermondsey Drill Hall now heard Pankhurst once more declare himself a Gladstonian. His programme was largely unchanged from 1883, and met with approval. At the end of September his Conservative opponent emerged; Colonel Hamilton JP.[10]

Richard was still called upon to support radical candidates in Manchester and on 2 October he addressed a meeting in Atherton in support of Caleb Wright, who was standing for Leigh. In this mining area, he focused particularly on the exploitation of coal reserves by the landowners without paying taxes on it and reminded 'the men of Lancashire' that they 'now had the opportunity of striking off their chains and making themselves free'. It went down well. The socialist overtones are clear, but Richard's actual declaration for that creed was still years in the future.[11]

Rotherhithe was never far from his thoughts, especially as the Conservatives had brought out a working-class candidate to challenge his claim on the workers' vote. *The Times* reported the publication of his programme, and noted in particular his advocacy of a graduated income tax, equalisation of death duties, church disestablishment, free education and a federal British Empire.[12] This represented some development of his policies since 1883, though the trajectory was familiar.

At this point, it was considered that Richard was going to win his seat. The old borough of Southwark was traditionally held by the Liberals, with only a blip in 1870. Now, as a result of the 1884 Redistribution Act, the constituency was divided into three divisions; Rotherhithe was one of these. Although it contained a park, its main feature was extensive docklands, connected especially with the Baltic trade. In contrast with Manchester in 1883, the Liberal Association was united behind Richard and it was believed that, with its 'advanced' leanings the constituency 'fit him like a glove'. The party 'rallied to him with wonderful enthusiasm', even though he came as a stranger. The *Manchester Guardian* believed that he had won over the association by his speech to them: 'Lancashire people know the platform power of Dr. Pankhurst. To the Rotherhithe folks it came somewhat in the nature of a revelation.' In competition with candidates who were 'of but moderate ability' he was 'an easy first'. Building on this good start, he was making 'troops of friends'.

The local papers gave good account of his public life, and 'excellent portraits have been given by way of bringing home his personality to the electors'. It was especially promising that he had won the support of upwards of 2,000 male temperance campaigners, demonstrating that his shift towards the local option was expedient, as well as perhaps a moral position. At a meeting of the Rotherhithe Free Church Gospel Temperance Society, held specifically to discuss this, he admitted that for twenty years he had opposed it, but believed that now the people had understood it and desired it, so that 'the measure was now ripe for being made into law'. The evening ended with edifying renditions of sacred works by the Free Church choir.[13]

Even Richard's appearance in support of the radical candidate for Camberwell did not appear to tarnish his reputation. This was the remarkable stepdaughter of John Stuart Mill, Helen Taylor, who as a woman was not legally eligible to stand, and who also chose to campaign in trousers![14] Indeed, it was a matter of comment generally that Richard included women in his team, and that they seemed to have 'almost as great an interest in the political contest as the doctor himself'. Note was especially made of his wife and the Misses Chafen and Chambers.[15]

Lincoln's Inn.

Richard Marsden
Pankhurst the barrister.
(Estelle Sylvia Pankhurst
Papers, 359, International
Institute of Social History,
Amsterdam)

The Manchester Brasenose Club. (Courtesy of Manchester Central Library)

St Luke's Church, Weaste, where Richard and Emmeline were married on 18 December 1879. (Courtesy of Rev. Jo Jarrett)

The Free Trade Hall. (Courtesy of Manchester Central Library)

Above left: J.S. Mill and Helen Taylor. (Courtesy of the LSE Women's Library)

Above right: Richard Pankhurst. (Estelle Sylvia Pankhurst Papers, 359, International Institute of Social History, Amsterdam)

Left: Ernest Jones.

Below left: Lydia Becker in 1873. (Courtesy of Oldham Archives)

Below right: Jane (Sophie) Quine/Craine. (Estelle Sylvia Pankhurst Papers, 359, International Institute of Social History, Amsterdam)

A young and confident Richard Pankhurst. (Courtesy of the LSE Women's Library)

Above left: Christabel Pankhurst. (Estelle Sylvia Pankhurst Papers, 359, International Institute of Social History, Amsterdam)

Above right: Sylvia Pankhurst. (Estelle Sylvia Pankhurst Papers, 359, International Institute of Social History, Amsterdam)

Above left: Adela Pankhurst. (Estelle Sylvia Pankhurst Papers, 359, International Institute of Social History, Amsterdam)

Above right: Harry Pankhurst. (Estelle Sylvia Pankhurst Papers, 359, International Institute of Social History, Amsterdam)

TO THE CITIZENS OF MANCHESTER.

Having now for many years taken an earnest part in promoting the cause of the people and of progress, I take leave, Fellow Citizens, to intimate to you that I propose at the next General Election, to present myself as an Independent Candidate for election as one of the representatives of this city, in Parliament.

A candidate for Parliament ought to hold firmly, as the foundation of his public life, the great, leading principles of free government and progressive politics.

These principles, though all of them important are, of course, not all of them equally capable of immediate application to practice.

I shall base my candidature on the maintainance of the following principles and lines of policy :—

NATIONAL POLITICS.

I. *Removal from the Constitution of all non-representative elements.*

Hereditary legislation is irrational, reactionary and hostile to liberty and progress.

In Government there ought to be no irresponsible, no irremovable power.

The representative principle must be accepted and applied without qualification or reserve.

The first work in this direction is obviously the abolition of the House of Lords, as an assembly of hereditary legislators.

II. *The establishment of the electoral and representative systems upon a truly Democratic basis.*

Hitherto we have heard much of democratic principles; we must now have democratic institutions.

To this end there must be instituted :—
(1) Universal adult suffrage.
(2) Equalisation of electoral power.
(3) Payment of —that is to say, indemnity to, Members of Parliament.

In one and the same nation there ought to be for all the adult members of the population, one and the same suffrage.

It is plain, too, that equal aggregates of voters should everywhere in the land be of equal electoral weight.

Ministers of State and Members of Parliament are equally entitled to indemnity for loss and expense incurred in the public service, and for precisely the same reasons.

III. *The Secularisation of all Political Institutions.*

This principle demands :—
(1) The disestablishment and disendowment of the State Churches.
(2) The abolition of oaths in connection with all political offices and positions.
(3) The cessation of all privilege or disability on the ground of religion in regard of all public institutions and public functions.

(4) The exclusion of all Ecclesiastic and Sectarian elements from public education in all its divisions.
(5) The establishment of a national system of primary instruction—secular, free, compulsory.

IV. *Nationalisation of the Land.*

At the root of privilege in this country lie the existing tenure and user of the land.

The policy under which the land is to be emancipated from its present political, social and economic thraldrom, involves the following propositions :—
(1) Land, being the gift of nature to all, its ultimate ownership is in society as a whole.
(2) Private property in land exists only by permission of society, which in right and duty, defines the limits of such property.
(3) The true and chief reason why society permits private property in land is, that it may be so used as to produce the greatest benefit to the entire community.

The ultimate ownership by the nation of the land, now as ever, the law of the land, must be turned from a barren theory into a fruitful fact.

National ownership of land is both consistent with, and promotive of, the productive cultivation and user of the land by individuals and bodies.

National ownership and individual right in land can be so accommodated, that the respective shares of the nation, and of the individual, in the production and value of the land, may be fairly adjusted and divided.

In land, it must be remembered, collective ownership is the old institution, individual ownership is the modern innovation.

V. *Grant to Ireland of a form of Local Self-Government, such as shall at the same time retain her in real union with Great Britain by means of a federal tie.*

The federative principle with its combination of local and central powers, furnishes the solution of the Irish question.

COUNTY AND CITY POLITICS.

The intimate relation and mutual dependence of local and central government, make it the duty of a parliamentary representative of the city, to keep constantly in mind the wants of the county and city.

In view of this duty the following lines of policy are indicated as, in the circumstances, just and expedient :—

I. *County Politics.*

The county needs for its efficient administration amongst other institutions the following :—
(1) Establishment of a really representative government.
(2) Provision for the local administration of justice.
(3) Utilisation on the largest scale of the water-ways.

II. *City Politics.*

The great business departments of the municipality only justify their existence by contributing to the good and economic government of the city.

The Markets, therefore, as one of such departments, should, as originally intended, be so managed as to derogate as little, and for as short a time as possible, from absolute freedom of trade.

The property should be cleared of charge.

The settled policy should be fair rents and free sale.

The government and administration of the municipality ought to be such as to enable the citizens to live, and consequently to sell so cheaply, as to attract customers from every quarter.

Much can and ought to be done by the municipality to improve the health and cheer the lives of the people.

They have not had their share of the public expenditure.

The social functions of municipal government have never yet been sufficiently considered.

INTERNATIONAL POLITICS.

The progress of civilisation has prepared the way for a great advance in the application of the principles of reason and justice to the conduct of nations towards each other, particularly in the following important directions :—

I. *Transfer from the Executive to the Legislature of the power of peace and war.*

This transfer, coupled with the vester in the legislature of the treaty-making power, would put an end to the dark and dangerous intrigues of secret diplomacy, and would at once lead to reduced armaments.

II. *International Tribunal.*

Permanent peace between nations is now a supreme international necessity.

Peace is the cardinal condition of international intercourse, inter-dependence, co-operation.

The time is ripe for the setting up among the nations of an International Tribunal. Appeal and submission to its powers may be at first optional, but must hereafter be compulsory.

The means are rapidly being provided for the institution of "The United States of Europe."

The establishment of an International Commonwealth is a not far distant possibility.

It is fit that one who appeals independently and directly to the people, should announce his candidature without the intervention of any Association.

I shall take the opportunity, Fellow Citizens, of from time to time, expounding and explaining to you in detail, the grounds on which I rest my claim to your suffrages.

We have reached a great crisis in politics.

Hitherto to be a Member of Parliament has, in most of the cities and districts of the country, been the exclusive property of the privileged and the rich.

The power of privilege is fast passing away.

The illicit and corrupting despotism of mere wealth in politics, must be stamped out, if public life is to be capable and pure.

With a civilisation so complicated and high as that of this country, it is vital to the future of the nation, that the career of the public service should be open; and that no organisation, no interest, no influence should be allowed to limit the liberty either of candidate, or of election.

For the people to freely choose from amongst candidates, candidates must be free to offer their services.

R. M. PANKHURST.

20th July, 1883.

P.S.—Those who approve of this candidature address : "Dr. PANKHURST'S Election Committee Room, 98, Albert Square, Manchester."

Campaign poster 1885. (Author's own copy)

Annie Besant.

Elizabeth Wolstenholme Elmy.

Alice Scatcherd (back row, 2nd from right) at the International Council of Women in Washington DC, March 1888. (Courtesy of the Huntington Library, San Merino, California)

Lorne House, 4 Buckingham
Crescent, Victoria Park.
(Courtesy of Maurice Barratt)

James Keir Hardie.

Leonard Hall.

Fred Brocklehurst.

Katherine Glasier.

Bruce Glasier.

Gorton Parliamentary Election, 1895.

Mr. HATCH'S RECORD.

Previous to 1886, UNKNOWN.

1889. Discovered CONTESTING GORTON. LOST.

DISAPPEARED for Several Years.

1892. Discovered contesting Gorton again. LOST AGAIN.

1893. Great COAL LOCK-OUT. Men, Women and Children STARVING. Councillor SUTTON writes HATCH for ASSISTANCE. Secretary writes:

"Hatch on the Continent, will attend to Miners' request in 3 months."

THREE MONTHS' STARVATION for the People. Councillor SUTTON writes again. NO REPLY. WAITING YET.

WHERE WAS HATCH?

Doubtless Studying BIMETALLISM as a means of FILLING EMPTY BELLIES.

1894-5. Period of GREAT DISTRESS in GORTON. PUZZLE: FIND HATCH.

June, 1895. Election commences————

HATCH DISCOVERED again CONTESTING GORTON

Commences work. District Visiting. 10 a.m.—Smiles, Shakes Hands, Praises Dogs. 1 p.m. LUNCHEON. 3 p.m. More Smiles, More Handshaking, Praises More Dogs. DINES. Attends Meetings. RECITES: "What I know about Socialism."

What Hatch does know about Socialism ◖

Each Day: Same Old Programme, Same Old Recitation.

STARTLING DISCOVERY Two Days before the Election: HATCH a BIMETALLIST!

ASK HIM WHAT IT MEANS!

WORKERS: Is this RECORD good enough for you? IF NOT, WALK to the POLL LIKE MEN, and

Put your X to PANKHURST

Printed and published by Mark Buckley, Ferns Street, Openshaw.

Above left: 1895 election poster. (Courtesy of Helen Pankhurst)

Above right: Richard Pankhurst late in life. (Estelle Sylvia Pankhurst Papers, 359, International Institute of Social History, Amsterdam)

ILP conference 1898 (Richard Pankhurst front row, 7th from right, Emmeline 2nd row, 5th from right). (Courtesy of Helen Pankhurst)

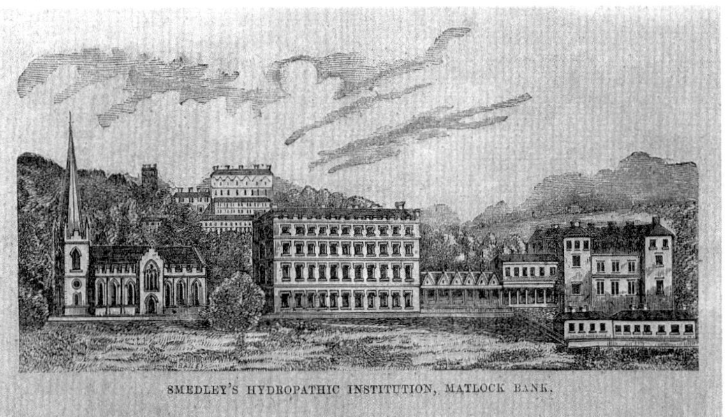

Smedley's Hydro, Matlock.

The Clarion Cyclists' Club House Ltd.

BANKERS' OR SECRETARY'S RECEIPT.

(To be signed by the Bankers or Secretary, and retained by Applicant.)

June 25 1897.

Received of R M Pankhurst the sum of One Pounds five Shillings, being the deposit of 2s. 6d. per Share upon an application for ten Shares of the Clarion Cyclist's Club House Limited

£1:5:0   For the Company

Clarion Club membership. (Estelle Sylvia Pankhurst Papers, 330, International Institute of Social History, Amsterdam)

Valewood Farm. (Courtesy of Allan Edgar)

Richard Pankhurst's grave in Brooklands cemetery. (Photograph taken by the author)

Emmeline in middle age. (Courtesy of LSE Women's Library)

Emmeline Pankhurst's grave in Brompton cemetery. (Photograph taken by the author)

Detail from Emmeline Pankhurst's grave. (Photograph taken by the author)

Malicious forces set themselves to stymie the Rotherhithe Liberal candidate. At their head was Colonel Hamilton himself, who began by referring to Pankhurst as a 'slum politician' because he went out and spoke to the poor in their own streets. He also tried to impugn his reputation as a successful barrister by claiming that he was content 'to take up those cases left alone by everyone else' and trying to convince the electors that Pankhurst was unknown in Manchester. He went on to attempt to persuade someone, preferably a workman, to travel from Manchester and denounce and discredit Richard. But no working man could be found who was prepared to do this.[16]

On 27 October a Manchester Liberal, Mr S. Capper, came to Rotherhithe to speak in *support* of Pankhurst. This was in response to a further and more serious attack by Colonel Hamilton. He had declared that Richard was that most abhorrent of creatures, an atheist. Mr Capper strongly denied this, citing the word of the widow of Paxton Hood, the Manchester minister who had written a favourable biography of that protestant Christian hero in the industrial north, Oliver Cromwell. This defence was reiterated by other Mancunians, notably Jacob Bright, MP for Manchester.[17]

Richard himself tried to divert attention to the important issues of his programme, proclaiming that 'nothing would induce him to descend from the height of his politics into the quagmire and swamp of mean and miserable personalities'.[18] He rehearsed again his policies in relation to the working man in Southwark Park on 7 November, and ended with a resounding declaration of support for William Gladstone and his campaign to win his seat in Scotland.[19] At this time, the religious smear perhaps seemed to him minor, and easily dismissed. Unfortunately it took on a life of its own. Hamilton exhibited no scruples, even, it was later claimed in the Court of Queen's Bench, boasting to some questioners: 'I do not care a snap of the fingers whether it is true or not: it will give me more votes than if I had all the Irish vote!'[20] Within a few days the slur was in the local press and handbills were being distributed at church doors and placarded all over Rotherhithe.[21]

Despite his consistent denials of having said anything that could be construed as an avowal of atheism, the local reaction was unpleasant. Stones were thrown at Richard, his hat was knocked off, there was blood on his face; the London crowds did not have the same deference for him that he was used to in Manchester. He tried to make light of the matter, and insisted that the most important thing was not winning but achieving progress. Emmeline too was pelted with market refuse, and her reaction was very different. She was mortified and furious, and feared he might lose the election, which she considered would be a disaster. She insisted that they go to church together to prove the detractors wrong: '*I* understand these people, *I* know what to do; you have always got your head in the clouds!'[22]

On the evening of 19 November he addressed a sympathetic audience at the Alexandra Temperance Hall. Buoyed up, he commented: 'I take it I am succeeding because of the abuse that is hurled against me.' He then launched into bitter invective in response to an attack by the Tory Lord Randolph Churchill, accusing him of being without honour:

> Whatever his title may be, he has behaved to me like a low, vulgar fellow … When he pours forth his foul Billingsgate against me, I am in good company. There is no man whom he has not abused … I take leave to say that Lord Randolph Churchill has done more to degrade Parliament and English public life than any man now living in England.[23]

And so it went on, relating how Churchill had similarly abused the Grand Old Man, William Gladstone, himself. The rant is remarkable, in that Richard seems to have really lost his temper for a while, but it must have made good entertainment for the crowd, who joined in with cheers, hooting, and some bright spark who opined that Churchill was 'Darwin's missing link'. Pankhurst's supporters on 21 November were so numerous and enthusiastic that they took the horse out of his brougham and pulled it themselves to his meeting in the Keeton's Road Radical Club. The following day they were busy pulling down the defamatory posters that Hamilton supporters had put up around the area.[24]

By the time of the nominations on 24 November the Conservative working-class candidate had dropped out and the race continued between Hamilton and a now hoarse Pankhurst.[25] Harking back to the defamation of his character by opponents, he became passionate in defending his own probity on 26 November:

> I have been a fighting public man. I have stood for my principles in dark days and in bright days. Everything I have done is open – all my public life lies open as the day. I say *all* my public life, and by my public character will I walk, and I shall not be led away by any kind of sinister suggestion or mean allusions, or personal invectives of any kind. My principles are those by which I live; they are principles which will make this country … powerful and happy. I will not abandon the noble aid I have from my principles and descend into the surging gulf of mean and slanderous personalities.[26]

There was bad news, however, as the Irish vote on which he was counting suddenly fell away when Charles Stuart Parnell, the nationalist leader, in the hope of concessions declared in support of Lord Salisbury and the Conservatives.

This change of tactic was one factor in the national Conservative victory that ensued; even in traditionally Liberal Manchester five of the six seats were won by Tories. In Rotherhithe, Colonel Hamilton was returned and the *South London Press* on 28 November 1885 claimed that the Irish defection explained this result.[27] There may have been some comfort in the relative closeness of the poll. Out of 8,455 electors, Hamilton got 3,327 votes, and Pankhurst 2,800.[28] His expenses amounted to £600; a heavy burden as £597 of it was borne by him personally.[29] It was probably at least a small comfort that the Rotherhithe Liberal and Radical Association presented to Richard an address, beautifully written and bound, which he kept in his personal papers.[30] They praised his eloquence, knowledge and personal character, and noted that: 'Your persistent refusal throughout the contest, under circumstances of the greatest provocation, to make use of, or reply to personalities obtained our heartiest approval and warmest sympathy ...' After expressing a belief that he would soon enter the Commons, they did not neglect to mention the support of Mrs Pankhurst and her 'noble spirit of wifely devotion and self-denying patriotism'.

It might have been wise to leave matters there, and allow the atheism charge to fade from popular memory, but Richard's principles got the better of him and he resolved to pursue an action at law against all those who had thus slandered him, beginning with Colonel Hamilton. Part of his reasoning was that he had lost the election in large part due to the rumour, now made public, that he had said in Manchester Town Hall, 'If there be a God I defy him, and if there be a Devil I am in a position to defy him too.'[31] There was also a broader motive: he wished to bring a test case to the new Newspaper Libel and Registration Act, to see if it could check the flood of slander and libel encountered by radical candidates.[32]

By 11 December the *Manchester Guardian* was citing a longer version of the atheism charge, which claimed that he had 'denied the existence of God and publicly defied God and the Devil'. Such beliefs would have rendered Richard ineligible to take the usual parliamentary oath of allegiance, and also would tar him as a blasphemer.[33] It probably did not help his cause that on 30 January 1886 he was a chief speaker at a radical meeting in Oldham at which the other most prominent participant was Charles Bradlaugh MP, notorious for his refusal as an atheist to take the oath of allegiance in parliament.[34]

Not content with pursuing his opponent, Richard also launched a case in Manchester Assizes against Stephen Chesters Thompson, an Ardwick brewer who was also a city councillor, and who had been the originator of the atheism claim. Pankhurst alleged that Thompson had slandered him in Chorlton Town Hall at a meeting in support of the Conservative candidate there, Arthur Balfour. It was explicitly stated that Richard's purpose in pursuing the case was 'not to recover damages, but that he might place himself right in the eyes, not only of his fellow-townsmen, but of his political and private friends ...' He asserted firmly that he had never made any public statement of his religious beliefs, despite questions during election campaigns asking him to do so, and added that in Rotherhithe 'he had constantly to assert that he was not an Atheist'.

The subtle and carefully reasoned answers that Richard gave as to his actual beliefs, which can be summarised as constituting an acceptance of the historical person of Jesus Christ as the true foundation of Christianity, seemed to a very hostile Justice Grantham not to be a denial of atheism, but rather a denial of 'the basis of the Christian faith and doctrine'. Agreeing that he had sometimes discussed religion, and describing himself as 'one of those who are called Agnostics, like Professor Huxley and Mr. Balfour', he asserted that he had always held the view that 'those things were beyond human comprehension'. He stated that he fully respected the religious views of others. However, his attitude may nevertheless have offended the devout. He allowed that at 'Carnarvon', whilst attending an arbitration, he may have referred to the Holy Spirit as 'the foggy member of the Trinity' whom he would like to cross-examine in the witness box. He contended that this was in the course of a lively and witty debate. The judge was not impressed and in effect found against Pankhurst and said Thompson had no case to answer.[35]

A further legal failure followed two days later when Richard attempted to prosecute the owner of the Tory-leaning *Manchester Courier*, Thomas Sowler, for his publication of the libel. Sowler denied any malice on his own part; indeed, he claimed he had not known about the report until he heard from Pankhurst that he was starting a libel action. Sowler claimed that, had Richard written to the paper to challenge the report, he would have published his letter; the same Justice Grantham picked up on this and directed the jury, who then found for the defendant, Sowler.[36]

Richard's loyal wife now took up the cudgels on his behalf, in what seems to have been her first public defiance of the law. She wrote to Justice Grantham in the strongest terms, including: 'It is to be regretted that there should be found on the English Bench a judge who will lend his aid to a disreputable section of the Tory Party in doing their dirty work; but for what other reason were you ever placed where you are?' She declared herself ready to go to prison for contempt of court, but the letter was simply ignored.[37] It is not known what her spouse thought of this sally on his behalf; her obvious fury suggests that she was not to be diverted from this course, whatever his fears might have been as to its consequences.

Even now, after what must have been vast expenditure, Richard did not give up and in June gave notice of further actions he was bringing against Thompson and Sowler in divisional courts in London.[38] Not only that, he also launched another action for libel against James Wighton, the Southwark printer who had produced the placards for Hamilton, but this action ended inconclusively when the defendant died.[39]

Richard's application to appeal against Justice Grantham's decisions was granted in Queen's Bench in December by Baron Huddleston and Justice Manisty. They concurred that the earlier hearings had been biased, and Justice Grantham was strongly rebuked for his summing up. Seeing the way matters were going, Chesters Thompson requested a settlement out of court, offering an apology and 40s plus costs. This was nothing like enough to cover Richard's expenses, but he accepted it because it proved his case. The apology was rescinded by Thompson in the press as soon as it was all settled.

Meanwhile, the *Manchester Courier* appeal began on 26 January 1887. Justice Hawkins had no sympathy for Pankhurst, yet the jury whom he directed to find against him were divided and eventually had to be discharged without a decision. The case was dropped with an agreement that the newspaper would publish an admission that the libel was false, and apologise for printing it.[40]

Two months later the final case, against Hamilton, was heard by Justice Grove. After much obfuscation by Hamilton, and eventually a retraction (which he afterwards denied in the press), the jury found in favour of Pankhurst. But again it was a pyrrhic victory, as he was granted only a miserly £60 in damages. Nevertheless, as Richard had hoped, these cases heard in Queen's Bench did apparently help to stem the 'torrent of libel and slander' against radical candidates.

The costs, financial and emotional, of pursuing all this litigation must have been huge. There was nothing left in the tanks by the end, and Richard responded to the calling of a further general election in 1886 by limiting himself to supporting other candidates, notably a pro-Irish Home Rule candidate, Frederic Harrison, for the University of London seat.[41]

In March 1891 Rotherhithe again adopted him as their candidate in the next election, which turned out to be in July the following year. However, according to *The Times,* a newspaper not noted for its liberalism, Colonel Hamilton had worked hard and won over many constituents of all stripes; his successor as the Conservative candidate needed to gain their confidence, but 'in Dr. Pankhurst he has not a formidable opponent'. It seems likely that the reportedly discreditable behaviour of the Pankhursts and other members of the Women's Franchise League over the Rollit Bill on 26 April 1892 may have deterred the Rotherhithe committee from adopting Richard.[42] It would appear that on this occasion discretion was the better part of valour and Richard did not in the end stand.

The Move to London and Legal Practice 1886–93

Meanwhile at some point in 1886, in the midst of all the litigation, the Pankhursts had moved to London. Emmeline had long expressed a strong desire to move to the capital so that Richard could develop his political career, and also in the meantime extend his legal work. Indeed he rented London chambers, though in fact most of his work continued to be based in Manchester, and he was forced to commute by rail, sometimes accompanied by his wife, but often alone. It was a stressful way of life, exacerbated by family and financial pressures. His letters from Manchester, quoted by Christabel in *Unshackled*, reflect his loneliness. He missed his wife; even after nine years of marriage, he wrote: 'You know how I love you and want to cherish your life. How splendid you were on Saturday – in all that unconscious loveliness! Dear heart, I hold you to mine!' He was also ever hopeful: 'We ought to feel that we are going through a preparing trial. So much is going on, in which we ought to have a part.' And in another letter: 'The time will come when more earnestness in politics will be vital to the State.' Throughout it all his philosophy remained constant: 'For nearly thirty years, day in, day out, in agonies and waiting, I have held to two principles – keep down private interests; work for great public ends.'

The conventional middle-class Victorian father's first priority was to earn a living to keep his family. For Richard Pankhurst this was to be achieved through his legal practice, both in Manchester and in London. It is hard to estimate how successful he was, but the impressive achievements of his early years as a student did not result in the sort of promotions he might have expected. He did not take silk or rise to the judiciary. While he seems to have pursued a steady career in litigation, towards the end of his life it was generally not impressive or high profile. The consensus at the time seems to have been that his radicalism prevented the offer of potentially lucrative briefs, especially when he joined the socialists in the 1890s. It also meant that he was prepared to act for those with whose causes he was in sympathy, while often not being paid the amount that would normally be expected. As Richard's political career became increasingly radical, the legal work that brought in good fees from establishment figures reportedly began to decline.

Besides exhausting and time-wasting commutes to Manchester, however, he frequented the Outer Temple Legal Club and established a practice in London at 222–225 The Strand, moving in 1893 to 5 New Square.[43] His London profile was further raised by attendance at the recently inaugurated Selden Society at Lincoln's Inn. It had been set up in 1885 to advance the study of the history of English law, especially through the publication of important works in legal history, beginning with the Pleas of the Crown from the medieval Eyre Rolls; this was right up Richard Pankhurst's street![44]

From The Strand he accepted the brief for a high-profile arbitration case before Mr Anderson QC in his chambers in Chancery Lane. Pankhurst and a Mr Smith represented the plaintiff, Manchester photographer Lachlan McLachlan, on 11 January 1886 putting the initial case for his client. It concerned rights over a giant photograph, 17ft by 10ft 6in, of 'The Royal Family at Windsor', which the plaintiff had prepared. He was suing William Agnew and sons, represented by William Agnew MP, Sir Joseph Heron, the Manchester town clerk, Mr Alderman King of the Manchester Corporation, and printer George Falkner for breach of copyright, claiming the vast sum of £30,000.[45] This complex case continued from January to the final publication of a decision on 9 August. It must have made a useful contribution to the Pankhurst family finances.

Richard was not always present at the hearing and on some occasions the plaintiff was represented only by Mr Smith. It is reasonable to assume that this was because Pankhurst was engaged in other legal matters, including his own litigation over the Rotherhithe election slanders, but also other cases in both Manchester and London. In the former he was chosen to represent the Corporation in serious and prolonged litigation with its own auditors, who had accused the Health Department of fraud. Alongside his colleague Mr. Cobbett, Richard triumphed after appearances in the Court of Queen's Bench, as the auditors' case fell apart and the worst that could be said was that there had been 'imperfect bookkeeping'.[46]

Pankhurst's appearances for the Manchester Corporation were more frequent in the later 1880s, dealing with technical matters such as sewage treatment, smoke abatement, gas nuisances and sanitary matters.[47] In June 1888 in the Court of Queen's Bench he defended Caminada, chief of the city detective department, and Mayor John Harwood, against the owner of the Victoria Hotel who was suing them for trespass, false imprisonment and assault, they claimed because he was in rent arrears.[48]

However, he did not always take the Corporation's brief; in September he represented the Barton, Eccles, Winton and Monton Board of Health in opposition to Manchester Corporation's plans to borrow a large sum to build sewage works at Davyhulme, which was outside the city boundaries. Those areas affected outside the city boundaries would not be included in the sewage scheme; they were the responsibility of the county of Lancashire. The impact in the city would be to clean up the River Irwell, at that time the chief conduit of the sewage. There would be an overflow into the new Manchester Ship Canal, which was not yet complete. It became clear that the other authorities wanted to be included in the Manchester scheme. As it stood, it was not sufficiently large to include them all. It was claimed that they had offered to pay for a bigger system, but had been refused unless they agreed to incorporation into the city.[49]

Richard did not neglect his role as a campaigning lawyer. On 23 August 1889 he published in the *Manchester Guardian* his argument for a proper, accessible criminal court of appeal, parallel to the civil appeal court. Explaining the history of earlier such attempts, he justified his call by explaining how the criminal law now included matters that had earlier been outside its scope, how there was more understanding that criminal acts were often the result of society's institutions and influences, and how there was now much more desire for certainty of guilt, especially where the death penalty was invoked.[50]

In London he was not afraid to challenge a judge. As defence counsel for one of a group accused of causing 'riotous proceedings' in Bermondsey Town Hall, Pankhurst took the judge of the London County Sessions to task for pre-empting the defence evidence, by presuming in effect to sum up in the middle of the trial. And he was not backing down:

> Dr. Pankhurst again intervening, the Judge said he would be heard and that the learned counsel was adopting an unusual mode of procedure. Dr. Pankhurst said he was only doing that which was done by all counsel in every Court in her Majesty's kingdom. He was no party to any arrangement [to prevent the judge from getting away quickly for another commitment], and objected to so many speeches from the Bench as irritating and interfering with the proceedings …
>
> The Judge. – Really, Dr. Pankhurst, I wish to treat you with every courtesy.
>
> Dr. Pankhurst. – And I desire to treat your Lordship with as much courtesy as under the circumstances I am able to do. (Laughter.)
>
> The Judge. – That remark is not called for. I have said nothing to justify it.
>
> Dr. Pankhurst. – Well, the fact is that I am not accustomed to so many speeches from the Bench during the progress of a case. It is calculated to disconcert one.
>
> The Judge. – Pardon me; I have made fewer remarks than most Judges do.
>
> Dr. Pankhurst. – I need not contradict you; the question is one of common knowledge to those acquainted with the proceedings of the Court. (Laughter.)[51]

The suggestion has been made that Richard's sarcastic approach in court sometimes redounded unfavourably on his case. Here we can see that propensity on display as he refused to defer to the dignity of the Judge. Yet it was not necessarily bad for the defence; after various adjournments, when the case was decided under a different judge Richard's client was found not guilty by the jury.[52]

Back in Lancashire, there were still lucrative briefs to be had; May 1890 saw the hearing in the Chancery Court of Lancashire of a case about fraud in the Salford Gas Department, in which Richard defended the latter.[53] He travelled back for other cases, such as applying for a licence for a new palace of varieties in Manchester, and acted for Barton, Eccles, Winton and Monton in the application of Eccles to be allowed municipal borough status. In this latter case he took the opportunity to explain the history of the area, not forgetting the origins of 'that remarkable edible' the Eccles cake in his efforts to prove Eccles worthy of incorporation.[54]

Briefs continued from Manchester corporation too; on 7 May 1891 the case was started in the police court against Hardman and Co., a Newton Heath chemical manufacturer being prosecuted by the corporation for pollution that was causing illness in local people. Pankhurst represented the corporation. In this case, a solution satisfactory to all parties was reached as the company made effective modifications to their practice that resulted in the safe disposal of the effluent.[55] At the same time, Richard was representing the corporation in an arbitration at the assize courts with regard to compensation offered to owners and tenants of properties as part of a council improvement scheme in Ancoats, Manchester.[56]

Corporation work continued to flow in the following year, when Richard was one of the counsel in an action against pollution by the Crumpsall chemical works of Levinstein and Co. It was claimed that local people were suffering from terrible smells and pollution that caused illness. In the event, the jury found against the company.[57]

Sewage disposal was a perennial headache for the Manchester Corporation, and in September 1892 a case arose over their attempt to purchase an estate at Rampton in Nottinghamshire for this purpose. Pankhurst represented the corporation in the hearing, explaining that the waste now amounted to 20,000 tons a year, which was set to increase as the city continued to grow. Naturally, the locals in Rampton objected at what they feared would be smelly and disease-ridden 'manure' being put on their land.[58] And it was not only Manchester that encountered this problem; Bury too was taken to court and, despite Richard Pankhurst's best endeavours to defend them, was fined a total of £50 plus costs for dumping liquid sewage in rivers.[59] The search for disposal sites was ongoing for Manchester, and in 1893 Pankhurst represented them in an enquiry as to the borrowing of £200,000 for the purchase of Chat Moss and the construction there of a sewage plant. In all such cases, he pointed to the example of Carrington

Moss, where the land had benefited by the application of treated sewage as manure.[60]

Yet alongside his mounting reputation as legal brief for the council, Richard continued to take on all manner of cases, some of which cannot have produced much income, but every little helped to meet his heavy household expenses. One example is his representation in the magistrates court of John Stott of the Greyhound Inn, Flixton, for the renewal of his licence. Despite some difficulty, due to May Stott, presumably some relation, being found drunk on the premises, the licence was granted.[61]

Money

Emmeline was probably well aware that Richard's professional income was not equal to the sort of life she wanted in London. On three occasions she decided to start her own retail business, namely Emerson and Company, twice in London and once in Manchester. Sylvia attributes this to her desire to have an independent income, but also to support the family and free Richard from his legal career so that he could concentrate on 'political efforts for the commonweal'.[62]

Even before the family moved to London, Emmeline stocked the first shop at 165 Hampstead Road with fancy goods, subliminally influenced by the ideas of William Morris. However, the business was at the wrong end of Hampstead Road and there were 'squalid market stalls' in front of it. It was a financial failure. Much of the stock ended up in the family home and was used for Christmas presents. The fact that Emmeline seems to have undertaken this and further incarnations of Emersons with equal failure, but with no demur from her unworldly spouse, is perhaps the most remarkable aspect of this adventure. Indeed, when she wrote to him about a worrying lack of customers, 'he merely reassured her that all would be well'.[63] It demonstrated that he was apparently unencumbered by the usual middle class paterfamilias's sense of the humiliation of a wife in trade.

That there was a long lease on the shop serves to demonstrate the lack of financial sense of the Pankhurst couple; with the failure of the business and also the tragic death of their young son, Frank, the family moved out, though the lease still had time to run and the premises were hard to let and often empty.[64] In 1888, nothing daunted, Emmeline not only rented a house in expensive Russell Square, but also re-established Emersons in Berners Street, soon thereafter moving to Regent Street in premises that were way beyond the Pankhursts' means. The hope that a more prestigious situation for the enterprise would turn it around proved vain and it floundered on, furnishing instead the Pankhursts' new home in fashionable style.

The house at 8 Russell Square was planned to allow Emmeline to establish a political salon to further her husband's political career. She initially argued that part of the large premises could be let to a doctor, but soon abandoned that idea. Its double drawing room was used for at homes and conferences. The splendid stock from Emersons created a tasteful setting; Chinese tea pots, Japanese embroidery and rugs from Turkey impressed the radical visitors. Emmeline, wearing elegant dresses she made for herself, was a charming and attractive hostess, who occasionally could be persuaded to play the piano and sing in her rich contralto. Richard, though himself reputedly tone deaf, took pleasure in his wife's singing; he often requested *The Bailiff's Daughter of Islington*, which had been a favourite with his father, Henry Francis.[65] A song about lovers divided by class, it ends with a triumphant reunion, and must have appealed to Richard's own romantic experience:

> Depart sorrow and welcome joy,
> Many thousand times and more,
> For now I have my own true love
> Whom I thought I would see no more.

Meanwhile, it appears that Richard was oblivious to all this expense. Perhaps he had some awareness that theirs was very much a second-class salon. Just around the corner, the famous novelist Mrs Humphrey Ward had held court for her relative Matthew Arnold, who brought in his train the Asquiths, the Tennants and the Huxleys, and the much sought-after American writer Henry James. By contrast, Emmeline was merely the wife of a provincial lawyer with neither wealth nor breeding. Rebecca West, though as a young journalist highly admiring of Emmeline, admitted that: 'A naive and ludicrous parody it must have seemed to those who really knew the world, or the real social functions of power, where great ladies shining with diamonds received at the head of wide staircases under magnificent chandeliers.'[66]

However, it seems highly unlikely that even a salon of that ilk would have impressed the high-minded Richard. When not supporting his dazzling spouse, sequestered in his library, 'its walls almost entirely lined with the Doctor's books', he was engrossed in his work. It may not have been important to Emmeline either to compete with the likes of Mrs Ward. As she had hoped, the Pankhursts were now able to host all the advanced thinkers of the day. Socialists, anarchists, free thinkers and humanitarians were all welcomed. William Morris, the Arts and Crafts designer who founded the Socialist League, and Malatesta, an Italian anarchist refugee, rubbed shoulders with William Lloyd Garrison, son of the advocate of the abolition of slavery, Peter Kropotkin, a Russian political refugee, and Dadabhai Naoroji, later the first Indian MP at Westminster.[67] Frequently present were Hodgson Pratt, a friend of Richard and a well-known worker for international peace, and James Bryce, British ambassador to the United States. Antoinette Sterling, an American contralto famous for singing 'The Lost Chord' and for not wearing corsets, was a visitor. Also from the US was the anti-slavery and women's suffrage campaigner Elizabeth Cady Stanton, whose daughter, Harriet, became close to the family.[68] Nearer to home, Manchester couple Jacob Bright MP and his wife Ursula were good friends, frequent visitors, and colleagues in the battle for women's rights. A contemporary of Richard, Ursula took Emmeline under her wing with 'an almost maternal love'.[69] The frequent presence of an exclusively francophone Henri Rochefort offered Richard the chance to converse in French 'with punctilious exactitude, his love of the precise word causing a frequent recourse to the dictionary'. So impressed was Emmeline, that she decided that her husband must have some French blood, so different was he from the usual Englishman; one of his forbears was a Dore, and now she recast this as Doré.[70]

This predilection to rewrite facts in a way that suited her world view has perhaps already been observed in her claim that she was born on Bastille Day. It may be the reason why in the censuses of 1881 and 1891 Richard's age increases by only nine and seven years respectively. By the time of the latter, he was being recorded as only 51, whereas in reality he was at least 56. It is not known who completed the census returns, but it was clearly Emmeline who dominated in family matters – even to the extent that Richard avoided the traditional male role of carving the joint by exclaiming: 'I am a helpless creature!' By the time of his death aged probably 64, when Emmeline registered the event his age was recorded as 58. Either the couple were so unworldly that they took no account of their birthdays and the passing of the years or someone was attempting to make Richard seem younger than he was.

It could be argued that this illusion was likely to be Emmeline's work. David Mitchell's books on the Pankhursts are often unfairly caustic in their assessments, yet there may be a kernel of truth in his opinion that Emmeline made the facts fit her idealised view of the family. She 'could never admit failure' and therefore: 'Her marriage had to be splendid, her husband a Galahad, her daughter a genius.'[71] And, writing with hindsight, both Sylvia and Christabel noted Emmeline's power in their parents' relationship. While Sylvia was often critical of their mother, the same cannot be said of Christabel. Yet she too records her 'spurring Father on in his political course, urging him to challenge the social and economic dragons in the people's path'. For instance, in his choice of a London campaign to enter parliament in 1886, she continues this theme:

Father would have been better advised to try a Northern constituency, but Mother, perhaps, was reckoning that she could more easily play the candidate's wife, and later the Member's wife, if Father's constituency could be within hail of the House of Commons. A seat in parliament was her first wish for him, that he might take the place in national affairs that she thought his due.[72]

What does seem certain is that both their heads were focused on matters other than financial. The couple had failed to read the conditions for their lease of the Russell Square house. This is especially surprising in the case of Richard, the lawyer. When the ninety-year lease ended in the winter of 1892–93, it was discovered that the final holder was liable for dilapidations over the whole period, which came to a large sum. Even before this, Richard had been forced by the sanitary authorities to replace the old drains; now he received a bill for redecoration of the whole house, strengthening of the balcony and repairing many aspects of wear and tear. He stumped up the money, which the family could ill-afford. Then he learned that the house was in any case scheduled to be demolished to make way for what was to be the Russell Hotel. But the Pankhursts' other-worldly lack of financial management was devastatingly exacerbated by the circumstances of their move to Russell Square. The tragic death of their son Frank had left the family prostrate with grief and precipitated the move in an attempt to provide a healthier environment for the family.[73]

'The Four Pillars of My House'[1]

Richard Pankhurst was well aware of the responsibilities of parenthood, in his own idiosyncratic way. In his writings he mused:

> How much of our character is given us in early life and quite beyond our control. Who can ever get over the moral education he receives in youth be it good or bad? Who can get over a thorough spoiling?[2]

Marrying and then becoming a father were essential landmarks in the evolution of a typical Victorian man, but it has to be said that Richard Pankhurst was not typical.[3] When he reached these points, there is no suggestion that he regarded them in the traditional way. The fact that he apparently acquiesced in Emmeline's attempts at business suggests a genuine and unusual commitment to equality in their marriage. And when children arrived, as they quickly did, he and his wife regarded them as mini-adults who would as soon as possible partake in their social and political crusades. Both his elder daughters recall his frequent use of set phrases, among which was, 'My children are the four pillars of my house!' This was conditional: it was Sylvia who claimed that he exhorted them almost daily, 'If you do not work for other people, you will not have been worth the upbringing.' Adela is even more explicit and very bitter:

> To what a treadmill he condemned us helpless, hapless children and his poor wife, with her talents, her gaity [sic] and her beauty. 'Working for others' was interpreted to mean, of course, adopting his political and religious views and sacrificing everything to them.[4]

Sylvia also relates that when they were 'still but toddlers' he repeatedly asked them what they wanted to be when they grew up. That a father of his class and generation envisaged his daughters working for a living was very unusual, but that he did so is attested by his urging that they should 'Get something to earn your living by that you like and can do.' Christabel also mentions that her father talked about education as 'youthful freedom from care, to be prolonged, until twenty-five years of age, when it would be best to marry or embark on a profession, or both'.[5] It was not going to be easy; his other exhortations included 'To do, to be, and to suffer!' and 'Drudge and drill! drudge and drill!'[6] This strong current of high expectations went way beyond the usual requirements of a middle-class girl.

In contrast with this was his romantic streak. In keeping with his love of poetry, Richard apparently insisted that his daughters had pretty names. Christabel (Harriette) was from Coleridge, 'the lovely lady Christabel whom her father loves so well'. For the second daughter, born in 1882, Estelle was Emmeline's choice, but Sylvia favoured her second name, which Richard playfully translated into 'Miss Woody Way'.[7] Adela (Constantia), born in 1885, was possibly named after a German warrior queen of the tenth century; she also indicates that he felt a fondness for her in that he called her his 'lively little cricket'.[8] And the boys, Frank and Harry, both bore the names of Richard's beloved father, Henry Francis, embodying the heritage of which the Pankhursts, including Richard, were so proud and its continuance into the future. According to Sylvia, Emmeline did not like the names Henry and Francis, and stipulated that she would only agree to them if the elder son was actually called Frank. This perhaps casts a little light on hidden aspects of the Pankhursts' marriage.[9]

Daily life with Richard was remembered fondly by Sylvia. She told her son that his grandfather 'would often ... sing the song from Shakespeare's *Two Gentlemen of Verona*, 'Who is Sylvia? What is She?' It is perhaps doubtful how mellifluous this rendition could have been as Richard was reputedly tone deaf.[10] This love of words and literature was woven into his life's fabric:

He husbanded every moment of his day. He rose early, except on Sundays, and read aloud or recited poetry to himself in the bathroom during his very systematic ablutions. He read as he walked to the 'bus, and in the 'bus to his Chambers. He bought the smallest editions of his favourite books, in order that he might carry them in his pockets. Milton was his foremost love among the poets, constantly consulted as a refreshment to the spirit.[11]

Indeed, that very volume was still in Sylvia's possession in the 1930s; it was three inches long with tiny type. He also had little black notebooks for jottings 'stowed away on his person'.

Emmeline took care of him as a good wife, a persona not usually associated with the later well-known suffrage campaigner. She brushed his coat before he went out in the mornings, and chided him for his bulging pockets, protesting 'with tears of exasperation in her voice: "Some surgeon will stop you in the street one of these days and ask you to leave him your body for dissection – you make such a sight of yourself!"' When he was especially well dressed for an evening, she put in his diamond studs 'preparing him lovingly for some function where he had to speak'. Her regard for him was manifest in the interview she gave for *The Women's Herald* on 7 February 1891 when she praised him for leading the way in promoting women's votes, and warmly recounted the encouragement he gave her in her public activities: 'In all women's questions I have his earnest help and sympathy.' His wife was a 'new woman' and he was proud of her.[12] He demonstrated also a strange dependence upon, or perhaps possessiveness over, her that emerges occasionally in Sylvia's account. She noticed that:

> When she [Emmeline] was away from home for a few hours, and the time had arrived for her return, he would rise from his work and pace to and fro, whistling always a single valse tune which had tender associations with his courtship, and from which, as his impatience grew, the melody would fade away.[13]

Yet neither parent displayed much emotional intelligence in their dealings with the children; that was the province of Aunt Mary, Emmeline's sister, who formed part of the household until she married. Sylvia recalls her comforting reassurance on several occasions, and notes: 'How little we, or she, in her unassuming gentleness, realized the measure of her great helpfulness to us.'[14] When the family was in London, from 1886 to 1893, and their parents went away to Manchester, the children were left in the care of the servants. They also went to the seaside at Clacton for 'some months' with Susannah and Ellen the cook. Their parents visited only occasionally. None of this was all that unusual in middle-class Victorian families.

When discipline and punishment were required, it was not Richard who imposed it, but Emmeline, often actually carried out by the servants. Sylvia relates how she was tied to her bed for a day by them for declining to take cod liver oil, and was before the age of 3 beaten by her mother for refusing to eat her porridge at breakfast. Perhaps Richard did not need to discipline; for Sylvia, it was worse than any punishment when he merely said in rebuke that she had 'a want of conscience'.[15] When she had offended, as far as Richard was concerned all that was required was an apology, and all punishment ended; 'benign forgiveness must erase all memory of the offence'. Christabel's memoir supports Sylvia's:

> I remember no rebukes or punishments from him, so they must have been rare, if any. At the same time, one felt how stern might have been his view of insubordinate conduct.[16]

Even the more hostile Adela concedes that, although she and Harry were 'terrified' of their father, he was 'as Sylvia depicts it, more gentle and considerate than my mother, who spoke impulsively and said very hard things in her anger, but cooled down quickly'.[17]

The immense fondness of Sylvia and Christabel for their father is an indication that he invested considerable time and thought into their upbringing. It was a deeply moral education, geared towards creating an awareness of social deprivation and political unfairness, and a strong desire to change the world and lead the way in redressing social ills. That this was regarded as much more crucial than any form of traditional education is indicated by the fact that their attendance in school was optional; they went late and spasmodically and when the school did not conform to the parental expectations, the girls were withdrawn. The alternative was sometimes a 'governess'; Miss Sowerby was an artist in London who, according to Sylvia, did not teach them and instead took the girls out to museums and places of interest. However, 8-year-old Christabel's letter to her father did report that Miss Sowerby was planning to teach her Latin.[18]

In London there was talk from Richard of schooling at a Marxist International School for refugee and destitute children, but Emmeline was horrified at the idea. He then came up with a proposal that they should attend the local board school, which was cheap, and argued that all children should go to the 'public' schools as they did in the United States; their mother objected that they were 'too highly strung' and would 'lose all originality'. Susannah, the nursemaid, backed up her mistress, saying that the local children there were 'rough' and the Pankhurst children would catch 'things' in their heads and all sorts of illnesses.[19] So the spasmodic education, which was not unusual for middle-class girls from homes of limited wealth, continued. The result was patchy, and ironically it was Adela, who felt that she had the least attention from her parents of all the daughters, who actually gained a more consistent schooling:

> Christabel was twelve years old before she understood subtraction but that was a deficiency in the way our father had educated her and Sylvia.
> I went to school when I was six and stayed until I was nearly sixteen

[after her father had died] and only left to let Christabel go to university and Sylvia to stay abroad after her art scholarship was exhausted.[20]

Yet Richard thought about his children a lot and Sylvia recounts how he brought them little presents, often books, when he returned from his chambers:

> For many years he brought a book home to us every night; history, travel, simple science, astronomy, botany, chemistry, engineering, fairy-tales, standard novels, reproductions of works of art ...[21]

They enjoyed the publications of Walter Crane, and sang the songs from *Pan Pipes* with Emmeline on Sundays, though even here there was the political angle of Crane's Socialist cartoons, such as 'The Triumph of Labour'. Fortunately, these were leavened with fairy tales by the Brothers Grimm and Hans Christian Andersen, and even a fold-out 'anatomical man'. Richard was imaginative in his bedtime storytelling, creating characters who lasted for several years; Nobs and Dobs were two boys who led lives of 'startling and absurd' adventures; Miss Popinjay adopted fantastic dress and was excessively vain, encountering many ridiculous mishaps. Accompanying these stories, Richard drew 'amazingly grotesque illustrations' that delighted his children.

Sometimes he spoke in more serious mode to them about his interests, declaring that 'Life is nothing without enthusiasms!' 'His rare eloquence, his love of knowledge for its own sake, his deep sincerity, his zest for life drew our young hearts to him.' He talked to them of Shelley's idealism and the poet's poignant grief when his children were taken away. He also read to them the poems of Whitman, in particular *Pioneers! O Pioneers!* which extolled those who made the American west with perseverance and enthusiasm, hard work and sacrifice, united in the great cause of creating a brighter future. This was a great theme of his life, and he hoped to inculcate it in his children.

When the children started their own newspaper, *The Home News*, Richard added the subtitle *and Universal Mirror* and contributed serious letters on significant subjects. The girls wrote about receptions at their home, noting 'Mrs Pankhurst looked elegant in a trained velvet gown' and 'the Misses Pankhurst wore white crêpe dresses with worked yokes', and equally importantly 'the refreshments were delicious, the strawberries and cream being especially so'. But the copy included weightier matters, as chronicled by an 11-year-old Christabel in the early days of the Women's Franchise League:

> Mrs Pankhurst held an At Home at her beautiful house on May 28th. There was a great number of people there. Dr. Pankhurst, as Chairman,

said in his speech that if the suffrage was not given to women, the result would be terrible. If a body was half of it bound, how was it to be expected that it would grow and develop properly. This body was the human race and the fettered half, women. He then, with many compliments, called upon Mrs. Fenwick Miller to speak. Mrs Fenwick Miller spoke of the attitude of the political leaders and the growing power of the Women's Franchise League. Some opponents tried to prove that women were naturally inferior to men, but our girls won degrees and honours at the Universities. Mrs Pankhurst wore a black sort of grenadine with train from shoulders, and looked very handsome indeed.[22]

Richard encouraged the children's efforts at self-education when the older girls, being out of school at the time, wrote lectures to deliver in front of an adult family audience. However, his well-meaning but clumsy and off-putting attempts to encourage them to overcome their shyness by saying 'Speak up' and 'Don't be self-conscious' were not the best-judged interventions. It was left to Aunt Mary to comfort them and assure them that they had done well.[23]

There was very little 'playing' in the family. None of the children refer to fun and games with their parents, though significantly Sylvia recalls the servants in this context: 'on rare occasions, at intervals of several months, we would have a wild romp, in which the servants would sometimes join – or perhaps it was they who began it'.[24] Later in life, when she had become the lover of James Keir Hardie, he was astonished when she confessed:

'You know I never played games!' 'Ah!' he said with infinite compassion and tenderness, 'that is what is the matter with you! You heard too much serious talk; children ought not to be brought up like that.'[25]

Richard does not seem to have taken much part in preparing for festivities such as Christmas either; this was the province of their mother. Sylvia relates how disappointed she was one year. Having dropped copious hints that she wanted a violin, on Christmas morning she was excited to discover an oblong box on her bed. Sure that it contained the desired instrument, she opened it only to find it was empty. Emmeline had thought fit to give her a box from her unsold Emersons stock as a receptacle for gloves!

Whereas their mother does not seem to have empathised much with the children, in her defence, it was she who had to cope with the difficulties presented by a lack of money; she was creative in making her own and her children's clothes, decorating the house and furnishings, and ensuring that there was food on the table. Admittedly, though, the actual management of the finances was the work of Susannah Jones, the nursemaid-cum-housekeeper.

Their father was more thoughtful about the children's needs and concerns, but with less time to devote to them due to the demands of his work and his busy schedule of meetings and speeches. He was very open to their questioning. Although like many Victorian fathers his private preserve was his library of 4,000 volumes, Christabel relates how the whole family sat there in the evenings, where he would be 'deep in a book':

> We schoolchildren had leave to do our homework at the big table and suddenly one or another would ask: 'Father, what is such and such?' or 'Who was so and so?' He was roused at once. Books were taken from the shelves, references and authorities were shown. The subject was illuminated in all its ramifications.[26]

He did not object when his daughters came in to quiz him about religious belief. By this time he had long lost his faith and was admitting to agnosticism. Christabel and Sylvia were concerned to hear the servants discussing whether their father was a believer. Ellen, the cook, said he was not, and that this would bring bad luck in this world and the next, but Susannah and the housemaid, Rose, claimed he could be heard praying in the bathroom every morning. In fact he was reciting poetry. The girls resolved to ask Richard about Christianity, and his manner of dealing with them, according to Sylvia's memories, is worth describing in full:

> He welcomed our questions, and answered them frankly, explaining that he had not spoken to us of this matter before, because he desired us to think and decide for ourselves. He gave us a brief outline of the Biblical version of the life of Christ, and of the Christian dogmas, expressing his own disbelief in the supernatural interpretation, and giving the two rival theories held by Agnostics, either that Christ was a persecuted reformer (as he himself thought), or merely a legendary figure, compounded from the stories of many martyrs. He showed us books dealing with this and kindred subjects, which we might read when we chose, and urged us to use our intelligence to investigate for ourselves. He gave us too some brief account of the origin of species and the evolution of mankind.[27]

He was perhaps not quite as open-minded as this may suggest, since Sylvia goes on to say that often after this he 'would say to us playfully, and yet in earnest: "If you ever go back into religion you will not have been worth the upbringing."'

Richard and Emmeline had five children in the space of eight years. Emmeline's favourite was Christabel, though Adela contends that Sylvia fulfilled that role for a long period – possibly in the aftermath of Richard's death, when Christabel was away in Geneva. Christabel was the only one breastfed by her mother; thereafter Emmeline seems generally to have progressively distanced herself from her offspring as the campaigning took over. Indeed, the final two, Adela and Harry, are not even named in her autobiography, being dismissed out of hand as 'two other children'. But before their arrival, the Pankhursts in 1884 produced a son, Francis Henry, known as Frank. His fate is one of the tragedies of their life.

Frank was by all accounts a sunny little boy, growing up with his fond elder sisters in London. When he was only 4, his parents were away on one of their business trips to Manchester when he developed what the doctor initially diagnosed as croup. However, it did not respond to treatment and his parents were summoned to return, Emmeline rushing back immediately, while Richard was obliged to remain in the north to complete the case on which he was engaged. It was realised too late that Frank was in fact suffering from diphtheria. When he died, Emmeline summoned her brother, Walter, from Manchester, then sent him north again to break the news to Richard. Both parents were heartbroken and never fully recovered from their devastating loss. Christabel believed that her father was especially affected: 'Fatherhood that begins in ripe years is doubly serious and Frank was his heart's core. The grief remained with him always and seemed to give him new tenderness for the children that remained.'[28] The stricken parents could not even bring themselves to put up a gravestone for the child.[29]

Emmeline had blamed the faulty drains at their home and moved everyone out into temporary accommodation, and then into the house in Russell Square. Richard urged the family not to forget Frank, but Emmeline could not bear to hear him spoken of, and she hid in her bedroom cupboard the two death portraits carried out by a lady commissioned for the task. Sylvia grieved alone and secretly, and did her own drawing of Frank, which she gave to her father. She considered it 'ugly' though Richard 'encouraged me kindly, saying that he could see Frank in my drawing very clearly. I felt an inexpressible throb of gratitude and sympathy; his understanding tenderness seemed like sunshine on my grief-frozen spirit.'[30]

Emmeline had some sense when she was expecting her last child in 1889 that he was 'Frank coming again', which probably explains why he was given the same names as his deceased sibling, Henry Francis, shortened to 'Harry'. Adela claims that she and Harry suffered physical neglect, blaming her mother in particular for her own poor health, weak legs and bronchitis. This is explained as very much rooted in Richard's demand for total commitment to the Cause.[31]

In contrast to the two elder daughters, Adela also recorded that she and Harry were afraid of the ageing Richard. Verna Coleman sums this up:

> 'Father was a more fearsome figure, more distant, humourless and cold, and often away'. Richard Pankhurst, so sure of all his political beliefs, was awkward with his children. Both Adela and Harry, whom she [Adela] loved protectively, were terrified of him, unable to comprehend his lectures on socialism, capitalism, religion and suffrage … Christabel, calmer and more understanding, saw her father as tender and still grieving for the lost Frank; Sylvia worshipped him. But the two youngest children, cowering before his impatience, did not realize that their father, now over fifty, was ill and overworked. And sad.[32]

Sylvia's portrait of these two small children likewise implies that they were emotionally neglected by their parents. And it did not help that from early on, perhaps from the age of 6, Adela rejected her father's agnosticism and resolutely but secretly held on to a belief in God, rebelling against one of his fundamental beliefs.

The experiences of Adela and Harry were very different from those of the two eldest girls. They were sad, even more so after 1893 and the family's return to Manchester, growing up in a household that now lacked the reassuring presence of either Aunt Mary or Susannah Jones, both of whom had left to get married. Too young to be involved in the ideological struggles of their parents, they were left in the nursery to bring themselves up. When a neighbour gave Adela a fox terrier puppy, Sylvia was indignant, and Richard's solution was to force Adela to share it with everyone. This too added to the sum of her grievances against her father.[33]

While the nurse, Susannah, had been loved by them, Adela perceived the other servants as unsympathetic, and attributed this to their unimportance in their parents' lives:

> My father's attitude to us was that we counted nothing at all beside the Cause and the servants soon grasped how little we counted in our parents [sic] lives … [They] slighted us all, giving us cold lumpy porridge and burnt potatoes, talking before us of murders and all kinds of horrors … They did not appreciate the equal terms on which we lived amongst them, but merely considered it as a sign that our parents rated us as of little worth. My father and mother, who could command respect from them, doubtless thought we, too, were properly treated, but that was far from the truth.[34]

Moreover, Adela implied criticism of her father when she remarked that he never suggested that Emmeline should give up her political activism to 'devote herself to her only son', Harry, who was 'pale and delicate, repressed and miserable'. The bullying these two younger siblings endured from their elder sisters is chronicled vividly, and went unnoticed by their busy parents. She concluded that she and Harry 'drooped more and more'. Sylvia confirms that the boy took to wandering on his own around the building sites of Victoria Park; Richard found his detachment 'incomprehensible'.[35] Even in death, Adela believed that her father had a baleful influence on her life; when she wanted to apply to study History on a scholarship at Oxford, Emmeline and Sylvia prevented her on the grounds that it would have been a betrayal of Richard, who had despised Oxford and all that it stood for. Adela also seems to have believed he would have taken special exception to a women's college.[36]

Later in life, Adela seems to have softened into a more adult understanding of her parent. She explained that his 'gentle personality permeated the whole of our family life'. But she also thought that he had sacrificed his family to his ideals, and his idealistic influence on them could never be wiped out. It is telling that one of the few 'games' in which she remembers they engaged was 'elections'.[37] Her summary of the ethos in the family home in the 1890s, as she perceived it, suggests that she was more aware of the political predilections of her parents and siblings than they realised: 'it was the family creed that socialism was destined to wipe poverty from the earth and to that end my whole attention was directed'.[38]

That there is much truth in Adela's view is demonstrated by the parental expectations of the older girls: 'My father treated his elder daughters as if they were grown up when they were only little children. He gave them an exaggerated idea of their importance and made them intensively self-conscious.'[39] From an early age, they were expected to participate in the political activities of their parents, helping at their gatherings by handing out refreshments, avidly listening to conversations and debates. The guests were many and fascinating. The children were especially intrigued by colourful characters like 'Mr Mulvi' (a maulvi was the term for a Muslim scholar), Queen Victoria's Indian servant, who wore a turban and flowing robes and who was teaching the queen 'Hindustani' (Urdu); Annie Besant, advocate for the striking match girls in 1889 wearing shockingly short hair and skirts that Emmeline abhorred; and Louise Michel of the Paris Commune, known as 'la petroleuse' by her enemies, who was so dark and wrinkled that she was like the bark of an ancient chestnut tree.[40]

In contrast to Adela's resentment, Sylvia in particular relished all this exposure to Richard's ideals: 'My father ... kept us on the high plane. We surveyed through his eyes the great movements of liberation and enlightenment.'[41] For good or ill, his influence had a strong impact on the whole family in one way or another for the rest of their lives.

As a wife and mother Emmeline was breaking new ground in her business and political life. She clearly felt the need to defend this, and on 7 February 1891 gave an interview to the *Woman's Herald*.[42] While not denying that she did not see her children very frequently, she argued that this was actually beneficial to them:

> I have four little children, who, I might say, are quite as happy, quite as well looked after, as any children. They are devoted to me, indeed, I think they appreciate me all the more because they do not see too much of me. I have an excellent nurse and governess to whom I can confidently entrust my children. I do not think the mother is the best instructress of her own offspring in any way; she is often too indulgent; the constant intercourse may, in my opinion, be the reverse of beneficial. My children look forward to my return as a treat; I have two days a week which I can devote entirely to them.

That Emmeline had the full cooperation of her husband was made eminently clear to readers:

> Our interview had come to an end when the drawing-room door opened and three charming little girls entered, followed by a nurse with the only boy, a baby of a few months. It was easy to see the loving devotion of the mother as soon as the children appeared; they ran eagerly up to her and were at once full of their plans and amusements, while the 'baby' crowed lustily to be allowed his place in the family conclave. It was a pretty picture, as Dr. Pankhurst, who also joined us, evidently thought, for he turned to me and said warmly, 'Does this not prove conclusively that neither business nor politics can in any way take from all that we desire and look for in a wife and mother!'

The Pankhursts were demonstrating a new model for family life, and Richard was fully on board.

CHAPTER 11

London Campaigns and the Emergence of Emmeline

In the years after the move to London, there were plenty of causes to keep the Pankhursts busy. Richard had earlier been associated with the journalist W.T. Stead in opposition to Britain's potential involvement in the Russo-Turkish war. Now in 1885 the latter began a campaign to expose the evils of child prostitution. He was supported by Pankhurst, who attended a conference for the protection of young girls.[1] Stead purchased a girl of 13 from her mother to prove how easy it was to do so. For his pains, he was tried and imprisoned, apparently not for the purchase, but for the purchase from her mother, who was not her legal guardian; this was her father. This set off a 'moral panic' across the nation. Working with Josephine Butler, the Liverpool campaigner for the rights of working women and prostitutes, Stead exposed the corruption and double standards of this aspect of the Victorian underworld. The corollary was the formation of the National Vigilance Association, which later mutated into the Personal Rights Association.[2]

As the editor of the *Pall Mall Gazette*, Stead was a leading champion of oppressed groups and it was perhaps inevitable that he and Pankhurst should become allies. Soon after the family had arrived in London, demonstrations by the unemployed were planned as a response to the depression of 1886–87. Many of the leaders, such as John Burns and Henry Hyndman, were prosecuted for sedition and incitement. Meetings in Trafalgar Square were banned, and attempts to hold them were met with violence. Richard could not ignore such oppression and through publications such as the *Gazette* he argued that there was a common law right to hold meetings in the square.

The events of 'Bloody Sunday' on 13 November 1887 provoked him into the extreme view that the law of precedent gave the right to use force against the unlawful violence of the state. He and Emmeline had appeared at a demonstration in Trafalgar Square, London, which was a protest against both the high unemployment rate and draconian law enforcement in Ireland. The government broke up the meeting using 2,000 police constables and 400 troops, resulting in the death of Alfred Linnell, who was trampled by a police horse on Northumberland Avenue, and 150 persons being injured.[3]

The Pankhurst couple attended Linnell's funeral a week later, ostentatiously travelling in the same coach as his family, which also transported trade unionist John Burns.[4] In supporting the new trade unions that were springing up among poorer workers, associated with the spread of Marxist socialism, Richard had put himself beyond the pale in the eyes of many in the middle and upper classes who were fearful of the new forces that were being unleashed. He worked with William Morris, Henry Hyndman, John Burns, Charles Bradlaugh, W.T. Stead, Annie Besant, Herbert Burrows and others to set up the Law and Liberty League, which defended public demonstrations and free speech against illegal action by the authorities.[5] This was the beginning of a new era in the Pankhursts' evolution as campaigners, as they inexorably began to move into the new left-wing of politics and to embrace the principles of socialism.

The Women's Franchise League

Although continuing to support the Manchester National Society for Women's Suffrage into the mid-1880s, the Pankhursts' move to the capital eventually changed their focus to the Central Committee in London. However, this was several years after they had settled there, when in 1888 there was a move afoot to allow other women's groups, particularly the Women's Liberal Federation, to affiliate with the women's suffrage campaign. Lydia Becker, now campaigning in London, was strongly against this. She believed that the movement should be above party politics, as it was the case that women were to be found among its ranks who supported both the Liberals and the Conservatives. She also feared that the women's cause would become subsumed in wider party issues and lose its discrete focus. At this point, Emmeline decided to join the London society so that she could vote with Becker, but it seems that at the December meeting at which the vote was taken she changed her mind and voted in favour of affiliation. The outcome was a serious split, in which Lydia Becker and Millicent Fawcett led those voting against the move into a section known as the College Street group (the Central Committee), which seems to have been supported by most of the regional societies. Meanwhile the Pankhursts, the Jacob Brights, Priscilla McLaren of Edinburgh and Alice Scatcherd of Leeds joined the pro-affiliation Parliament Street group (Central National Society) and began to liaise with the Liberals.[6]

Richard and Emmeline and their friends had hoped that this new arrangement would lead to the adoption by the Parliament Street group of a definite policy by which married women would henceforth be explicitly included in the suffrage Bills presented to parliament. Up to now they had been excluded, sometimes by implication because of the law of coverture, particularly the aspect that prevented them from owning property and thereby fulfilling any property qualifications, an important aspect of eligibility to vote. After 1882 when married women gained wider property rights[7] they might have expected to be included in the proposed suffrage Bills that were brought in, except that coverture was deemed by some to exclude them still, and some Bills were presented that stated this explicitly. This was abhorrent to the Pankhursts and their allies, and it was not long before they resolved to do something about it.

According to Sylvia, they were pushed into taking action by a fear that a proposed Bill to give the vote to only unmarried women might actually succeed because a majority in the Commons had pledged to support it. Under the auspices of Ursula Bright, they met in London to decide how to proceed. At the AGM of the Parliament Street group on 21 March 1889, Florence Fenwick Miller, seconded by Richard Pankhurst, successfully put forward a resolution condemning what they termed 'the coverture clause'.[8] Despite this, the executive committee decided to include the invidious clause to exclude married women. Richard wrote to Harriet McIlquham, who was to become a close associate, on 5 April, expressing his commitment to the ideal of the married women's vote:

> Your earnest sympathetic words are a great help. It is such words that encourage in the arduous struggles of public life. All who stand for causes that have not yet won a front place must make sacrifices ... We must go on insisting that the principle of the movement must be boldly asserted. No compromise is our cry.[9]

The upshot was the formation of a provisional committee that would set up a formal society, later named the Women's Franchise League (WFrL). MPs were approached to take charge of a new Bill, which specifically included married women within the wording of the original 1870 women's suffrage Bill drawn up by Richard Pankhurst. However, the MP who was to propose the Bill, Richard Haldane, drew up his own very similar version, which was introduced into the Commons on 2 August 1889. The key words for the WFrL were that: 'No woman shall be subject to legal incapacity from voting at such elections [Parliamentary, Municipal, Local and other elections] by reason of marriage.'[10]

In July 1889 the Pankhursts' last child, Harry, had been born in the house in Russell Square. Sylvia's story about the genesis of the Women's Franchise

League, that it began in a discussion around Emmeline's bed when she received visitors on 23 July, a couple of weeks after Harry's arrival, has been dismissed by some as inaccurate. It seems to reflect Sylvia's usual desire to put her family at the heart of all new initiatives in the women's movement. The correspondence of Elizabeth Wolstenholme Elmy does show that there was discussion about a new society from earlier in 1889.[11] However, Sylvia's account of a preparatory bedside meeting is plausible as the WFrL was formally established on the following 25 July at the home of the Tebbs in London. The executive then met on 7 November to appoint its officers, with Harriet McIlquham as chair, Elizabeth Wolstenholme Elmy as official, paid secretary, Alice Scatcherd as treasurer, and a committee that included Richard and Emmeline Pankhurst, Harriet Stanton Blatch (whose mother, the American Elizabeth Cady Stanton, was a corresponding member), Florence Fenwick Miller, Josephine Butler, Cunningham Graham, Clementia Taylor, Jane Cobden (daughter of Richard Cobden) and Lady Sandhurst.

On 25 November the league was launched at a public meeting; a distinguished guest speaker was William Lloyd Garrison, the United States campaigner for the emancipation of slaves. Fittingly, the new body was founded on 'Garrisonian' principles; pragmatism was abandoned in favour of adherence to principles.[12] There was to be no compromise, and the league drew ever closer to the infant labour movement. In 1890 the WFrL held a conference at the Leeds Law Institute, chaired by Alice Scatcherd. She set the tone by opining that the two key issues before the country were 'the labour question and the women's question'. The league viewed these two as linked; women's freedom was seen as dependent on their economic circumstances.[13]

The activists were assiduous in spreading their ideas and working to gain members. Four series of public and drawing room meetings were held in London between January and July 1890, numbering thirty-six in all. Naturally, the speakers included both Richard and Emmeline Pankhurst. Meanwhile, in the north of England, Alice Scatcherd and Agnes Sunley held several public and club meetings. Early on in 1890, the WFrL also organised three discussions at the National Liberal Club; Richard Pankhurst led the second, probably at this time still viewing himself as on the fringes of the Liberal fold. Jacob and Ursula Bright joined on 20 May 1890, when the committee tried to add to its strength by the co-option of extra members.[14] Ursula in particular soon became prominent on the committee, forging links with the Women's Liberal Federation and persuading Emmeline to join it.[15]

Despite an apparently auspicious beginning, the WFrL was soon rent by disagreements, particularly centred on Elizabeth Wolstenholme Elmy. Maureen Wright, her biographer, claims her as the shaper of the league's policies as they evolved, amounting to the 'conscience of radical suffragism', and nicknamed by her as 'the young giant'.[16] But she soon came into conflict with the other leaders of the league in a protracted power struggle.

The Pankhursts wished to bring in Sir Charles Dilke, with whom they had established a friendship because he was a high-profile supporter of both women's rights and the labour movement, with which they were increasingly in sympathy.[17] However, he was *persona non grata* in many circles owing to a notorious and scandalous divorce suit. Elizabeth Wolstenholme Elmy strongly resisted the Pankhursts' attempts, apparently not only due to a moral stance, but also because she did not want women's suffrage to be mixed with causes that did not necessarily put women's rights first. Sandra Stanley Holton states in *Suffrage Days* that the Pankhursts had no time for the scandal-mongering and hypocrisy, remaining loyal to their friend.[18] Interestingly, Sylvia believed that her father's view was that 'the man's public work should not be prejudiced by the case'; he and Emmeline had called on Dilke in the midst of his court case and had encouraged him to 'live it down'.[19] Indeed in a letter of 31 June 1886, Richard was offering advice on how Dilke should proceed with the case, expressing a view that the first hearing was conducted unfairly and that Dilke was innocent of the charges against him, adding: 'I exhort him to be of good heart in waiting for a better time.' He had sent an article on these lines for publication to the *Daily News* and the *Pall Mall Gazette*.[20] Elmy also harboured misgivings about Jacob and Ursula Bright, believing them to be embroiled in the perceived plot to reinstate Dilke in respectable circles. She was frustrated by the attempts of the Pankhursts to 'force Mrs Bright on the Committee against [her, Elmy's] persistently expressed wish'.

Elmy also clashed with Florence Fenwick Miller over accusations that the former was not effective in her role in the league, and there were dark intimations in an anonymous pamphlet circulated at this time, suspected to be the work of Fenwick Miller, that an impoverished Elmy had misappropriated WFrL funds.[21] Even the influential and wealthy Alice Scatcherd rubbed Elmy up the wrong way by the demands she made of her as secretary, and Elmy complained that she and her assistant, Romola Tynte, had been treated brutally and as a result had become ill.

When on 22 May 1890 Elmy resigned as secretary, officially due to 'her health and strength being unequal to coping with the work' (and finally actually left on 25 July when the committee refused to reinstate her) she was temporarily replaced in her role by Emmeline Pankhurst and Countess Schack. It was then more permanently undertaken by Harriot Stanton Blatch, alongside the increasingly dominant Ursula Bright. It has been claimed that Richard Pankhurst's annotations to the 1890 Annual Report demonstrate the WFrL's desire to erase Elmy's importance in the organisation.[22] It may be that a serious, but unexplained, quarrel with her husband, Ben Elmy, exacerbated his personal irritation with the problematic secretary.[23]

There were other weaknesses. The league never grew beyond a few hundred members in London, Leeds and Lancashire, and there was little close contact between them. Its organisation was weak and loose; for example, the role of chair rotated in executive meetings, and attendance was irregular. In 1890–91 its income was a mere £350. As early as 1890, in the Annual Report, it was appealing to members to at least pay their subscriptions because 'they have exceeded the funds at their disposal'. It also wasted its energies in fighting the other suffrage groups.[24] Nevertheless, the WFrL still agitated for Bills to include explicitly the married women's suffrage, as demonstrated in one of the earliest examples of Emmeline speaking up in a meeting. This took place on 22 April 1891 when a vote was to be taken in the Parliament Street group as to whether to do so. The more radical proposal was defeated. The account in the *Manchester Guardian* described the scene:

> ... signs of the approaching storm were visible in the whispered conversations and evident excitement among a knot of ladies at the back of the hall ... Before the resolution could be put Mrs Pankhurst rose and excitedly moved an amendment which 'let the cat out of the bag.' It was the old grievance of the married women's franchise, which led some years ago to the formation of the Women's Franchise League.[25]

Meanwhile, the league extended its scope and adopted a wide range of causes, seeing itself as the radical wing of women's suffragism. Evidence of Richard Pankhurst's influence in this is furnished in a letter from Lilias Ashworth Hallett to Millicent Garrett Fawcett, reporting that at a meeting at Mrs Jacob Bright's between the Parliament Street London suffragist group and the WFrL 'as Dr Pankhurst showed signs of his intention to boss the whole business they (the Parliament Street people) had backed out and declined further union'.[26] The international conference on the position of women 'in all countries' organised by the WFrL at Westminster Town Hall on 16 and 17 July 1890, offered two evenings of speeches and discussion. It included delegates from France, Italy, Denmark, Sweden and the USA.[27] Again Richard's influence in the league is apparent; he had suggested combining the gathering with a London conference on international peace and arbitration, which duly took place. This was not an isolated example of the internationalism of the league. In May 1893, for example, Alice Scatcherd and Ursula Bright attended the Council of Representative Women in Chicago as WFrL delegates.[28]

As time went on, the leaders also developed strong contacts with socialism. To begin with, the Pankhursts favoured the Fabians, whom they joined in October 1890; Richard became president of the Manchester branch. As much as four years earlier he had addressed their conference, advocating that William Morris should train up some of 'his young socialistic fellows' to go into parliament.[29] At home the Pankhursts were reading the *Fabian Essays*, along with such subversive writings as Kropotkin's *Fields, Factories and Workshops* and Blatchford's *Merrie England*.[30] This served to alienate suffragists in other organisations even further; on 2 April 1892, Mr Levy wrote from the National Liberal Club in Whitehall to Ursula Bright in response to a request that he speak against the upcoming Rollit Bill.[31] He expressed the view that the WFrL would have supported the Bill

> if the Women's Franchise League had not become a mere annex to the Fabian Society, as was painfully apparent at the last conference. The opposition to the Bill is, of course, inspired from that source, and is dictated not by any desire, pure and simple, for women's enfranchisement, but in the interests of Socialism.[32]

The WFrL campaigned for equality for women in divorce, inheritance and the custody and guardianship of their children, co-education, and trade unionism, the defence of oppressed races, and the abolition of the House of Lords.[33] It is possible to perceive the influence of Richard Pankhurst in much of this agenda. The conference held in the Pankhurst home at 8 Russell Square on three consecutive evenings in December 1891 dealt with three main areas: the economic position of women; political rights and duties of women; and the programme of the League and the Bills it had promoted. Richard himself presided over the final session. He obviously still supported fully the original focus of the organisation, and Sylvia relates how this defender of international peace was much less pacific than many of the women campaigners: 'Why are women so patient? Why don't you force us to give you the vote?' Then playfully clawing the air with his long fingers: 'Why don't you scratch our eyes out?'[34] The fragmentary records of the league suggest that by now Richard's role was more about drawing up agendas for conferences and documents, rather than attending actual meetings. He did, however, chair the meetings at his home on 15 February 1892 and at St James Place on 3 June 1893.

Gradually, the league fell apart; Elizabeth Wolstenholme Elmy's resignation in 1890 had led to her formation with Harriet McIlquham of the rival Women's Emancipation Union. Lord Haldane, a frequent visitor to the Russell Square home of the Pankhursts, having agreed to sponsor the league's Bill along with Sir Edward Grey, failed to take any steps to action the measure, and when the former told Emmeline and Ursula Bright that it was just a principle and would not be enacted for fifty years, Emmeline refused to deal with him further.

The mainstream women's suffrage movement, represented in the Commons by William Woodall, MP for Hanley, struggled to get their more limited Bill debated; government business took up almost all the time allotted to private members' Bills. However, in 1892, Sir Albert Rollit, a Conservative MP, independently managed to secure a slot for his Bill to enfranchise women who had the vote in local government elections. This did include some married women, but most could implicitly be left out due to the laws of coverture. Every suffrage group apart from the WFrL, including Elmy's Women's Emancipation Union, supported it. Even a committee set up by the WFrL to hold a demonstration in Hyde Park was led by its secretary, Mary Cozens, into support for Rollit's Bill.[35]

However, the WFrL leaders, including Richard and Emmeline Pankhurst, denounced it as 'enfranchising middle-class women and spinsters' while denying the vote to married women, and women lodgers, 'thereby adding a new disqualification to the working women of the nation'.[36] At a meeting in St James's Hall in London in support of this measure, Richard Pankhurst proposed to amend the Bill, 'urging that no measure for women's suffrage was worthy of support which did not embody the principles of full legal enfranchisement for all women'. He was opposed by the famous Fabian and writer, George Bernard Shaw. According to Elizabeth Wolstenholme Elmy, the WFrL, having called on working men and women to turn up to oppose the Bill, mustered 200 supporters who were led by the socialist Herbert Burrows.[37] The latter had already interrupted the speeches so often that he was threatened by the chairman with ejection from the meeting, when he led the way in storming the platform and overturning the reporters' table. *The Times* explains in detail:

Mr. Burroughes [sic], in the midst of a great disturbance … made his way rapidly towards the platform, with the intention, as he declared afterwards, of sitting there quietly until the speaker had done, and then of answering him. His friends thought he was being ejected and followed him up with a rush. The people on the platform, seeing the sudden movement, thought the platform was being charged. The men jumped up to act on the defensive, while the women moved hurriedly towards the rear. The reporters' table, at which some 15 or 20 reporters were seated, collapsed under the rush, and coats, and hats, and note-books were instantly trampled under foot. The people on the platform, headed by Mr. St. Ruth, one of the leaders of the meeting, resisted the onslaught on the platform of Mr. Burroughes and his followers, and for a few minutes there was a hand-to-hand fight. The massive brass railings in front of the platform were torn down, and a remarkable scene of confusion and excitement ensued for some ten minutes. The advantage lay with Mr. Burroughes and his followers, who stood on the platform cheering.[38]

At this point the chairman declared the meeting over, yet the confusion continued. Many of the audience left, but Shaw managed to speak up in favour of the Rollit Bill. Practicalities now impinged upon the proceedings: 'The new chairman then announced that the motion and amendment would have to be put at once, because otherwise a cost of an extra ten guineas would be incurred for the hall.' Despite the objections of 'an excited Scotchman', the motion and amendment were put and Richard Pankhurst's amendment objecting to the Bill was carried 'by an overwhelming majority'.

Sensational accounts of violence were published by the papers, not least *The Times*, whose headline, 'RIOT AT ST. JAMES'S-HALL', made the most of the division and tension within the movement. The incident caused Harriot Stanton Blatch to resign from the WFrL. Richard Pankhurst too was apparently out of sympathy with such extreme measures, though pleased at the passage of his amendment. He wrote to James Levy, chair of the meeting, explaining that he had neither sought nor supported the rush on the platform, and denying incriminating words attributed to him. In his reply to Richard, Levy undermined the legitimacy of the WFrL amendment, claiming that it had only passed because many supporters of the original resolution had left, leaving the WFrL activists in the majority. In the event, the Rollit Bill failed to pass the Commons.[39]

Meanwhile, the WFrL was languishing. It was not helped by the fact that the Pankhursts moved back to the north in the spring of 1893, and on 22 November 1893 a decision was made to amalgamate with the Manchester National Society for Women's Suffrage, and Dr and Mrs Pankhurst were to represent the League at the MNSWS annual meetings.[40]

That year, at the World Congress of Representative Women in Chicago, Ursula Bright explained the league's broad programme, and its links with the labour movement. For others on the executive, this last was becoming a major focus, and this was particularly true of Richard and Emmeline Pankhurst, as expressed in Richard's anti-capitalist utterances. Speakers were sent out to socialist groups to enlist their support, despite the fact that many of them were unsympathetic to women's suffrage, believing in the prime importance of class struggle. When the Pankhursts moved back to Manchester they found a new home there among the embryonic Independent Labour Party.[41] In September 1894 they finally resigned from the WFrL.[42]

A successful amendment to the Local Government Act of 1894, which granted the local vote to married women on the same terms as for single women, effectively removed the question of coverture from the local suffrage demand. This provided a fig leaf for the WFrL, who had been active in achieving it and claimed the credit for it. However, it had been supported by all the suffrage societies, and it provided an opportunity to work together that later resulted in the reunification of the movement in 1897. By this time the WFrL was only a shadow of its former self.[43]

While WFrL efforts in London weakened, however, in the north Alice Scatcherd continued the fight. Christabel notes that she was a frequent visitor to the Pankhurst home, and 'a great nursery favourite'. She is also memorably described by Sylvia as

> a tall, bony Yorkshire woman of Morley, near Leeds, of substantial means and assured social position, she repudiated as badges of slavery, and refused to wear, either a wedding ring or the veil with which every would-be well-dressed woman covered her face in those days. (Mrs Pankhurst then never went out without her veil.) Because this middle-aged lady wore no ring, hotel proprietors many times refused to admit her, when she appeared with her husband, despite her appearance of indubitable respectability, and her staid, unfashionable dress, completed by large, low-heeled, elastic-sided boots.[44]

Soon, however, Ursula Bright, supported by the Pankhursts, began to find fault with her, attributing her shortcomings to the menopause, which 'makes her irritable and weary at times', although acknowledging that she was 'a very fine woman and a most valuable worker'. Largely as a result of Scatcherd's efforts, in the north of England the WFrL was active for almost a decade after its formation in 1889.

By the time that the WFrL finally faded away at the end of the 1890s, the College Street and Parliament Street women's suffrage societies had reunited in the National Union of Women's Suffrage Societies under Millicent Fawcett, and both Richard Pankhurst and Jacob Bright had died. But there is a strong line of thought that the league had been a precursor of the Women's Social and Political Union, founded by Emmeline in 1903 and popularly known as the Suffragettes, in its assertiveness, its unwillingness to compromise on policy and its leanings towards the labour movement. It was part of a broad socialist current in the pre-First World War era, which Richard Pankhurst had helped to create.[45]

Final Years in the North, 1893–98

By 1893 both Richard and Emmeline were ill, due to the stresses and strains of financial embarrassment, the constant travelling to Manchester, and perhaps disappointment at the failure of the Women's Franchise League. Richard spent a few weeks at Smedley's Hydro, probably at Matlock in Derbyshire, where he would have taken advantage of a variety of hot and cold water treatments in this spa town, as well as undergoing a regime designed to modify his 'diet, clothing and habits of life'. Exercise was strongly recommended. Smoking and alcohol were to be avoided.[1] There was some improvement, but he never fully recovered. Unbeknownst to the family, he was suffering from stomach ulcers and was often in pain. Emmeline decided that the time had come to return to the north. The second Emersons was given up as a costly burden and the whole family moved to Lancashire.[2]

Even while they were based in London, Richard, sometimes accompanied by Emmeline, had made frequent sallies north to carry on his forensic career, as well as to attend functions such as the Manchester Grammar School annual dinner and the Athenaeum Lecture and Debating Society jubilee.[3] Indeed, it was in 1892, shortly before his return to live in the area, that he had joined the most influential and prestigious of all the Manchester clubs, the Literary and Philosophical Society, which counted among its members such scientific eminences as James Prescott Joule and Henry Roscoe. The decision to return to the north was not as much of a break to him as it must have been for his children, who do not seem to have travelled there at all in the eight years of residence in London. The capital was the place where the two elder girls spent a large part of their formative years.[4] And the move north was the time at which their Aunt Mary, the point of stability in family life and a comforting presence to the older children, left the household to train as a teacher of dress cutting in technical schools, and soon after married.

The Family in the North

The wrench from life in London was perhaps mitigated for the children because they moved, not to Manchester, but initially to the seaside resort of Southport, where it was hoped that Emmeline would recover her strength. Richard too may have taken advantage of the presence in the town of a Smedley's Hydro. However, Emmeline languished away from the excitement of city life. On the other hand, the children experienced a sense of liberation in the small, rented apartment at 45 Talbot Road, just near the impressive main parade, where they spent more time with their mother than ever before. Adela in particular remembered this as an extremely happy interlude, where 'my father and mother were kind and cheerful'.[1]

It was perhaps a desire on Emmeline's part to have less responsibility for them that it was decided that they would attend Southport High School for Girls. She had always opposed any suggestion that they should go to a school, but in Southport she relented, and even acceded to little Adela's demands to go with them. The experiment was a success, particularly for Sylvia, who loved the school. Richard did not entirely hand over his daughters to the charge of the principal and his wife, Mr and Mrs Ross. He 'stipulated that we should not take religious instruction'; Sylvia read a history book instead, while actually listening with fascination to the Scripture lessons. It seems that Richard, as a local dignitary, distributed the prizes at the school in May, but it was not long before the family was on the move again.

Emmeline was so depressed by the summer of 1893 that she could barely bother to take a short walk to the Southport shops. The family moved to a farmhouse in Disley, Cheshire. For reasons that are difficult to discern, Emmeline enjoyed her time in this rural backwater, 16 miles away from Manchester, and helped with haymaking, went blackberrying and took the children out for days in a pony and trap. Richard bought the family a donkey. Christabel and Sylvia now had lessons from a governess with two local girls. At Disley, another mainstay of the family's well-being found a new calling; Susannah Jones married the keeper of the golf course, and after she had seen the Pankhursts safely settled in Manchester she returned to live in a 'poor little cottage in the midst of Disley Golf Links'. Meanwhile, Emmeline had recovered her enthusiasm for life and was ready to return to the fray in the big city.

The family came again to Manchester in the spring of 1894 and, after a short spell in temporary accommodation in the city at 173 High Street, Oxford Road, the house they chose was in the extremely prestigious new development of Victoria Park at 4 Buckingham Crescent, grandly named Lorne House, and now on Daisybank Road. Much like the house in Russell Square in London, this property was above the Pankhursts' means, but was intended as a venue for the salon over which Emmeline would preside.[2] At this time, the four houses of Buckingham Crescent were surrounded by gardens with lilac, laburnum and red hawthorn trees, and fields beyond the boundaries. Christabel explains that, although the children's hearts were heavy at moving to Manchester, they were 'wonderfully happy' when they moved into Buckingham Crescent:

> The picture now in my mind of those Manchester days is of the library, with flowered gold-and-brown paper and booklined walls. Mother reading, writing or sewing at one side of the big, glowing fire. Father at the other side, deep in a book. He stretches out his fine, sensitive hand, now and again, to show that he is thinking of us all and enjoying our companionship.[3]

Adela, a little unusually, praises Richard on the subject of his daughters' education in this period:

> My father was quite incapable of denying us anything in his power to give us, simply because we were girls and educationally, our opportunities were as good as if our sex had been male. We went to an excellent school; the Manchester High School, but there was no great compulsion to learn placed upon us.[4]

The High School was advanced in that it offered an academic education to the daughters of the middle classes, yet the Pankhurst girls left before they reached the maximum age of 18. One reason for this may have been that the fee-paying school was too expensive, but it is also clear that formal education was not a high priority in the family. It cannot have helped either that the headmistress,

Elizabeth Day, had 'unsuccessfully begged the Governors ... not to admit us, on the ground that our father was a Republican and an Atheist'.[5] True to form, Richard again excluded his offspring from Scripture lessons. Sylvia was badly bullied over this, and was desperately unhappy at the school. Perhaps due to the fact that she did not make a fuss, it does not appear that her parents noticed. Adela too was miserable there, partly due to the prejudices of her parents; she felt socially isolated because they forbade her to continue a friendship with a little girl whose father was a Conservative councillor. She also relates the story of her friendship with an Irish girl who verbally attacked Sylvia for being horrible to Adela: 'Your face would frighten a crow off its nest,' the friend exclaimed, and told Sylvia to: 'Go and boil your head and play with the gravy.' Sylvia immediately reported this to her parents; they were shocked, and Richard indignantly asked Adela: 'Could I really like a girl who used such expressions?'[6]

The children were excluded in general from the social life of their peers, and were expected for ideological reasons to join children of the working class in outings with the Clarion Cycling Club and attend parties organised for the children of the poor.[7] The cycling club helped to ensure the popularity of Robert Blatchford's socialist newspaper, the *Clarion*. Christabel, eager to get her wheels from her time in Southport onwards, finally succeeded in 1896. Her father 'shrank from the thought of his young daughter riding among the traffic', but was finally persuaded by the two eldest girls in concert, and they joined the club together. Christabel was given a new, speedy Rudge Whitworth, costing over £30, a very large sum for the penurious family; Sylvia, less committed to the whole venture, had to make do with a bike that was not only second-hand, but also apparently home-made by a comrade out of gas pipes! The parents do not seem to have noticed the unfairness of this arrangement, and the upshot for Sylvia was, to say the least, trying:

> It was of curious design, low-geared and rather too small for me; but it did not occur, either to Mrs Pankhurst or to me, that the machine was placing upon me a considerable handicap, when, in rather poor health, I attempted to keep pace with my elder and more athletic sister.[8]

The sisters spent every free day cycling and they enjoyed their Sundays with the club in the fresh air of the countryside. Their father reluctantly accepted their new-found hobby, though Sylvia felt he regretted that it took them away from home and 'the public interests so dear to him'. Part of this may have been due to Clarion leader Blatchford's attacks on the work for peace and internationalism of their parents' close friend and leader of the Independent Labour Party (ILP), James Keir Hardie.[9]

While the older girls were enjoying the society of young cyclists and were included in the political activities of their parents, Adela and Harry were languishing. In 1896, at the tender age of 11, the former experienced some sort of breakdown or burnout and ran away from school. When she was brought back she refused to speak and was off school for a year. Richard attempted to restore her spirits by reading poetry to her; Emmeline played the piano. She also records that her parents became more aware of the bullying she was subjected to by Sylvia in particular and: 'Father began to take a stiffer line with his elder daughters.' With more attention, Adela did recover slowly, but remained emotionally fragile.[10]

Christabel enjoyed the High School far more than her sisters, and made a friend whose home life seemed to her far superior to their own, which she said (according to Sylvia) was 'nothing but politics and silly old women's suffrage'. When Christabel was banned from playing the dancing master in a school production of Molière's *Le Bourgeois Gentilhomme* by the hostile Miss Day, Richard was detailed by Emmeline to plead with the headmistress. His failure led him to exclaim: 'There is no justice in this place!' Since Christabel had shown some talent and commitment to dancing lessons outside school, her mother had resolved that this should be her career. She therefore was contemptuous of the High School and its teaching and kept her daughters away at any opportunity, such as helping at a fund-raising bazaar. Richard was more ambitious for the academic success of his children, and when Christabel was 16 he pronounced that as she had 'a good head' she should be coached and matriculate. Emmeline cried and objected that 'she would not see her daughters brought up to be High School teachers'. Eventually Christabel abandoned the notion of a dancing career, but neither did she or Sylvia become teachers.[11] Sylvia was allowed to train as an artist, and Christabel eventually in 1906 gained a law degree at the Victoria University of Manchester, having been the only woman on her law course and gaining first-class honours.[12]

From Liberal to Socialist

Pankhurst, while an increasingly radical Liberal and moving steadily towards socialism in his final decade, continued to put policy and moral worth above party. At the annual meeting of the Manchester Working Men's Clubs Association on 13 June 1887, held in Manchester Town Hall, he referred to the recent death of Mayor Matthew Curtis. Despite the fact that the latter was a Conservative, he acknowledged that Curtis was a man with 'two characteristic qualities of an Englishman – intense practical activity and genuine public spirit … He had passed away, leaving us the tradition of the life of a true civic soldier.'[13]

By March 1891 Richard had firmly nailed his, so far relatively moderate, colours to the socialist mast when he was elected president of the Manchester and District Fabian Society.[14] It was not long before he became associated with other, more left-wing, organisations and indeed had already begun to introduce his children to the world of socialism. At the age of 8, Sylvia's first public meeting in the company of her parents was in London, to hear Social Democratic Federation leader H.M. Hyndman 'in a small, dingy hall'. The movement could not afford a better venue. No sooner had the chairman delivered his introduction than Emmeline insisted on leaving the hall; it turned out that she had found a bug on her glove and could not bear to remain. Though fierce in her crusades to improve the lives of the people, there were limits to Emmeline's tolerance of the 'hands-on' approach to the poor.

The socialists were a trial to Richard in other ways; he did not join the Social Democratic Federation of Hyndman, according to Sylvia because he found its focus on economic considerations to be too limiting. There were interminable internal squabbles and expulsions that he found distasteful and as a result there was little activity on large public issues. On top of all that many of the leaders, including Hyndman, were hostile to women's suffrage. But in her father Sylvia observed a commitment to the real issues and together they plunged into the dark alleys of the city and embarked on what for Sylvia became a lifelong mission to work among the desperately poor.

Having established initial links with the socialist movement in London by joining the Fabian Society, and also befriending in particular the working-class agitator James Keir Hardie, in the years after their move to the north the Pankhursts committed wholeheartedly to socialism.[15] It is claimed that they had first seen Hardie in 1888 at the International Labour Conference and again at the Paris International Socialist Conference in 1889. When he fought successfully as an independent for a seat in parliament in 1892, this ex-miner from Scotland was 'ardently admired' by the Pankhursts.

A miners' strike from July to November 1893, actuated by an attempt to reduce wages, galvanised Richard into a series of polemics in the press and lectures against the employers in mining areas such as Clayton and Bradford in Manchester. He advocated that government, in the guise of the county councils, should take on ownership of the mines and oversee their running by groups of miners.[16] Meanwhile, Hardie had introduced a Bill in the Commons that embodied a centralised plan for the ownership and management of the mines. In both cases, the aim was to empower the workers and ensure fair wages.

Hardie's Independent Labour Party (ILP), a forerunner of the twentieth-century Labour Party, was set up at the Bradford (Yorkshire) conference in January 1893. The direction of the Pankhursts' travel was clear when they chose to attend. At the conference Hardie dominated all the key decisions, arguing successfully against the demands of Manchester socialists, led by Richard Pankhurst, in favour of the 'Fourth Clause'. This would have prevented ILP members from voting for a sympathetic radical (or perhaps even Conservative) candidate in local elections.[17] It seems that here Richard was taking the uncompromising stance he had advocated in the WFrL.

The ILP put up its first candidate in the person of Frank Smith. Despite the contentions over the Fourth Clause, a 'warm friendship' between Hardie and the Pankhursts had sprung up and was cemented during the hard-fought by-election in Attercliffe in July 1894 when the Pankhursts travelled to Yorkshire again to join Hardie in support of Smith. They wrote ahead that they were coming 'to take part in the fight in favour of Labour and against the tyranny of Liberalism'.[18] On arrival they accompanied Smith to the nominations, at which Richard seems to have played a prominent role. He subtly used it to make a point about the unfairness of the system, which required a huge deposit beyond the means of working-class candidates:

> At twenty-five minutes past twelve Mr. Frank Smith, accompanied by Dr. Pankhurst, arrived. He had three nomination papers ... On the Town Clerk reminding the Labour candidate that a deposit of £100 was necessary to meet the returning officer's expenses, Dr. Pankhurst rather ostentatiously produced bank notes ... and handed the required amount to the Mayor.[19]

On 30 June it was noted that the ILP candidate was holding no fewer than fifteen meetings at which the Pankhursts spoke alongside many socialist luminaries.[20] That evening, relaxation was in order; it was reported that at 2am the ILP contingent were in the Victoria Hotel 'enjoying a quiet smoke in company with Dr. Pankhurst'.[21]

On the day of the poll Emmeline took her place with trade union leader Ben Tillett and Keir Hardie in addressing workers in the dinner hour.[22] The election passed off peacefully, but there was a sad incident when Frank Smith, Keir Hardie and Dr Pankhurst were driving through the town; 'a little boy ran full tilt against the wheel of their carriage and was knocked down'. The child, with serious head injuries, was carried to his home nearby, whilst Ben Tillett rode off on a bicycle to get medical help. Taken to the children's hospital, it was thought the child would fortunately live. Frank Smith came a poor third in the contest.[23]

It was not until September 1894 that Richard made his move to socialism fully official by an announcement in the press. Emmeline, despite the misgivings of her friend Ursula Bright, who believed that the ILP were 'too violent and contemptuous of other people's methods'[24] and could not succeed, was slightly ahead of him in that she allowed herself to be put up by the ILP as their candidate for the Manchester School Board as early as July. She appears to have had a considerable amount of help from her husband in producing her manifesto; when informed of her adoption by an ILP committee member, the latter stated: 'I took the liberty of reading the programme sent me by the Doctor, judging you are in full sympathy with it, and to show to the Executive Committee that you are far in advance of the programme adopted by the joint committee.'[25] This does not necessarily indicate that Emmeline was not wholly on board with the ideology of socialism, but it does show that her enthusiasm and application was strongly influenced by her husband. Adela recalls that: 'Socialism appeared to my mother as a beacon of light for humanity. Trusting in my father, for whose wisdom she had such reverence, she gave herself heart and soul to the labour movement.'[26]

In council elections in Manchester from September onwards, Richard could be found supporting ILP candidates.[27] And his socialism was not exclusive to the ILP; on 29 July he was present at the International Socialist Congress organised by the Social Democratic Federation in the Free Trade Hall. The satirical *Spy* magazine reported caustically that he cheered free schools, free medicine and free doctors, but was 'silently sorrowful' when free law was promised.

Also at this period Richard began to speak for the ILP. He led a discussion on it in the Owens College Debating Society; it is perhaps due to his influence that women were allowed to attend, for only the second time. His enthusiasm for women's rights was not shared by all socialists. Although Hardie was in favour, others in the socialist movement at this period prioritised male workers' rights and feared that women's rights could detract from their focus. Richard's speech demonstrates how far he had travelled from Liberalism:

> The fundamental policy of the Independent Labour Party was to establish a system of society from the economic point of view. That system was Socialism, and it was to be established upon the collective ownership of the means of production, distribution, and exchange ... To private property in the means of production ... was due the misery and degradation of the civilised world ... His great hope for the future of the empire was in the workers and the women.[28]

He included a major attack on the property-owning class ('a band of marauders'), and in particular on one of its most prominent defenders, the arch-Conservative Lord Salisbury. But perhaps this was all too radical for his audience, as they voted thirty-three to twenty-three against his resolution that all friends of the people and of progress should support ILP principles.

It was not long before he was advocating the formation of a, with hindsight unfortunately named, 'National Socialist Party' at a Manchester meeting. He greatly impressed his new comrades:

The Doctor was in his finest form ... Amongst the many beautiful and ennobling thoughts that he uttered was 'that the earth is new to every generation. Do not let us bring forward institutions that will set back the emancipation of man.'

Inspired, the meeting enthusiastically and unanimously agreed.[29]

The different timing in the decisions of husband and wife with regard to officially declaring for the ILP may be explained by their personalities; it is clear that both were tending in this direction, but whereas Emmeline was impulsive and decisive, Richard was often more cautious and thought long and deeply about his beliefs and the actions that should follow. Christabel believed that he was also held back by his fear of the opprobrium of his fellow lawyers, city councillors, businessmen, and wealthy clients. He was afraid for his livelihood. Moreover, she quotes his words questioning whether he had 'life and strength left to fight the position', perhaps implying that he knew that his health was failing. Once decided, he proved himself strong in his commitment. Christabel is ringing in her endorsement: 'Gallant as ever, he held his head high and faced the new storm that broke upon him as the first man of his sort and standing in the city, perhaps in the whole country, to join the Labour movement.'

Richard's worries were well-founded; this was not without consequences. The Pankhursts ceased to be invited with the great and the good of Manchester to official functions at the Town Hall.[30] Worse, Richard found that clients withdrew their briefs, and the city council did not call on him for much of their legal work. He had plenty to do, fighting the causes of trade unions and political organisations, but it seems such work was often unpaid.

Christabel explains in her memoir that both parents had high hopes of the labouring classes and the new party in terms of gaining women's rights, and also in redressing other political and social wrongs:

Father ... hoped that this growing party might succeed in ways where the old parties had failed. Even more perhaps than in its principles, he had hope in its personnel. The common people, to Father's generation, seemed almost, if not quite, a different creation. Some reckoned them innately inferior. Others, of whom Father was one, were tempted to think of them, or at least hope them to be, possessed of an innate quality which would enable them, were they once free and powerful enough, to reform the world and its ways. He idealized them, as did Mother.[31]

Emmeline's role began to change in these years. Encouraged by the ILP's acceptance of women in politics, which contrasted with the hostility of the Social Democratic Federation of Hyndman and the indifference of the Fabians, she began to take on a new prominence in campaigns.

The Pankhurst household was educated in the ideas and issues of Labour politics through Hardie's *Labour Leader*, Robert Blatchford's *Clarion*, and the Manchester *Labour Prophet*. Sylvia noted that their home became 'a centre of Socialist agitations' where ILP speakers, including Hardie, were accommodated on their visits to the city. Hardie was a hero to the whole family. Richard, Sylvia claimed, 'with a tremble of enthusiasm in his voice' had praised 'the brave stand Keir Hardie had made in Parliament'; he called himself 'the member for the unemployed'. By 1895 Richard was close enough to him to advise him about the management of the *Labour Leader* and wrote expressing concerns for his health.[32] Sylvia describes Hardie at length in her 1931 work, *The Suffragette Movement*, in particular noting 'his eyes, two deep wells of kindness, like mountain pools with the sunlight shining through them; sunshine distilled they always seemed to me'.[33] Hardie and Sylvia later became lovers and her description testifies to the fondness she continued to feel for this much older man.

Bruce and Katharine Glasier, a young couple, very much in love to judge by their private diaries, were also included in the Pankhursts' circle. The former began as a lowly Scottish shepherd boy, but his wife was a Walthamstow minister's daughter who had studied at Newnham College and who insisted on putting BA after her name, even though at that time Cambridge did not award degrees to women. They were spartan in their lifestyle, which contrasted with Emmeline's devotion to a beautiful home and gowns, albeit often made by her own hand. Katherine and Bruce gave very cheap lectures and accepted 'the poorest of hospitality'; Katherine made her own dresses out of green serge, 'cut with aspirations towards Burne Jones'.[34] It seems that Bruce first met Richard Pankhurst in April 1896 at an ILP conference, as he humorously described:

I was pleasantly seated between Dr. Pankhurst and the Newcastle delegate. The Doctor and I got on famously. We conferred together and acted in concert. The Doctor always deferred to me on points of law and procedure, and I was guided invariably by his judgment on matters of propaganda. Thus our position was impregnable. Mrs Pankhurst had, I noticed, some misgivings at first about this coalition of our twain

> intelligence; but remembering that the Doctor and I were the only two
> people in the Conference who had read Dougal Stewart's *Philosophy of
> the Human Mind* and the judicious Hooker's *Ecclesiastical Polity*, she
> became somewhat reassured.[35]

The Glasiers stayed overnight with the Pankhursts at 4 Buckingham Crescent on a few occasions when they had speaking engagements in the Manchester area. The first recorded was on Saturday, 9 November 1895, when Bruce noted in his diary that they were treated to 'Bkf [breakfast] in bed in morning!' This unlooked-for luxury resulted in further stays the same month, but the diaries thereafter do not record further overnight stops, though daytime visits continued.[36]

Other visitors included prominent female speakers for the ILP, such as Caroline Martyn, who was 'tall and pale' and 'wore sandals and a long whitish grey robe of would-be Grecian form' of which Emmeline definitely did not approve. Tom Mann, secretary to the ILP, made Emmeline smile at his exuberance and romped with the children. There were German socialists; at the end of May 1896 Wilhelm Liebknecht came accompanied by Eleanor, daughter of Karl Marx. A large meeting was held by the socialists to welcome them, and Pankhurst presented an address to Liebknecht.[37]

Socialist meetings for Manchester adherents saw apparently regular attendance by the Pankhurst family. The Manchester ILP central branch met, perhaps predictably in this period of idealism, in 'a poorly-lit, evil-smelling room over a stable', in a side street off Oxford Road.[38] It was not all earnest speeches and international celebrities. Christabel was detailed to dance at many ILP events, and Sylvia records that sometimes the two sisters danced an Irish jig together for the wholesome entertainment of the socialists.

Elevating the Poor

Even before the return to the north, Richard had formed an association there with the Manchester Ancoats Brotherhood. On 31 January 1890 he stepped in to replace Thomas Ellis MP, detained at Luxor on the Nile by sickness, in giving them a talk. The Brotherhood was an institute for the poor founded by Charles Rowley, who brought to them the best examples of music, art and science; he was a friend of the pre-Raphaelites and ran shops that sold prints of the great masters. For Richard this was the start of a mission to offer political education to the lower classes that continued for the rest of his life.

In the New Islington Hall he considered the topic of Society and Sovereignty. The tickets were limited to 250, but 'the demand for them is so great as to be embarrassing'; this may have been in part also due to the 'very pleasing selection of music' offered by Mr D. Smith and friends after the talk. Richard's successful and popular lectures continued in the autumn and winter of 1894 with a series on the duties of citizenship, primitive society, the development of law and ethics, and national and international citizenship. His stated aim was 'to diffuse sound views on broad lines upon the great organic questions now under discussion in our own and other countries'.[39]

The whole family began to spend Sundays with the Brotherhood, and Sylvia in particular was taken by her father to the places where the working classes lived, 'the dingy streets of Ancoats, Gorton, Hulme and other working-class districts'. Her description of Richard in these streets is vivid:

> Standing on a chair or a soap-box, pleading the Cause of the people with passionate earnestness, he stirred me, as perhaps he stirred no other auditor, though I saw tears on the faces of the people about him ... The misery of the poor, as I heard my father plead for it, and saw it revealed in the pinched faces of his audiences, awoke in me a maddening sense of impotence ...[40]

When the Pankhursts adopted socialism, this was not just theoretical. Richard and Emmeline became dedicated to elevating the position of the poor in practical ways. In July 1893 he led a committee to convert an existing school into a 'doss-house' for working men in Manchester's worst slum, Angel Meadow, a scheme based on developments in London. This was a new departure; Richard's hands-on involvement hitherto had been limited to educational activity, but now he got down to the realities of poverty. This may have been partly due to Emmeline's influence. Despite her aversion to bugs on gloves, as a result of her election as the ILP candidate in Openshaw as a Chorlton-on-Medlock poor law guardian in December 1894, she threw herself into the day-to-day lives of those unfortunate enough to have resort to the workhouse. This, in the early days of women's inclusion in local bodies, was her first public role without Richard and she pursued it apparently with the full blessing of her spouse.

The winter of 1894 saw the beginning of a period of severe hardship that lasted until the following year. Unemployment was very high, and there was no help for the able-bodied poor, even though the government acknowledged their distress. Richard came into his own, forming a committee for the relief of the unemployed, which also included as treasurer Dr Martin of the Chorlton poor law guardians.[41] Using funds raised from street collections and advertising in the local press, there were food distributions that fed up to 2,000 people a day. Emmeline negotiated in the market for donations of food; other ILP members cooked it and handed out soup and bread.

In February 1895 Richard allied with a young socialist, Leonard Hall, the son of a doctor, to lead deputations to the municipality and the boards of guardians, demanding that they form committees to address the needs of the people, give local boards of guardians the powers and money to provide help for the able-bodied, find work for the unemployed at trade union rates, and acquire land for them to work.[42] Emmeline agitated within the board of guardians on similar lines. Her resolution had just suffered a defeat when Richard and Leonard Hall arrived at the head of procession of unemployed workers clamouring for action. The board, ever wary of anything that might raise the poor rates, refused to accede to their demands, and one member uttered something about 'undeserving poor', provoking Richard's riposte that this was 'an insult to human nature'. There were claims by the board that the protesters had been forced or bribed to join in. When Hall reported all this to the unemployed outside, matters became dangerous and the guardians then agreed to send a deputation to the city council supporting demands for work and other help.[43]

While this was occurring in Manchester, in Leicester (and elsewhere) there was a lockout in the boot and shoe industry. The Pankhursts rushed there to lend their support to the workers and Richard pleaded their cause through the press.[44] Meanwhile, Keir Hardie demanded in parliament that the government should open workshops for the men. As Sylvia put it: 'Like the bit and brace, Keir Hardie and the Pankhursts seemed wrought to work in unison.'[45]

The next month, April 1895, saw the gathering of the ILP in conference at Newcastle. 'Our exhaustless friends, the Pankhursts' were duly in attendance, and it was noted in the *Clarion* by Leonard Hall that: 'In moving the adoption of the [financial] report Dr. Pankhurst's classic eloquence swells our bosoms with legitimate pride.' Richard, 'the legal lion of the party', uttered 'brave words, apt and true' when he asserted 'there has been noble self-denial in the raising of the funds, and equally noble self-denial in the expenditure of them'. He did not stop there, but later, during discussion of the party's agricultural programme, he successfully 'urged the necessity for a "State Land Department"'.[46] Only a few days later, on 2 May, the National Administrative Council (NAC) of the ILP resolved to invite twelve people from all over England to join them; Dr Pankhurst was on that list.[47]

Later, when matters had somewhat eased, in September 1895 Emmeline read a paper at the North-Western Poor Law Conference at Ulverston on the powers and duties of poor law guardians in times of distress. The speech was written by her husband, and bore his hallmark historical and legal explanations, as well as setting out measures to be adopted in the future, should such hardship arise again. These were on the lines of those demanded in Manchester in the winter of

1894–95. They were regarded as extreme, 'even fantastic', in their benevolence. But it seems that Emmeline presented the matter so well that influential people supported the Pankhursts' arguments. This enhanced her position on the Chorlton board and she was empowered to make numerous practical changes that improved the lives of the workhouse inmates, not least providing seats with backs for the old and underwear for the young girls.

ILP Candidate – The Gorton Election of May 1895

When a general election was called for July 1895, Richard was adopted by the ILP to stand for an industrial suburb of Manchester, Gorton, which included Emmeline's poor law district of Openshaw. This had been under discussion as early as January, when Richard wrote to Keir Hardie agreeing to stand for the ILP, but asking for a safe seat as he had fought twice in 'forlorn hopes' and would do so 'no more'.[1] A series of open-air meetings were held in the time-honoured way of the working classes, and Richard addressed in his speeches the issues close to Mancunian hearts; apart from the general principles he held about sharing wealth and the ownership of land and mines, he discoursed on a dispute between the dockers and the Manchester Ship Canal directors about wearing the union badge, describing the attitude of the latter as 'ridiculous and tyrannical'. There was a new coherence to these policies; now they were all about changing the basis of society 'from an individualist character to a collectivist character'.[2]

He was one of twenty-nine ILP candidates, who were greatly feared in particular by the Liberals. Suggestions were made by the latter for a deal to persuade the ILP to withdraw a candidate in another constituency, if they were to agree to vote in Gorton for Richard. There was a debate in the press, much as there had been in 1883, about whether Liberal supporters should vote for the 'Red Doctor'. As it happened, the ILP at a meeting in the Douglas Hotel in Manchester on 9 July 1895 voted to reject this approach.[3] Early in July it seemed that the Liberals would run a candidate in the person of James Brierley, which the ILP argued would split the vote and allow in the Conservative, Ernest Hatch.[4] Pankhurst was clearly disconcerted by this development and wrote to Hardie that if the ILP were to successfully promote the withdrawal of Brierley, he would win 'by a large majority'. Nevertheless if this did not occur he heroically offered:

> I shall fight and hope to beat both candidates. In any case as I have before been sacrificed to my principles I am perfectly ready for the same reason to be once more sacrificed if the need arises.[5]

In the end Brierley withdrew; as a radical, he explained that he and Pankhurst supported the same policies and he agreed that if they both stood Hatch would be elected.[6] Furthermore, the outgoing Liberal MP, William Mather, urged Liberal voters to elect Richard, and even helped with his expenses.[7] Hatch, fearing the ILP threat from the popular Pankhurst, once Brierley had withdrawn raised that old spectre, the accusation that Richard was an atheist. The latter immediately sent letters to him and his agents and party threatening legal action under the Corrupt and Illegal Practices Prevention Act of 1883.[8] This apparently quashed the attack.

The Irish vote was still a consideration, and Emmeline went to meet T.P. O'Connor in Liverpool to persuade him to lead them in support of Richard. She did not succeed. The Irish were sympathetic, but as Catholics they disapproved of socialist opposition to religion, and also were worried that a weakened Liberal vote would hamper the delivery of Gladstone's Home Rule policy for Ireland.

Pankhurst attempted to appeal to both the workers and the Liberal voters. To the former he offered nationalisation of the land, the mines and the railways, old age pensions, and an eight-hour day. He had elaborated on this last at the annual meeting of the Working Men's Clubs on 2 May, showing an awareness of the limitations placed on workers by their current long hours:

> For his own part he thoroughly approved the Eight Hours Bill as an act of economic justice, a social duty, and a public good ... Working men would have some time and some energy left after eight hours' work to devote to the higher interests of mind and body.[9]

To the radical Liberals he offered Irish Home Rule, Church disestablishment, the local veto on licensed premises, and the abolition of the House of Lords. However, a major stumbling block was that he was too closely associated with the extremism of the ILP. And he did not hide this at all. Indeed, he proclaimed it. Keir Hardie had behaved in ways that were beyond the pale for many: he had worn a cap instead of the usual top hat to go into parliament and arrived accompanied by a brass band; he had stated his republicanism and linked congratulations on a royal birth with condolences for a Welsh colliery disaster; he had hinted at royal adultery in speeches that had had to be expunged from Hansard. Yet Richard praised him:

> When Keir Hardie stood up in the House of Commons for the people, with a faithful, earnest, manly appeal, he stood alone ... are you not going to send other men to support him? [10]

Emmeline, fond though she was of Keir Hardie, was aware of the danger a too close association with him might mean for her husband's candidature, and 'knit her brows fiercely' when opponents described 'the man with the cap' as Richard's 'leader'.[11]

The election was run on a shoestring. Richard had warned the ILP that he could not afford to pay for his own campaign, and the party assured him that it would finance its candidates. A finance committee was established to run elections, and Richard was among its members. Campaigning was done on new, cheaper lines; instead of issuing circulars for meetings, announcements were chalked on pavements. Advertisements were placed in the press and requests were made at meetings appealing for donations.[12] The family threw themselves into the fray. Emmeline, with Christabel and Sylvia carrying Richard's colours of yellow and black, was busy canvassing in Openshaw, visiting the homes of voters, delivering addresses on a soap box that were designed to appeal to the conventional wisdom about husbands and wives, but were also probably sincere: 'You put me at the top of the poll [for the board of guardians]; will you not vote for the man who has taught me all I know?' Emmeline even braved the public houses of the town to appeal to 'men with glistening eyes and thirsty lips' to come out and vote for her husband.[13]

A heartfelt letter published in the *Manchester Guardian* on 6 July summarises the high esteem in which Pankhurst was held in certain Manchester quarters:

> As Mr. Leonard Hall has stated, in a letter which does him great credit, that he will not contest the North-east division, the I.L.P. now, of all the Manchester Parliamentary sections, has only one candidate in the field – Dr. Pankhurst for the Gorton division ... Anyone listening to the worthy Doctor must feel the grand human sympathy throbbing in his honest heart, and those who know him more intimately know full well what sacrifices he has made for the practical realisation of his schemes for the amelioration of the wretched state of existence of our

poor weaker brothers and sisters. It was chiefly due to his exertions and initiative that thousands of poor destitute creatures were fed in Stevenson Square and elsewhere during the last severe winter ...

E.G. Taylor, 34 Ackers St., Oxford St., Chorlton-on-Medlock
5 July 1895

Yet it was disheartening that while many expressed love and appreciation for Dr Pankhurst, they opted to vote for the Conservative, Mr Hatch, because they considered Richard had no hope of winning this time. Even before Gorton polled, Keir Hardie had lost his West Ham seat, which served to confirm this belief.[14] Indeed, every ILP candidate in the election failed in the poll.

In Gorton there were thought to be Liberals who had abstained, but in any case the Liberal majority had been in decline; it stood at over 1,800 in 1885, fell to 457 in 1886, and was down to 222 in 1892.[15] There was a larger swing towards the Conservatives than in any other area of Manchester and Salford. Hatch gained 5,865 votes at a cost of £1,375 in expenses; Pankhurst gained 4,261 votes with a mere £342 in costs. Although he bitterly berated the Liberals as closet Tories, Richard was 'smiling and gay' at the post-count meeting, declaring that this was not defeat, it was 'victory postponed' and assuring his weeping daughter, Sylvia, that: 'There is life in the old bird yet!' She nonetheless was devastated, and was later scolded by her mother as having 'disgraced the family' with her tears.[16] It seems likely that Richard was heartened by the fact that of all the ILP candidates he had achieved the highest number of actual votes. His 4,261 compared very favourably with Fred Brocklehurst's in Bolton at 2,696, Ben Tillett's in Bradford West at 2,264, and Tom Mann's in Colne Valley at 1,245. Even Hardie himself in West Ham South only polled 3,975.[17] It was in the light of this that the *London Evening Mail* gratifyingly noted that: 'Karl Marx and Keir Hardie pale into insignificance beside Dr. Pankhurst.'

Perhaps he was secretly relieved that he would not have to brave the stresses and strains of debating in the Commons, particularly in view of his health problems. Or perhaps he was one of those who see themselves as a lonely crusader without an army, 'sustained only by the righteousness of the cause and the kinship of a scattering of rare spirits', much like his hero J.S. Mill. Stefan Collini points out that this attitude of Mill's 'flattered his intellect, provided a sense of purpose, explained away failure'.[18] Yet Richard did have one redoubtable fighter on his side; his determined wife, who after all this drove alone in a pony and trap to the Colne Valley to support the candidacy of Tom Mann, and on her return through Gorton was stoned by Tory thugs who had spent the evening celebrating their victory in the pubs. 'Tired as she was, her nerve was unshaken.'[19]

Pugh points out that Pankhurst's intervention in the Gorton election of 1895 did eventually bear fruit; thereafter the Liberals did not run a candidate in the constituency again. When the political tide changed in 1906 and the Conservatives fell out of favour, the new Labour Party was able to reap the reward of victory; the ground had been prepared by Pankhurst's unsuccessful attempt eleven years earlier.[20]

Meanwhile, Christabel at least believed that this period was the happiest in the family's history, though acknowledging that her father must have experienced frustration when his high ideals seemed unattainable:

> We were very happy in our private family life. Those were the best of all the years. If politics and movements did mean forgoing some things that other people's children had, those other children had not our Father and Mother, our interesting life. Our lot contented us; we were proud of it.
>
> Father sparkled for us as much as – or more than – for his friends. His courtesy in his home was complete and his loving ways invariable. Mother was queen – 'Where's my lady?' was always his first word. Some of the poor people took to calling her Lady Pankhurst with a vague idea that this must be her title. He never in our hearing addressed her by her first name, but always by some word of endearment …
>
> Only his wife knew all Father's regret that he could not give more effect to his ideals, could not do more to overthrow the social evils which men of all ranks and parties now are openly condemning and attacking.[21]

He nevertheless continued to do his best, working assiduously on sub-committees of the NAC such as the one set up in January 1896 to investigate accusations against James Tattershall, the candidate for Halifax, of breaking party rules. At the crowded annual meeting of the Manchester ILP on 16 February 1896 Richard's prominence was clear as the chief speaker, alongside Keir Hardie. He chose to attack the government in its focus on foreign affairs, to the detriment of the condition of the workers. Indeed, he referred to the government as a 'foreign affairs association' and 'an army and navy club'. His conclusion was that only the ILP could furnish a remedy for the deprivation of the poor.[22]

In April at the ILP annual conference Richard was elected onto the NAC itself with fifty-two votes, which put him fifth out of thirteen.[23] At the subsequent NAC meeting in London he 'urged strongly' that the ILP should contest North Aberdeen with their secretary, Tom Mann, as the candidate. At this same meeting, Pankhurst was elected with Hardie to attend an International Socialist Congress. Not content with that, he also gave notice of a motion for the next meeting on the appointment by the NAC of land, industrial and political organising committees.[24]

Nevertheless, sitting increasingly uneasily with his new-found socialist beliefs, Richard was to be found as late as February 1896 giving a lecture to the Manchester Statistical Society on Company Law, and in particular on limited liability and joint-stock enterprises. He declared that 'though defects and abuses naturally existed, the system was sound and honest'. The admiration he expressed for the 'men of high powers and proved eminence in all walks of manufacturing and commercial ability' demonstrates that his socialism was very much of the British type; the idea of ownership by and for the people was not a concept he seems to have embraced universally, or at least in all company.[25]

His interest in legislation and clarity of insight into the detail continued unabated, as demonstrated by his letter to the *Manchester Guardian* of 20 March 1896.[26] In this particular case he was concerned about new legislation regulating companies; he presented areas where amendment was needed and exhorted the House of Lords, where the bill had just passed its second reading, to pay 'earnest attention' to its provisions. He likewise maintained his links with the Manchester Law Students' Society, chairing their annual meeting in October 1896 as a vice-president.[27]

Perhaps surprisingly, Richard also still found time for the Manchester Arts Club, one of the earliest clubs of which he had been a distinguished member. On 23 April 1896 they held a meeting chaired by Pankhurst to celebrate Shakespeare's birthday. A large audience gathered to hear him discuss the similarities between the Bard's works and Greek drama, both of which represented 'the universal in human nature and in human life'. He believed that Shakespeare was superior to Sophocles, in that his characters were deeper and more complex, and that: 'His high heart beat ever in unison with ... the music which goes forth ceaselessly from the mighty harmonies of the universe, of nature and of man.'[28] Fittingly, the evening was accompanied by music directed by Dr Henry Watson that was 'Shakespearean in character.'[29] Perhaps this was for him a little light relief after all the heavy politicking that was his normal fare.

Boggart Hole Clough

By the time of the meeting of 3 July 1896, held in Manchester, the NAC was preoccupied with the prosecution of socialist speakers at a local outdoor venue, the unpromisingly named Boggart Hole Clough. This was a 63-acre site at Blackley, north of Manchester, and the dispute featured the consolidation of Emmeline Pankhurst in her first leading role as a public political campaigner. As was now increasingly his wont, Richard was active mainly behind the scenes and in court. The issue blew up in 1896 when Manchester Corporation acquired the Clough; for several years the socialists had used the site for meetings on the workers' day off, a Sunday. Now the leader of the Parks Committee, Councillor Needham, decided to put a stop to them.[30] The appeal of the Clough as a place to meet is clear from a description afforded by the *Manchester Guardian*:

> The meeting … took place in the cleft in the hill on the left side of the Clough, entering from Harpurhey. It is a natural amphitheatre, of which the ridges made by the wind and the rain form the seats, rising in tiers on either side, to the top of the fissure.[31]

The onset of the dispute was preceded by a major May Day demonstration by workers in Peel Park, Salford.[32] There were banners, bands and six speakers' platforms, and the attendance was 'strong in numbers', filling the cricket and games pitches. It featured many local trade unions and branches of the ILP and other socialist organisations, including the Clarion Cycling Club and the Labour Church. The Manchester ILP banner bore the motto 'Neither riches nor poverty, but justice'. Emmeline spoke of the power of labour from one platform, and the crowd approved of her assertion that 'the time for words is past, and the time for action is come'.

Richard occupied a separate platform, and proposed the first of three major resolutions, which greeted workers all over the world and advocated labour representation on all nations' legislative and administrative bodies. He saw socialism progressing in all countries, including in Britain, demanding land nationalisation and an end to monopolies. These words may have resonated less with his hearers than his next statements:

> The capital of the country had accumulated to an extent never before known, productive power was never greater or more effective, and wealth was enormously increased. Why was it, therefore, that there was so much poverty in England, so much want of employment, and so many people struggling to keep themselves from falling into indigence? … The answer was that the capital of the country was exploited by the few to the injury and the prejudice of the many … It was because the wealth which the workers earned was not justly divided amongst the workers who earned it.[33]

He went on to expound some of his usual policies about nationalisation of the land, but added to this the necessity of working people having political power.

He therefore stated his belief that MPs should be paid so that workers could enter parliament:

> It was necessary that side by side with the command and control of the industrial machine they should have the command and control, by their votes and their members, of the political machine ... They must stand firm to the principles they were met to enforce, because the cause of Socialism was the cause of humanity.

Many of those in power believed that the time had come to stop the march of this dangerous ideology. In May, John Harker, a Trades Council member, was taken to court and fined 10 shillings for speaking in Boggart Hole Clough. It probably did not help him that he had stood against Needham in the previous council election. The prosecution claimed that the crowd of around 400 who attended had caused damage in the park, and there had been complaints from nearby residents. Harker was defended in court by Richard Pankhurst, who argued that there was no legal basis for banning orderly meetings, and tried to disprove the claims of damage. Richard was then instructed by the ILP to take the case to a higher court. An appeal was launched via the *Clarion* to raise the funds to pursue it and other cases that were expected to ensue.[34] The movement was boosted on 30 May by the visit of the 'veteran Socialist' from Germany, Wilhelm Liebknecht. Hyndman's SDF had organised it, and Richard Pankhurst of the ILP was the main speaker to welcome him. All socialist organisations were encouraged to attend.[35]

The outcome of all this agitation was a defiant reaction by the ILP and their supporters to what they regarded as the suppression of free speech. A stream of speakers, including Emmeline, famously wearing a pink straw bonnet, attracted thousands to Boggart Hole Clough. Each week the male speakers, defended in a crowded court by Pankhurst, were fined and when they refused to pay up they were imprisoned. It cannot have helped their defence when they referred to their opponents as 'bald-headed, egotistical, bombastic old fossils'![36] An attempt by the judge to get agreement that the meetings should be suspended pending an appeal lodged by Richard was rejected by the defence. Soon prominent ILP members Fred Brocklehurst and Leonard Hall were incarcerated. The newspaper report of the latter's release includes Emmeline's description of the conditions under which they were detained. Prison was not for the fainthearted:

> She knew that in Strangeways he [Hall] had been placed under great indignities. The prisoners there did not get enough food; strong men waited for their meals, prowling round their cells like hungry wild

> beasts. – (Shame.) She had heard that Mr. Hall, who was in a basement
> cell and had asked for another blanket, had been told – and this was
> all the reply he got – that the people outside were complaining of the
> heat. – (Shame.) Mr. Hall could read the prison regulations through the
> blanket which he had.[37]

Furthermore, Brocklehurst on his release claimed that he had been ill in prison, but was refused admission to the prison hospital for treatment.[38]

By 21 June, the crowd in the Clough on Sundays had reached an estimated 10,000. Emmeline lectured pointedly on the life of William Cobbett, the radical grandfather of the corporation's prosecuting lawyer.[39] Bruce Glasier, who attended at a distance to assess the situation prior to his own appearance as a speaker the following Sunday, wrote in his private diary that the crowd was estimated even higher, at 15,000.[40] 'The scene at the Clough [was] a magnificent sight. Not daring to go too near … I could not hear Mrs Pankhurst's speech but her words rang clearly through the dell … she passed out of the gates with an enthusiastic crowd in her train.' The continued prohibition and prosecutions gave rise to 'indignation meetings' in other venues, such as that held in the New Cross district of Manchester, and another in Stevenson Square a few days later, both attended by the Pankhursts and their allies and up to 15,000 people. They both spoke, although according to the press coverage it was Emmeline who seems to have been the more prominent and clearly had a great deal of popular support.[41]

On 3 July Emmeline appeared with Mrs Smalley, Mrs Bennett, Mrs Harker, Mrs Mellor, and Bruce Glasier in the Police Court over their participation in the Clough on 21 and 28 June. The NAC meeting that was convened at 11 am on the same day in York Street, Manchester, voted to leave to attend the trial.[42] Bruce Glasier noted the scene in his diary:

> We all sit in a row – Katharine [his wife] has a seat in Press box. Hardie,
> Mann, Smart, Curran, Stacy and Martyn look on from side. Court
> crammed. Hundreds in all below and outside. Cobbett prosecutes and
> brings forward witnesses. Mrs Pankhurst and I hew their evidence to
> pieces. Great amusement. Case adjourned …[43]

The judge wished to see what would happen on the ensuing Sunday – dealing with a middle-class lady was quite a different matter from sentencing mostly working-class men. Indeed, it was stated by the prosecution that the wives had been sent to speak by their husbands, who feared arrest and thought their wives would not be imprisoned.[44] Not only had Emmeline spoken, she and the other women had also broken by-laws by taking a collection in specially prepared bags.

The crowd attending the hearing was so great that many had to remain outside. It was claimed that some of them were drunk and foul-mouthed, and included 'a gang of "scuttlers", and drags and cyclists'. Officially defended by Richard, Emmeline also spoke out herself very ably, calling and questioning witnesses in her own defence. The case against her was, after several adjournments, eventually dismissed; the conviction of a middle-class lady, wife of a member of the Bar of the Northern Circuit, would have caused a public outcry, even though she quite plainly declared she would continue to speak in the Clough.[45]

When the NAC resumed its meeting at 4.30pm on 3 July the discussion concerned a possible appeal to the House of Lords with regard to the imprisonment of Leonard Hall, Fred Brocklehurst and others. Richard seemed to adopt the role he had gained in so many other organisations, as legal adviser to the council: 'Dr. Pankhurst stated that an appeal to the House of Lords ... would cost a considerable sum of money, and there was little likelihood of it being successful.' In a similar role, he joined Russell Smart and Tom Mann in scrutinising a draft constitution for the ILP that had been submitted by the chairman, Keir Hardie.

They resolved to ask all ILP branches for money to help Manchester to continue the fight for free speech in other ways, and Richard was detailed to prepare a leaflet requested by the Sheffield branch, explaining the events at the Clough. A demonstration in support of those on trial was planned in Manchester's Stevenson Square. It may be significant that Emmeline featured among the speakers on platform 1; Richard was on platform 2.[46]

By 5 July, the crowds at the now regular Sunday meetings in the Clough were estimated at between 25,000 and 40,000 people, and the dispute had attracted the attention of Sheffield MP A.J. Mundella, who had addressed a letter to the Sheffield ILP on the occasion of their declaring their support for the Manchester branch in their struggle. It was Emmeline who presided at this huge gathering and read out the minister's letter, which promised to intercede with the Home Secretary against Manchester Corporation.[47] So great was the crowd that not everyone could hear, but she could be recognised from her trademark pink bonnet, which was so often pressed into service that she had to renovate it regularly.

When Leonard Hall was released from Strangeways prison on 11 July, Richard drove over with Bruce Glasier to meet him, and warned the prison governor that the continued detention of Hall's fellow prisoner, the unwell Brocklehurst, was illegal and that the governor would be accountable for his safety. That gentleman was apparently unconcerned, even amused. He offered to pass on to his superiors any complaint Richard might choose to lay.[48] Following old radical tradition, each release of prisoners was marked by a big celebration and reception. Brocklehurst's was detailed in the sympathetic *Manchester Guardian* of 20 July 1896:

Mr. Brocklehurst was liberated early in the day, but in the evening there was a sort of reconstruction of the scene, and Mr. Brocklehurst made an imaginary exit from the prison shortly after seven o'clock. He appeared in an open carriage at the upper end of Southall-street, and was driven past the prison gates. The demonstration had been advertised, and there was an immense crowd in the street, made up largely of women and children ... With him in the carriage were Mr. Leonard Hall ... and Dr. and Mrs. Pankhurst. A procession, headed by a brass band, was formed and went along Great Ducie-street, Victoria-street, Market-street, Piccadilly, and Lever-street, to Stevenson Square.

As always, the square was the site of a large meeting that included speeches and resolutions. Hall and Richard Pankhurst were noted among the speakers.

The excitement of the Clough meetings was captured in an article in the *Clarion* of 1 August 1896, when Julia Dawson penned her report:

I should like to tell you all about the gigantic meeting at Boggart Hole Clough; about the burning enthusiasm of the 40,000 or 50,000 assembled; about the red-berried women; about the triumphal car, in which sat Dr. and Mrs. Pankhurst, Ben Tillett, Bruce Glasier, Mr. James Johnston, J.P., and other comrades brave and true, on whom all Manchester seemed to be setting such admiring eyes; about the tramcars crowded with Socialists, and running every two minutes the whole of the afternoon; about the hundreds of Clarion cyclists, and the thousands of pedestrians, all making for the one sanctified spot; about the enthusiasts on the top of the 'buses and trams waving the red flag aloft ... about the hearty hand-clasps from comrades who 'discovered' me; and about the way in which our cup of joy was bubbling over as we realised that salvation had so surely come to Manchester.

By now the Clough meetings were often chaired by Emmeline. They featured such big national figures as Keir Hardie, Bruce Glasier and Ben Tillett who drew the huge crowds.[49] On one of the Sundays early in July the Pankhurst family drove with Keir Hardie and Emmeline's sister, Mary Goulden, to the Clough in an open barouche. Emmeline and Hardie walked from the gates to the meeting place, cheered by the huge crowd. Her speech was effective and the audience was appreciative. But when there was also a call for 'Dr Pankhurst' she side-stepped his absence from the platform by talking about how he had led the democratic movement for twenty-five years. By this time, though he attended in support, Richard had taken a back seat in the proceedings. It may be that he was again suffering from the stomach ulcer that eventually killed him. However, it is also true that his appearances in court demanded much of his energy and attention.

The struggle continued, though the council was embarrassed by the notoriety of their policy. When the prosecution in court claimed that the meetings were attended by 'people in clogs, and known thieves from Angel Meadow', Manchester's worst slum, Richard advertised for witnesses to testify to the good behaviour of the crowd.[50] He threatened to subpoena unwilling witnesses, who included the town clerk, the mayor and the chairman of the Parks Committee, all of whom had visited the Clough to see what was going on. Some 431 other witnesses agreed to testify to the good character of the crowd; the court process ground to a halt. While Richard may have held back in the Clough, he was still evident in court. The *Clarion* on 18 July 1896 referred to his latest appearance as 'flinging his irresistible spirits, Niagaran eloquence, and invaluable professional equipment unreservedly into the fight'.

The council tried to impose a new by-law banning public meetings in the parks, unless the Parks Committee specifically authorised them. It was made clear that the ILP would not get this permission, demonstrating that the policy was driven by partisan objectives. However, the Home Secretary eventually intervened and imposed a new by-law binding the Parks Committee to approve any reasonable request for a public meeting.

This was a triumph for the ILP, and to rub salt into the wound at the next Manchester council election the ILP ran five candidates; Harker and Brocklehurst were elected and Councillor Needham lost his seat. It appears that Richard also stood for a time as the candidate for Bradford ward. At a meeting on 23 September, it comes as no surprise that he chose to speak about the right of free speech. Indeed, this topic was a key focus of all the ILP candidates. He went on to advocate the municipalisation of the tram system, as the gas and water already belonged to the city. Good housing too was an object of his attention; it should be offered at suitable rents for the workers, 'with a supply of hot and cold water and baths'. That he took his candidacy seriously is illustrated by his letter to the NAC of 1 October explaining that he was unable to attend because he 'was prosecuting his candidature for the Manchester City Council'.[51] However, it seems that in the end the seat remained uncontested; Richard did not go to the poll. The duties of a councillor were onerous, carried out conscientiously as they would have been by Richard. He still needed to maintain his family by his court work. And he was not a well man.

For Emmeline, Boggart Hole Clough was a watershed moment; she was now a political leader in her own right. It was she who was invited to speak at ILP meetings, and to support Keir Hardie in his campaign to win a parliamentary seat in Bradford, Yorkshire, in a by-election in October 1896. In contrast,

Glasier, perhaps gaining a rare glimpse of a hidden and more pessimistic aspect of Richard's character, reported in his diary in November when he visited his chambers that the latter was not boosted by victory: 'Dr. does not look in very cheery spirits. His practice must have suffered extremely from his recent prominence in the Clough agitation and ILP movement.' They discussed the possibility of claiming damages for Hall's and Brocklehurst's imprisonment, though Richard doubted this could succeed, exclaiming that: 'The law is not made to protect the people but to oppress them.' He also feared that chasing money would tarnish their cause: 'All the glow of martyrdom would be taken away from our struggle by the glow of gold.' Now well into his sixties, Richard must have seemed like an *eminence grise* to 37-year-old Bruce. He concludes: 'A good old chap is the doctor.'[52]

A lighthearted skit on the Boggart Hole Clough events was enacted by the Law Students Society, who had often benefitted from Richard Pankhurst's lectures on aspects of the law. Indeed, a year before this, he had been elected as the society's vice-president. In their annual mock trial at the Assize Courts:

> 'Mrs Chorlton Board', 'Dr Blank Burst' and the Chief Constable of 'Smokeyopolis' figured in a claim by 'Swear Hardie' for £100,000 damages for a torn shirt, and the pain and suffering caused him by an assault in 'Winterhill Clough'.[53]

There were serious personal consequences of the Clough affair. During this period of intense political activity the apparent breakdown of the Pankhursts' youngest daughter, Adela, occasioned considerable anxiety on the part of her parents.[54] And there were increasing financial problems due to Richard's role as defence lawyer in the Boggart Hole Clough cases, which deterred influential clients from employing his forensic services. As Glasier surmised, this was exacerbated by his prominence in the ILP as a member of its NAC.

The following May Day, 2 May 1897, Boggart Hole Clough was chosen as the site for what was intended to be the biggest workers' celebration of all. A great procession assembled in Stevenson Square in the centre of Manchester to walk to the site. At its head was 'a large body of cyclists' from the socialist Clarion Club, then the Demonstration Committee, and many trade and other societies, churches, and political organisations, including the Social Democratic Federation, the Ancoats Brotherhood and the ILP. Each carried their banner, and several bands accompanied the procession.

Just as they set off, it began to rain, and those many participants without waterproofs were quickly soaked. On arrival at the Clough the expected five speaking platforms had not been erected. The crowd arrived to a 'desolate' scene, where 'a keen wind bore the rain across the high ground and down the sides of the slope in drenching showers'. The participants struggled to find the designated speaking places, until at last some staves with numbers were put out. People had begun to leave even before the event had properly begun; the speeches were mostly brief and to the point, despite the multiplicity of socialist resolutions that had been agreed beforehand. Number 1 area featured Richard Pankhurst, who spoke eloquently to what was estimated to be the largest group. Though more brief than usual, he referred to the contrast between rich and poor in Britain and how it should be addressed with 'a fair day's pay' for 'a fair day's work'.[55] But the event was a damp squib in all senses.

Immediately on the heels of the Boggart Hole Clough affair, the Pankhursts became embroiled in another dispute in Belgium occasioned by the imprisonment in Antwerp, followed by deportation, of trade unionist Ben Tillett, who by now had the respectable position of alderman on the Manchester Council. He had been attempting to recruit British seamen there to the International Federation of Ship, Dock, Wharf and Riverside Labourers.

Richard and Emmeline (with her sister, Mary) were actually on their way 'for a tour of the continent' but agreed to divert to Antwerp along with James Sexton, the leader of the National Union of Dock Labourers. This was in response to a call by their friend Tom Mann, leader of the International Free Labour Association, that they should jointly address an open-air protest meeting in Antwerp. Sexton, writing in the *Clarion* of 12 September 1896, perceived the humour in the events that followed:

On arriving at Harwich, I met Dr. Pankhurst and Mrs. Pankhurst, with the historic summer bonnet, which, true to its earlier traditions, played havoc with the peace of mind of the Belgian police, who are but human.

Warned off by those police, when in Antwerp they collected about a hundred unemployed men. They were twice dispersed by the force, upon which they moved to the Monopolieken, a tavern by the docks. Again stopped by the police (described by Sexton as 'little gendarmes with big, fierce moustaches') the agitators were interrogated at the police station. Released on condition that they refrain from further action, they regrouped early the next morning in the Francfurt, and Sexton gave an address that *The Times* described as 'an inflammatory harangue to an audience of 200 dockers', but which Pankhurst by contrast claimed was 'an orderly meeting' about which 'no possible objection could be taken to anything said or done'. Sexton was arrested mid-flow.

Sexton continued: 'The Doctor had … loaded up his legal mind with the Belgian Constitution; and, lor! how he did chuck at the Belgian authorities in bucketfuls [sic], in which he was ably assisted by Mrs Pankhurst, who acted the part of interpreter.' When Richard argued his right as a barrister to be present at Sexton's questioning, he was refused. He immediately lodged a formal protest, but the unfortunate Sexton, who by then had managed to speak at five meetings 'in order to show his contempt for Continental bumbledom', was deported that evening on the basis of a Belgian law authorising the expulsion of trouble-making foreigners.

According to Sexton, many of the police were sympathetic, having their own dispute with the authorities over pay; the persecution of the socialists was at the door of the employers. The police were in fact invited to join the international movement. And Sexton also claimed that all 5,000 of the dockers in Antwerp did so.

Amidst rumours that the British Foreign Office had intervened in the matter against the trade unionists, it was reported that the Pankhursts were free to continue after this interlude with their continental holiday. It is not clear that they did so, however, as Richard's missive on the matter to the *Manchester Guardian* just after this bore the address of his Manchester chambers, 10 St James's Square.[56] Perhaps the affair had exhausted him; his ill health was an increasingly significant fact of life. It was noted in the annual report of the ILP for 1896–97 that he had attended only two out of a possible five meetings of the NAC, which were held at various venues around the country. Along with that of Fred Brocklehurst, this was the poorest showing on the list. Both of course, as well as being in poor health, had been embroiled in the exhausting Boggart Hole Clough agitation that may in part at least explain their failure to attend.[57]

Pankhurst was still a celebrity in the ILP. In December he was top of the bill in opening a Leeds ILP bazaar, ahead of local leader John Lister of Shibden Hall. The socialists were fundraising by selling 'useful and ornamental articles' and the event was enlivened by 'Dramatic Tableaux Vivants, Chamber Concerts, Shooting Jungle, Electrical and Mechanical Novelties, Gipsy, and Phrenologist'. It was not all worthy speechifying.[58]

CHAPTER 14

Maintaining the Family Income

It may have been expected that Richard Pankhurst, the gold-medal winning student of the 1860s, would have excelled in his career and been elevated to the status of Queen's Counsel and then to the judiciary. This failed to happen; perhaps he lacked the ambition to climb that particular ladder, in favour of his political campaigns. His daughters disagreed about his attitude to his legal career; Sylvia believed that he loved the work, that he thought it 'a fine profession', it is implied because he was 'able to help many people by it'. Adela strongly argued that 'he hated his profession and his heart was in politics … The legal profession was merely the abnoxious [sic] means by which he earned a living.' Perhaps harking back to his father's early career, according to Christabel he 'would say, half whimsically, that he wished he were an East India tea merchant or something which would not mean conflict between purse and politics'.[1] What is certain is that his growing extremism eventually put obstacles in the way of his promotion, and even, as time went on, prevented his being employed by many of the wealthy and powerful Manchester establishment.[2]

The bread-and-butter employment went on much as ever in the early 1890s; a question of pollution in Bury, the refusal of a music licence to a new Palace of Varieties, a dispute about a new wall blocking the light, and cases concerning patents and bankruptcies sum up the sort of fare on offer. However, some cases were more notable. There is an irony in the one that Pankhurst took on in the spring of 1894 when he was appointed defence barrister for that same Chesters Thompson whom he had sued after the Rotherhithe election. Thompson had been accused of misappropriating moneys belonging to his brewery, and by January 1895 was being interrogated in the bankruptcy court, Richard's particular area of expertise. The matter was finally settled, successfully for Chesters Thompson, two years later.[3]

A considerable part of Richard's employment well into the 1890s was concerned with matters relating to the Manchester Corporation. In 1891, while still living in London, one of the many corporation matters to take him away from home was a local government inquiry into insanitary dwellings. This was triggered by the city's application for an improvement scheme in some of the most unhealthy areas.[4]

The biggest project in Manchester that had engaged Richard's support, his personal involvement and his professional services was the Manchester Ship Canal. As early as 1883, a year after the first meeting convened by Daniel Adamson to discuss the canal project, Richard had been speaking in its favour during his first attempt to enter parliament for Manchester. As a member of the Chamber of Commerce he saw it as a means of reducing 'the burdens under which commerce operated'; a way to get around the duties imposed on Manchester goods by the port of Liverpool.[5] He at some point became a shareholder. Adamson had been keen that the scheme was accessible to smaller investors. It was reckoned that once the canal was operating fully, shareholders could expect as much as 18 per cent profit on their stake. Richard must have been hopeful that the venture could improve his family's financial position.[6]

Early in 1893 the project was expected to be completed by the end of the year, but a further £2 million was needed in addition to the £3 million already raised in loans by the City of Manchester. This resulted in a power struggle between the directors and shareholders, and the local corporations, especially Manchester, which had been attempting to dictate all the terms. It was hoped to raise the money from other local corporations such as Salford and Oldham. The policy was announced at a special meeting of the shareholders in the concert hall on Peter Street. There was some fear of opposition from the Manchester Corporation and a parliamentary challenge to the further borrowing; Pankhurst expressed his hope and belief that this would not result in 'a combat' and hoped that 'a large policy of mutual consideration would unite the two parties'.[7]

At a meeting of shareholders in August 1893 Pankhurst featured on the platform. By this time, Manchester had come up with the £2 million, and representatives from that city and also from Salford and Oldham had joined the board of directors. Richard proposed the vote of thanks 'in very eulogistic terms' to the new chairman of the board, Lord Egerton of Tatton, and his colleagues.[8] On 30 December 1893 he made a speech to the County Quarter Sessions for Salford in support of an application for a certificate to declare the Ship Canal completed and ready for the reception of vessels. Describing this as 'a historic occasion' after a process that had been 'every step of the way … a battle against the obstinacy of nature, and the opposition of man'. It is interesting that, though he heaped praise on the leaders of the venture, the chief engineer, the shareholders, the local people, the public servants, he neglected to mention the vast army of labourers, perhaps 1,000 of whom died in the process of construction. This was probably due to the fact that his employer on this occasion was the Canal Company. But he ended with his usual resounding flourish:

> The Manchester Ship Canal majestically marks a new epoch in the life of this community, and by its true magnificence as a proof and precedent of engineering power and industrial energy, as also by its important relation at once to ocean service and inland navigation, inspires us all with new hope for our country's future.

> *Floreat flumen navigerum Mancuniense!*[9]

This was followed two days later with a ceremonial sail by the canal directors and others along the new waterway. The Pankhurst family were on board, and Sylvia in particular was impressed by the technological achievement of the Barton swing bridge.[10]

Despite being opened by the Queen on 21 May 1894 with great ceremony, including a twenty-one-gun salute, early on there was concern that the canal was attracting less trade than expected.[11] Richard was at the forefront of calls for concerted action by Manchester merchants to increase its use. On 6 June 1894 he wrote to the *Manchester Guardian* encouraging the shareholders to discuss the issues at their conference, arguing that 'the many-sided power of this district needs but to be organised and directed to the attainment of positive practical objects connected with the canal to add another splendid instance to the roll of the great commercial triumphs achieved by the men of Lancashire'. At the meeting itself, he called for one director to lead in grappling with the high costs of transit, so that the problems could be ironed out.[12] By the time of the annual meeting, matters had been improved, he opined, by the appointment of 'a permanent competent chairman'.[13] Discussions as to how best to drum up trade for the canal continued for the rest of the year.

Further trouble blew up in the following year, when the canal directors decided to lock out all the dockers who wore a button badge as members of the National Union of Dock Labourers. Richard and Emmeline, now in opposition to the canal owners and directors, met with the union leaders, general secretary James Sexton and Salford branch secretary, T.M. Purves. They found that the unionised workers had never asked for more wages, nor objected to working with those who were not in the union, nor interfered in any way with them.

The letters sent to the directors by the union were 'conciliatory and courteous', whereas those from the directors were 'curt, summary and dictatorial'. Blackleg labour of an inexperienced nature had been imported to replace the offending dockers; they were described as 'all sorts and conditions of men from all parts of the country, including the tramp and casual wards of workhouses'. In his letter to the press about this issue, Pankhurst ends with the cry: 'Who is to bear this great loss? How long is this directorial despotism to continue?'[14]

Ultimately, after a great deal of hard work, the canal venture was a huge success. It was arguably the greatest engineering project of its era, and the largest navigation in the world. In the years after 1900 Manchester was considered the third port in the realm. But this happy development did not occur until after Richard Pankhurst's death and his canal shares did not come good in time to save the family finances, being estimated as worth just over £300 in 1898.

It is notable that as a socialist Richard was increasingly vocal at this time in support of trade unions. His position added to his alienation from some powerful interests in the local economy. He appeared at the meeting of the General Railway Workers' Union in the Co-operative Hall in Ardwick in September 1895 and his speech illuminates his attitude by this date:

> He said the principle of the organisation of labour was changing the whole character of modern civilisation, and was grounding society on a solid, stable and permanent basis … He was glad they had been able to achieve two great points for the lurrymen. The first was a fixed standard of working hours. The standard now was 60 hours a week, but he hoped the time was not far distant when it would be 48 and no more …[15]

Going on to describe an agreement between the Ship Canal Company and the 'lurrymen', he opined that the latter were protected against overwork. He did not miss the opportunity also 'to advocate the representation of the railway workers in Parliament and the nationalisation of railways and mines'.

When in November a Manchester council seat came vacant in All Saint's ward, the Conservative candidate was chair of the Manchester Steam Ship Lines Association; it was argued that he would be especially useful as a council representative on the canal's administrative body. Perhaps surprisingly, the now-socialist Richard Pankhurst supported this candidate's election as 'a most desirable step in the interests of all'.[16] Here is proof that, even as an ardent socialist, he sometimes still put principle – or suitability – before party.

But despite his socialism, he was never without favour as a lawyer representing Manchester Corporation. Increasingly, as the city boundaries were extended through the acquisition of 'out-townships', Manchester was concerned with the unglamorous but vital problem of sewage disposal. At a local government inquiry on 15 March 1894, held to examine Manchester's request for a loan of £100,000 to complete a drainage and sewage scheme, Richard represented the city.[17] He did so again the following year, acting with two Manchester QCs on behalf of the corporation against the township of Stretford, which was trying to win the right to put more of their own sewage into the Manchester main outlet sewer running through their district.[18] In 1896 he was still of sufficient standing with Manchester Corporation that he was awarded the brief to buy for the city the Trafford Park estate for the general recreation of the public. The bid failed and the area became an industrial estate, and a significant part of the Ship Canal's ultimate success.[19]

Pankhurst was not always on the side of the Corporation; in his final years he defended the Clayton Aniline Company Ltd in the Police Court against the council in a prosecution under the 1875 Public Health Act. The company was accused of allowing black smoke to belch from their chimney; Richard's case was not that they had not done so, but that the agreement between Manchester Corporation and Clayton township when the latter was incorporated into the City of Manchester allowed for it. He also put the case that the manufacturers had done everything possible to reduce the smoke. However, in January 1897, the finding was against his clients.[20] He perhaps acquired somewhat of a reputation in these types of cases, as he appeared again in November defending the Crumpsall Vale chemical manufacturers, Ivan Levinstein and Co. Ltd. and also Thomas Hyland and Co. in Beswick, in both cases for the same offence.[21] These were minor briefs, acting for companies that faced regular fines of a few pounds, heard in a minor court. They cannot have been very lucrative.

It is not unconnected with this that his socialist beliefs were increasingly apparent. His appearance in February 1896 at a public meeting in favour of a proposal that the corporation should run its own telephone company, hoping that this might become a widespread idea and provide cheap and efficient telecommunications across the whole country, reinforced the idea that he was increasingly committed to public ownership.[22] His vehemence in defence of the poor was marked when on 29 September 1896 he spoke up at a meeting he attended with Emmeline. It had been organised to oppose the corporation's intention to build lodging houses for 1,000 persons, who would be incomers, on land that had been purchased to provide housing for the poor of the city. Richard was hugely indignant, describing as 'Manchester atrocities' earlier evictions of families from homes that were scheduled for demolition, without the corporation replacing them with new dwellings. He did not moderate his language:

Their action left one under the belief that they could not be trusted, because they were ... prepared on technical grounds to turn onto the streets whole families, and hurl them into distresses which brought on disease and early death. It amounted to constructive murder to do so.[23]

Or according to his daughter, Sylvia, it meant at the least 'the moral death of the masses'.[24] It is likely that Richard's public admission of socialist beliefs, and his accession to the ILP leadership, combined with this sort of extreme language, increasingly played its part in limiting his options for employment.

CHAPTER 15

Final Years

On 6 October 1890 Richard Pankhurst, as always interested in new ideas, had attended a meeting of the Manchester Cremation Society, chaired by his old teacher R.C. Christie, now Chancellor of the Victoria University. The society was encouraged that they now had 230 members, yet disappointed that more headway had not been made in raising awareness among the general public of this new, hygienic method of disposing of bodies. But they had succeeded in forming a company to raise cash and build the first crematorium, opened in 1892. Richard was elected to its council and purchased shares in the enterprise.[1] He was never to take advantage of the services it offered; eight years later he was buried, apparently in the conventional manner, in Brooklands cemetery in Sale.

He continued to expand his activities for a time as the 1890s wore on. Having been elected a member of the oldest and most prestigious of the Manchester's gentlemen's clubs, the Literary and Philosophical Society, on 23 February 1892, his first known contribution was in February 1897 when he offered an uncontroversial critique of the Patent Office and suggested how it might better help inventors and the public.[2] So far, so unexceptionable, but all was not well.

Richard was enduring severe abdominal pain and it was hoped to alleviate his condition in clean air and healthy surroundings. It seems that Emmeline too was unwell, and according to Richard's letter of 11 April 1897 to Tom Mann it was because of doctor's orders to her that she must 'go into the country and keep quiet' that the whole family moved the following week to Valewood Farm in rural Mobberley in Cheshire. He added that: 'Mrs Pankhurst's health has never been right since Boggart Hole Clough.'[3] Nevertheless, an income being still crucial, he continued to work. He walked each day to the little Cheshire Lines railway station to commute into Manchester, often accompanied by his eldest daughter who was enrolled in the city on an eclectic mix of courses in logic,

French and dressmaking.[4] The rest of the family enjoyed their rural interlude, which continued till sometime in the autumn.

Meanwhile, Richard was to be found acting for the Manchester Ship Canal Company in May 1897. This was the final stage of an appeal about the payment of rates on dock buildings and warehouses against the Overseers of Salford. The outcome was a compromise.[5] Two months later Richard was on the platform at the Ship Canal Annual Meeting and spoke about his optimism for the future of the enterprise, appositely adding that: 'He believed that the tide had turned.' Nevertheless, he still exhorted 'the merchant princes of Manchester' to emulate the merchant princes of medieval Italy and give their business to the canal in 'the true spirit of citizenship'.[6]

The NAC Minutes give some indication of the state of Richard's health. On 5 January 1897 he had sent apologies that he was unable to attend 'owing to illness and business engagements'.[7] He slipped out of view in the leadership of the movement, and his place was taken by his ardent wife. Emmeline maintained her links and was voted onto the NAC in Birmingham on 12 April 1898, a clear sign that her political star was in the ascendant. She joined the Publishing Committee and met with the Organising Committee in Bradford on 5 May 1898 as the representative for ILP public officials in Manchester.[8]

When he felt better, Richard was still active in the cause of socialism as far away as Southport, presiding at a meeting on the beach in May 1897, held after the conclusion of a Miners' Federation gathering in the recreation ground. His friend, Keir Hardie, spoke in favour of the nationalisation of coal mines and an eight-hour day.[9]

Closer to home, when living in Mobberley, the Pankhurst family were engaged in raising money for the imprisoned Leonard Hall and his family. On Whit Saturday, 12 June 1897, Emmeline offered to provide 100 picnic teas at 1s each to the ILP and the Clarion Cycling Club. It was reported that there was strong representation from as far away as Rochdale, Oldham, Ashton, Warrington and Manchester. A generous £10 19s 3d was raised.[10]

Pankhurst was also committed to support the workers during disputes; he spoke up many times for the engineering workers during a six-month lockout, arguing for their claim of an eight-hour day. On 18 July 1897 he travelled into Manchester to address an ILP meeting in Alexandra Park in their support, describing the employers' action in characteristically strong terms as 'vindictive and wantonly wicked', whilst the engineers were 'the most splendid industrial force history had ever known'. He asserted that an eight-hour day should be the maximum for all workers. This was repeated ten days later in a meeting of 10,000 men in St James's Hall in the city.[11]

As municipal elections approached, in October 1897, Richard was well enough to preside at an indoor meeting in Bradford ward in support of ILP candidate J.E. Sutton at which Tom Mann spoke. There was a large, sympathetic crowd, who were apparently easily managed, and Richard is not reported to have made a speech.[12] He did speak up, however, shortly before the election in support of the ILP candidate in West Gorton; against a background of industrial unrest, he did not mince his words:

> It was quite impossible for the serious and clear-minded workers of Gorton to misunderstand the battle in which they were engaged. It was a fight which was intended by the employers to result in starving the worker into servitude and slavery. That being so he could not comprehend how a working man still kept on voting for his master.[13]

Richard engaged in a further, ongoing, campaign for the construction of houses for rent to working-class families. Then in December of that year, Emmeline and Richard travelled together to Leek in Staffordshire; Emmeline addressed the Leek Labour Church on the afternoon of 12 December on Poor Law Administration; Richard followed this up in the evening with a talk in the Temperance Hall on Social Ideals. Both occasions were treated to 'special singing' by the Potteries Clarion Glee Choir.[14]

The ongoing question among socialists of various stripes, the Social Democratic Federation, the Fabians and the ILP, was whether they should amalgamate and form one great socialist party. In April 1898 Richard was still plugging away. At the party conference, supported by Bruce Glasier, he made his view known that he 'admired the spirit that sought unity by fusion' but that he did not think the time was ripe. 'Federation should precede fusion. Later on the federated bodies would become one Socialist party.' The conference agreed, and federation was the approach that continued to prevail until the turn of the century.

In a different way of challenging the power of the establishment, since the early years of the decade Richard had backed efforts to recover footpaths closed by landowners, and to get land opened up to the poor for their convenience and leisure. The Peak and District Preservation Committee was fighting for a public footpath over Kinder Scout, and the Pankhursts joined expeditions to walk the proposed route, in the face of obstruction from the landowners, led by the Duke of Devonshire. From 1894 Richard was the 'honorary counsel' for the committee.[15]

It seems that this was only the most famous in a string of similar agitations at the time. There had been a campaign over Winter Hill via Smithills Moor, near Bolton, Lancashire, in which Pankhurst represented the walkers. This was about more than footpaths; it was said in court that: 'The lack of liberal support is largely attributed to the somewhat hasty action of the Socialists in precipitating the movement,' suggesting that there were political and anti-landowning motives also in the mix. The newspaper reports of the hearings provide fascinating evidence of local life at the time. Unfortunately, despite a plethora of depositions to prove long-standing usage of the path, and a marathon four and a half hours' summing up by Richard, the judge found in favour of the landowner, a Colonel Ainsworth.[16]

There was better news in the Peak District; in May 1897 the walkers succeeded in establishing a legal right to use the footpath over Kinder. They celebrated with a mass walk that included stops for speeches. Richard referred in his to 'the most striking aspect of modern human life … a fierce hunger for nature … in the wild … for mountain, moor and stream' and this was closely linked to 'the health of the masses'.[17]

On 14 October 1897 Richard attended the fifty-eighth annual conference of the Union of Lancashire and Cheshire Institutes, but his participation seems to have been limited to proposing the vote of thanks to the council of the Union.[18] He played a similar role at the Manchester Statistical Society meeting of 11 November, when the topic was the English Poor Law. Perhaps significantly, now it was Emmeline, also present, who participated in the lively discussion that followed.[19]

Although a sick man, Richard entered the fray against Manchester Corporation in the autumn of 1897 over their attempts to escape prosecution by the local government board for piping semi-treated sewage into the Manchester Ship Canal. The council wanted to build a culvert to take the effluent instead into the Mersey between Warrington and Liverpool. Pankhurst led an outcry against the scheme. Supported by Emmeline, in letters to the press he argued for a year against it, from financial, practical and environmental points of view. He sarcastically contended that the Ship Canal was already so filthy that the sewage, semi-treated by chemicals and with sludge removed, in fact improved the quality of its water. And he laid down the need for a higher standard of purity for the effluent, which the powers that be did not accept.[20]

Advocating that twenty-five sanitary experts should be convened to advise the Rivers Committee on the matter, he favoured the use of a chemical method for the disposal of the sewage. His proposal was ignored. Moreover, he suggested that the council was issuing misleading propaganda in favour of their scheme. So effective was he that the council offered that if he laid off, he would be awarded the brief to get the necessary act through parliament, with a fee of £10,000. This weighed with him 'not a straw'.[21]

When the council called a Town Meeting on 24 September to approve their scheme and apply for an Act of Parliament for the new culvert, Richard took full advantage of the opportunity to explain his opposition. He pointed out that when the proposal first arose, the Rivers Committee had not had proper advice. He suggested that they should have rejected the claim of the Local Government Board to have the power to impose fines on the council if they did not act immediately; they had been bounced into taking the quickest option rather than having proper, considered consultations. His sarcasm at their weakness was patent:

> He was there unhesitatingly to say of the proposed scheme that it represented three things. It represented, first, scientific impotence and despair ... How sad it was that this great city, with Victoria University, with high culture, and scientific opportunities, greater, perhaps, than those possessed by any city in the world, should say, 'We give up; science can do nothing; let us go down a culvert miles and miles away to the sea.'[22]

He went on also to cite the incapacity, cowardice and lack of common sense of the corporation, and the pusillanimity of the committees dealing with the case. He was even bold enough indirectly to attack the advice to the corporation of Sir Henry Roscoe, professor of Chemistry at Manchester University. And he asserted that the culvert scheme was wantonly extravagant. He was not alone in his stance; many of the others who spoke denounced the scheme, and when it came to a vote it was resoundingly rejected. The Lord Mayor and the Rivers Committee therefore set in train the organisation of a public poll on the matter. In the end the scheme was abandoned when the ratepayers voted almost two to one against. The family was very proud of Richard's victory, but he privately confessed to Emmeline his regret that he could not do more to realise his ideals or eliminate 'social evils'. Probably aware that time was running out for him, he was unable to take pleasure in the smaller steps towards achieving his vision.[23]

This was not his only crusade against the Corporation. In the summer of 1897 there was a scandal concerning the Watch Committee over their mismanagement of the police that involved underhand dealings, and a laxity of discipline in one division of the force. An ex-police superintendent had been accused of being drunk on duty, consorting with prostitutes, taking bribes and tipping off brothel keepers before police raids. It could not have been a more damning record. When an enquiry found the reports to be true, the Home Office reviewed the case and decided that the appointment of officers should no longer be in the gift of the council's Watch Committee, but instead in that of the Chief Constable. In September Richard joined a Citizens Indignation Committee set up by the Manchester business community to agitate in the forthcoming local elections against the return of any candidate associated with the Watch Committee.[24] When they held a meeting in October, Richard was outspoken:

there was extreme danger that the Corporation of Manchester was going deliberately to sever itself from the service of the city, and that the great body of citizens would lose all confidence alike in the deliberations and in the conclusions of the Corporation. They were extravagant ... and they were combining together to pass each other's minutes without discussion ... There was abundant evidence of what he stated to be found, for instance, in recent proceedings of the Parks Committee, the Rivers Committee, and the Watch Committee.[25]

The committee considered its work done after the elections, when many of those implicated were no longer on the Watch Committee, though Richard argued for further action as the council was still appointing old members by a ballot system, and apparently excluding ILP councillors, such as Brocklehurst and Sutton, from the body.[26]

In contrast to his recent opposition, he acted for Manchester Corporation in the Chancery Court of the County Palatine, opposing the granting of a licence for liquor to the Palace of Varieties. The case ground on and was to be taken to the Court of Appeal in London.[27] However, this was the end of his participation in it; two months later, he was dead. But not before he had been retained as counsel for the corporation in the prosecution of the superintendent of the cleansing department, R.D. Callison, over financial irregularities.[28]

A Traumatic Death

Sylvia Pankhurst furnishes the most detailed and vivid account of her father's death.[29] Although only 16, she had to manage the crisis alone with the servants and the younger children, 13-year-old Adela and 8-year-old Harry.[30] No one in the family was aware of how serious Richard's condition was; in the first half of June[31] Emmeline had travelled abroad to take Christabel to stay with Noémie, her old friend, in Switzerland and the parents had not really made their children aware of his illness. Sylvia, however, relates an incident during 1897 in Mobberley that illustrates his suffering:

Walking to the station with my father one morning, I was distressed to see him stop short, obviously in pain, and press his beautiful hands among the sharp thorns of the hedgerow. 'Why are you hurting yourself, Father?' I exclaimed in alarm. He answered: 'It is to counteract the other pain.' When in a little while he had recovered himself, he was solicitous for my distress, assuring me, with gentle endearments, that it was only a passing attack of indigestion of no importance. After that he often paused a few moments when out walking, and though we understood he was in pain, he made light of it, and no thought of danger entered even the threshold of our minds.[32]

The project to take Christabel to Geneva was preceded by much excitement, and it seems that Emmeline did not anticipate any immediate danger to her husband until the day of departure. Saying their goodbyes before Richard set off for his office, she was 'gripped by a sudden fear' and hugged him, uttering endearments. She charged Sylvia to 'Look after Father'.[33] He too may have realised that his days were numbered, since at the moment of parting he 'could scarcely bear to let his wife go'. Yet this was more than a feeling of that moment, as: 'He was always sad when she was away, as she often was in the evenings at meetings now; always restless if she were late in returning.' Christabel, who gained possession of her father's letters to her mother, affords further insight into this period of separation. Letters went back and forth, and his final missive to her was poignantly loving, but it may also hint at some discord between the couple: 'When you return, we will have a new honeymoon and reconsecrate each to the other in unity of heart. Be happy. Love and love, Your husband, R.M. Pankhurst.'[34]

Sylvia also relates how his work now put Richard under great strain. Employed by Manchester Corporation in the enquiry into financial irregularities by R.D. Callison of the cleansing department, he was finding the work exhausting and was 'worried and tired'. Every night after his return from his chambers he was sequestered with Norbury Williams, the City Auditor, in discussions about the case. Sylvia sensed a sadness and 'a clinging affection' about him that made her uneasy. It was during an adjournment of the case that Richard met his end.

On the day when his final crisis began, Saturday, 2 July, after working as usual until midday, Richard sat down to lunch with the remaining family. In the middle of the meal, he picked up a strawberry, instructed Sylvia to serve the children and left the room. She found him in Emmeline's drawing room 'huddled uncomfortably in a small armchair, his every line denoting agony'. When Sylvia suggested a doctor, he turned her down. She hastened to report that he was ill to the servants, who were eating, but they dismissed her concern – having perhaps seen it all before. Sylvia eventually got him into bed with a hot water bottle, although she still did not realise the seriousness of the situation.

The next day, shocked by 'the awful change in him', Sylvia resolved to get Doctor Yates, who eventually came and dismissed her from the room. The servants by now were 'all solicitude'. Assured by the doctor that her father would soon be well and that she should not worry, she administered the oxygen he ordered. Richard's mind wandered in and out of lucidity 'helpless as a little child'. The doctor, advised also by Doctor Dreschfeld, attended every two hours, though when he was late Richard repeatedly asked for him and feared he would faint and would not be able to be revived.[35] Sylvia's main thought was that they must get him better before her mother returned as: 'Mother must not see him like this! … Mother could not bear it!' When a nurse was suggested by the doctor, Richard refused and begged Sylvia and the servants to help him. An operation was considered but rejected as impracticable due to blood clots in his stomach.[36]

On Monday, 4 July matters were so serious that the doctor suggested Richard telegraph Emmeline to come home; he dictated to Sylvia: 'I am not well. Please come home.' The next day Adela and Harry were finally allowed to see their father, and 'gazed in awe at his changed face'. Sylvia and the cook stayed with him: 'The time crept on, and as I stood holding the tube [for oxygen], which seemed a line of life to him, he turned away his head as though to gaze at something … Father was dead.' According to Sylvia, the doctor had known for some time that Richard had a stomach ulcer. He had not told him so as not to worry him. The ulcer had perforated his stomach.

Meanwhile, Emmeline received his telegram and hurried home in the belief that it was Harry who was ill, and that Richard had worded his message so as not to worry her too much. It was on the train from London to Manchester that she learned the truth, when she saw a black-bordered newspaper read by another passenger. She arrived home to find that the family had rallied round; her brother Herbert and her sister Mary, as well as the children's former nursemaid, Susannah, were present in the house. Her shock and grief were profound. Emmeline could not bear to be alone so she and Sylvia took to sleeping together and shared sleepless nights. All of them were deeply affected; they had lost 'the lodestar of our lives' and did not know which way to turn.[37]

The Funeral

The funeral, arranged by Messrs Kendal, Milne and Co., the same company who had made Emmeline's wedding dress nineteen years earlier, was held the following Saturday, 9 July. Richard was laid to rest in Brooklands cemetery with his parents, Margaret and Henry Francis. It was a beautiful summer's day, 'full of brilliant green and golden sunlight'.[38] His plain oak coffin, hidden by a plethora of red and white wreaths and the ILP's large cross of red carnations and geraniums, was drawn on an open car by two bays, and was accompanied by a procession that included many of the movements in which he had been active. Black was not much worn, but the gentlemen had black ties, and in the Victorian tradition many people sent their carriages to swell the ranks as a mark of respect. The streets were lined with people who turned out to pay their respects, the men with their heads uncovered. The cortège left from Victoria

Park, and proceeded by way of Oxford Street and Stretford Road, headed by a large ILP deputation and Emmeline and the children, with other members of the Pankhurst and Goulden families. Only Christabel was absent, still staying in Geneva. They were accompanied also by 400 representatives of the Clarion Cycling Club, pedalling in a seemingly endless stream, and wearing white rosettes. They included many ladies wearing white blouses and coloured hats. At Old Trafford the chief mourners boarded a train to Brooklands. The rest proceeded by road and arrived around 3.30pm.

On arrival at the cemetery, the cyclists stood bare-headed as the hearse passed through their two lines. A dense crowd of around 2,000 predominantly working men, women and children attended the burial. The organisations with which Richard had been associated were represented; the Manchester legal profession; the Manchester Court of Bankruptcy; the Manchester Coroner; the Manchester Law Students' Society; the Manchester Chamber of Commerce; the Manchester Council and Corporation; the Portico Library; the Manchester Athenaeum; the Arts Club; the Manchester Statistical Society; the Manchester School Board; the Union of Lancashire and Cheshire Institutes; the Owens College Associates; the Chorlton Board of Guardians; the ILP, both local and national; the William Morris Labour Church, Leek; the Bradford Labour Church; the *Clarion*; the Manchester Warehousemen and Clerks' Schools; London County Council; Ancoats Healthy Homes Committee; the Peak District and Northern Counties Footpaths Preservation Society; the Women's Franchise League. Of particular note was a Mr W.H. Chadwick, described as 'the old Chartist'.

There was no religious ceremony, but after the coffin was lowered into the grave in the Church of England area of the burial ground, there were a few moments of silence. A number of speeches in praise of Richard's work and devotion were made at the graveside. Fred Brocklehurst, standing on a small, raised platform at the head of the open grave, explaining that he had not known Richard in early life, referred to his long-term interest in social questions. He noted his great probity:

For thirty-five years Richard Marsden Pankhurst lived in the full blaze of Manchester's public life. It was a period long enough to test the greatest of reputations and to try the character of any number of men. Perhaps the vastest tribute which could be paid to their departed friend that day was to say that he came through the ordeal unscathed. For the whole of that long career he had lived a perfectly blameless life … Manchester would never need to feel ashamed of the character and conduct of one of her most brilliant sons.[39]

Bruce Glasier, whose nose was put out of joint because he had been asked to speak by Emmeline and was apparently feeling upstaged, found the speech 'very formal ... without the least feeling or tenderness'.[40]

Alice Cliff Scatcherd then praised Richard's support for all aspects of the women's movement, for which he was 'an inspiring memory'. She opined that any progress women had made towards freedom was 'very largely due to his influence'. Leonard Hall also spoke at the graveside. He mentioned the high positions Richard might have reached, but that 'he died absolutely a poor man' because of his dedication to public causes. Glasier did not much like this speech either, noting that Hall 'steps in front and delivers an aggressive and rather ill flavoured harange [sic]'. Glasier himself, aiming to say only 'a few simple words', believed he spoke for the ILP when he described Pankhurst as 'one of the most beautiful figures of their time'. The Rev. T. Horne (chaplain to the Chorlton workhouse) gave a particularly passionate oration declaring 'the nobility of citizenship which he [Pankhurst] exhibited ... his stupendous grandeur of character'.

After a last look at the coffin, the crowds dispersed, presumably much cheered and inspired by the rhetoric they had heard and the example of Richard Pankhurst's spectacularly 'blameless' life. Glasier concluded his diary entry on the funeral: 'The whole affair imposing and orderly – save the speeches, which with perhaps the exception of my own few words, were, I think, very unsuitable.'

He and his wife were clearly a great support to Emmeline, as he goes on to say: 'I call afterwards upon Mrs Pankhurst. She appears not to know what her position will be, but she asks Katharine and myself to come and spend an evening with her.' And indeed, Emmeline's letter of 12 July to Katharine, on black-bordered paper, refers to the latter's 'loving words' and that she was 'deeply grateful to Mr Glasier for his Kindness'. She invites the Glasiers to come and see her with their little baby soon, so that she can discuss with them 'what to do with books, papers, etc.' as she was struggling with them 'for I will have no strange hand touch them'.[41]

Some of those at the funeral probably went on to attend a memorial meeting at Boggart Hole Clough on the following day, this time 'by special sanction of the Corporation', despite the fact that it was organised by the North Manchester ILP. There was disturbance when their right to hold the meeting was challenged, the claim being made that it was a political event, but order was eventually restored and the meeting endorsed the resolution of regret at the loss of Dr Pankhurst and his 'noble qualities of citizenship' and self-sacrifice by raising their hats.[42]

James Keir Hardie, absent from the obsequies as he had travelled to Scotland to console his wife on the death of her mother, in the *Labour Leader* reflected the feelings of many, particularly on the radical left of the political spectrum. He believed that they had the comfort of knowing that Richard had 'left behind a memory for integrity and courage which is priceless … A scholar, a gentleman, a brilliant conversationalist, a faithful friend, an affectionate father.'[43] For his gravestone Emmeline chose a line adapted from Walt Whitman, whose works Richard had read to his children: 'Brave, noble, true and my loving comrade'.[44]

Fred Brocklehurst added to his graveside comments in an article in the *Manchester Evening News,* stressing how Richard was ahead of his time in his support for popular education. He acknowledged how his dedication to radical causes, republicanism, socialism, hostility to organised religion, and opposition to the council over the culvert scheme, were at the expense of his professional career and occasioned considerable self-sacrifice. He praised his brilliance as a lawyer, singling out particularly his work in international law, and: 'As an orator, notwithstanding the defect of his voice, he never failed to thrill and impress an audience.' The comments Brocklehurst added about the more private man are revealing: he was 'the most charming of conversationalists, and the kindliest of friends'. And his power was rooted in his honesty and courage, which was recognised even by those who disagreed with him profoundly.[45]

The words of Leonard Hall at the graveside were not reported, but on 16 July 1898 he published a piece in the *Clarion* that reflected his great sadness at the loss of his comrade:

> There is a big lump in my throat as I try to write this. During these latter years I had the privilege – and it has been a keen pleasure and steady encouragement to me – of Dr. Pankhurst's friendship and intimacy; I started by esteeming and ended by loving him. A brighter, braver, truer, higher-souled man never lived. He never even knew what pettiness or meanness was. Nobody ever saw him in the dumps … He was uniquely charming and winning as a companion – not a touch of vanity or affectation anywhere about him … he was always as lively as a boy of 14 – without a shadow on his mind, and ranged with his customary vivacity, versatility, and flow of information and classical allusion from one topic to another, easily holding the field in the dozen friendly cross-table duels at the Arts Club, where we lunched …

He related his last meeting with Richard, when they parted in Albert Square, Manchester; Richard had just bought from an old book stall a copy of the *Life of George Stephenson*, with the hope of finding some ideas on economics. He probably never read it, as the next day he fell ill. Hall summarises Pankhurst's influence: 'for 35 years the leader of the reform vanguard in this city … I don't think our dead comrade was ever appreciated even by his own party at half his great worth …'

CHAPTER 16

Legacy

Obituaries were published in organs of the press right across the political spectrum. *The Times* focused drily on Pankhurst's legal background, educational work and support for the middle-class National Reform Union, as well as the co-operative movement, referring only in passing to his association with the ILP and his attempts to enter parliament.[1] It mentioned the associations to which he contributed; the NAPSS, the Royal Statistical Society and the Association for the Reform and Codification of the Laws of Nations. His work for the Manchester Chamber of Commerce, especially on the bankruptcy laws, was noted. It was an impersonal and perfunctory account of such a passionate life.

By contrast the *Clarion*, the socialist paper run by Robert Blatchford, headed by a flattering pen-and-ink drawing, began with a lament at his passing: 'The cause of Socialism has lost a powerful advocate, and the Democracy a loved and valued friend.'[2] Describing the details of his last days, and then explaining his early life and his legal career, it went on to extol his commitment to socialism and his eloquence as a speaker in its cause. It listed those for whom he spoke up: the citizens of Manchester, members of socialist organisations, trade unionists, the unemployed, those who fought for free speech, Irish nationalists, and the 'proletarians of all countries, for whom his sympathies, his energies, and his life were spent'. The words of a Manchester socialist who knew him personally were then cited: 'This evening it is hard to believe that Dr. Pankhurst is dead – that we never more shall have the much-needed encouragement of his friendly presence and stirring voice.' The unnamed 'Manchester correspondent' went on to review Richard's ideological progress:

I have known the Doctor for many years. All along he was on the side of the people. Before modern Socialism took its present broad, tolerant, definite form in this country, he was far in advance of the Liberal party, to which he at one time belonged, and he made his presence felt among the Liberal chiefs of Manchester. He was indeed a sharp thorn in their comfortable cushion. He had no sympathy for the wire-pulling methods of expediency, and never swerved in the slightest degree from his advocacy of justice and honesty in dealing with the workers.

When he could not move the Liberals to change course, he joined the burgeoning socialist movement, but it was recognised that this came at a cost:

Had he been a selfish, grubbing, professional man with an eye only for the main chance he might have secured promotion even to the judicial bench. And he would have made a wiser, more just judge than some of their lordships that I wot of. As it was, there was no professional advancement for him, and his self-denying espousal of the cause of the people was only made at great sacrifice of both means and personal comfort.

The *Manchester Guardian* noted the messages of condolence sent to Emmeline and the family. The first, from the Manchester and Salford Trades and Labour Council, sounded a personal note referring to her loss of 'a kind husband and a loving father'. It appended to this also the loss felt by the industrial classes of their 'true friend and sympathiser' and 'fearless advocate of the rights of freedom'. This was followed by the words of the Ancoats Brotherhood, which described: 'The energy, the enormous enthusiasm he displayed, both with purse and pen and on the platform,' and their sense of his loss as a lecturer at their meetings.

Even the Liberals of the city, who might have been expected to be somewhat cursory in their remarks, were at pains to express their 'deep sense of the loss sustained by Manchester' and recorded their 'appreciation of his invaluable gifts, devoted … to promote the political, social, and intellectual advancement of this district and of the nation'. They referred to Richard's demise at their meeting on 8 July, and drew up a eulogy that was to be shared with his widow. At their annual meeting in April 1899 they included Richard Pankhurst's name in their commemorations, but only as one of a list of secondary figures. They were all overshadowed by the death of William Gladstone, the great Liberal leader, which had occurred in May 1898, and even more so by the presentation to the Town Hall of a bust to commemorate the radical John Bright. They were, however, generous enough to their wayward member to concede that: 'By the decease of Dr. Pankhurst the public life of Manchester has been deprived of one of its most able and self-sacrificing men, one whose voice and aid were ever at the service of the weak and struggling.'[3]

> The Manchester Council, in the words of the Lord Mayor, noted his
> passing as 'a man of sterling honesty – of great uprightness and integrity,
> and of great sincerity. He was a man who had played a conspicuous part
> in the history of Manchester ...'[4]

That most prestigious of Manchester clubs, the Literary and Philosophical
Society, included a fulsome account of his life in their Report for 1898. It drew
attention especially to his legal career and achievements in the fields of patent
law, scientific jurisprudence and legal reform. However, the writer believed that
his involvement in politics prevented his achieving 'the highest distinction'. It
noted that his career began at a period when the law was undergoing a process
of change and modernisation, and described him as 'ever among the extreme
reformers' who by the 'boldness of his ideas, and the clearness of his views, had
a very great influence on current thought'. Going on to refer to his educational
interests, attempts to enter parliament, and marriage to 'Miss Emmeline
Goulden, of Seedley'. It concludes:

> However great the public disfavour his extreme views gained him,
> his brilliant ability as a speaker and thinker, and the charm and
> kindliness of his manners in private, never failed to secure for him the
> personal regard of those who met him. Into all work with which he was
> concerned Dr. Pankhurst threw an extraordinary amount of vigour, his
> temperament being undoubtedly conducive to his untimely decease.[5]

The Minutes of the ILP NAC recorded their sense of loss at a meeting where
Emmeline was present on 23 July:

> Resolved:- That the members of the National Council of the Independent
> Labour Party tender to their colleague, Mrs. E. Pankhurst, their
> respectful sympathy in her great affliction consequent upon the loss
> of her distinguished husband, Dr. Pankhurst, whose brilliant advocacy
> of, and faithful adherence to, the reform movements of the past thirty
> years have endeared him to reformers of all shades of opinion. We, of
> this Council, mourn his loss as that of a dear friend and comrade.

The resolution from the Manchester branch of the ILP was naturally fulsome in
its appreciation, recording their 'high appreciation of the self-sacrificing life of
their beloved comrade Dr. Pankhurst', and deeply regretting the loss to socialism
occasioned by his sudden death.[6]

The annual report of the ILP was even more emotional:

One blow which has fallen upon us during the year must be present in
all your minds. Dr. Pankhurst, the friend, comrade, adviser and inspirer
of so many of us personally and of all of us collectively, was stricken
down, suddenly and unexpectedly. In him the Party lost one of its truest
and most devoted members – few know what immense sacrifices he
had made for the cause – and one who would, almost certainly, have
been returned to the next House of Commons, where his abilities would
not only have won for him the admiration of non-Socialists, but would
have been of incalculable benefit to his party and to the people of this
country. Not merely his personal friends, but all who appreciate the
difficulties in our path, must regret his untimely death.[7]

Ironically for a lawyer, Richard left no will. There were a few share certificates
with an estimated worth of £930 13 9d., which was insufficient to cover his debts.
It is interesting to see what Richard had chosen to invest in: his portfolio included
the Manchester Ship Canal, which at just over £300 in value was his most
significant holding; the Investors Co-operative Society Ltd; the Brasenose Club
Building Co. Ltd; the Manchester Masonic Hall Co. Ltd; the Royal Courts of
Justice Chambers Co. Ltd; Manchester Portico Newsroom Library; Manchester
Crematorium; various railway-related shares; several banks; cattle and bread-
making businesses; a brick company; the Southport Guardian; the British and
Foreign Patent Co. Ltd; a land company, and a West Indian plantation syndicate.
Quite a few of these were worthless, however, as they had been wound up, or were
not fully paid up.[8]

Within a week of Richard's death there were calls through letters to the press
for a fitting tribute in his memory. The socialist Alfred Winks explained that:
'One main common sentiment suffused everything he [Richard] said and did.
"I love the common people," was his emphatic phrase, oft repeated.' He believed
that money should go to Owens College, 'whose brightest star he was', and ended:

Let no money be wasted on gilt and marble; let something be done for
the propagation of the principles of truth and justice he so dearly loved
and so bravely espoused. This, and only this, I firmly believe, would
have met with his own approval.[9]

In no time at all a meeting was held in the Arts Club on Albert Square to
consider the fund-raising. It was an illustrious gathering headed by Sir William

Bailey of Manchester Ship Canal fame, and perhaps surprisingly including Stephen Chesters Thompson, Richard's nemesis in the Rotherhithe election.[10] The Jacob Brights, unable to be present, offered to join the committee. Political enemies such as his opponent in the Gorton election, Ernest Hatch, donated to the fund in commemoration of a man whom they praised for his integrity and honesty and the sacrifice of his pecuniary interest to the public good. Manchester newspaper editors C.P. Scott (*Manchester Guardian*) and Harry Sowler (*Manchester Courier*) likewise gave £10 and £5 respectively to the fund. Indeed, the *Manchester Evening News* on 16 July 1898 commented particularly on the diverse nature of the donors:

> Holders of all sorts of opinions were present, united for once in the desire to pay honour to a man who held the most advanced views and fearlessly expressed them. Some of the subscribers opposed Dr. Pankhurst tooth and nail during his life-time. They fought him on public platforms, in the press, and in the law courts. But in the presence of the great leveller they forgot all differences …[11]

The amounts ranged from a modest 3s from 'three workmen' to an enormous £50 donated by Jacob and Ursula Bright and £25 each given by the suffragists Rose Hyland and Alice Scatcherd.[12] The Watch Committee, with whom Richard had crossed swords the previous year, were less enthusiastic in their support of fundraising in his memory. Two Sunday concerts were proposed in the Comedy Theatre in Manchester; the committee allowed the first because it consisted of sacred music performed by the Moody-Manners Opera Company. However, the second, by 'Snazelle', a magic lantern entertainer, was 'described as secular' and the committee deferred their decision for a week, yet in the end they relented and agreed.[13] With smaller amounts coming in from the many supporters, the fund reached about £200 within a day and an appeal was soon launched to the community that was gratifyingly successful. By 17 August it had reached the princely sum of £934 17s 0d, and eventually it topped £1,000.

Meanwhile, everything – furniture, paintings and books – in 4 Buckingham Crescent was sold off; the family moved to a more modest house in Nelson Street. Blatchford suggested an appeal for them in the *Clarion*, but Emmeline did not want the poor to pay for an education for her children that they could not afford for their own.

Unfortunately, the heavy-handed and patronising manner in which the money dedicated to Richard's family was administered was irksome to Emmeline, and would certainly not have pleased Richard. She regarded the money, not as a relief fund, but as a consideration due to both her husband and herself for all the public work they had done. Unfortunately, the committee of male administrators did not regard it in the same light and questioned her right to use it as she saw fit, wishing to spend the money on Harry's education rather than that of his sisters. Naturally, Emmeline was not placated: 'I believe and my husband thought it too that it is quite as important to give opportunity of education to gifted girls as to boys. I am carrying out his wishes in what I am doing.'[14]

As Richard would have wished, in addition to the help raised for his family, at the meeting of the NAC a further fundraising initiative was agreed in his memory, to promote 'the social and political work to which he was so whole-heartedly devoted'. It was also decided to use the fund to publish 'propagandist literature' to support the work of the organisers and render it 'more permanent and effective'.[15]

Other tributes included a lecture, 'The Life and Times of Dr. Pankhurst', delivered three months later to 700 of the Manchester and Salford ILP members by Fred Brocklehurst. He extolled Pankhurst's contribution to education, touched on his religious views and the expression of his 'religious enthusiasm in the fruitful field of politics', and characterised his political creed as 'the principle of democracy'. As in other declarations about Richard's life, Brocklehurst acknowledged his sacrifice of time, money and position for principle, and pointed to him as 'a splendid example for the youth of the city'. In Richard's memory £7 was collected on the spot to help fund a socialist lecturer and organiser. The proceedings were also enlivened by excellent singing from the Socialist choir. A further commemoration in a portrait and quotation on socialist Christmas cards produced by the Socialist Co-operative Trading Society Ltd, with which a very select few were honoured including Katharine Glasier, Keir Hardie, Tom Mann and George Bernard Shaw, attests to Pankhurst's popular appeal.[16]

The ILP held a public meeting in the Free Trade Hall in Manchester on 22 October 1899. James Keir Hardie was in attendance, as was the Manchester Socialist Choir, who 'rendered appropriate selections of music during the proceedings'. The chairman, Tom Cook, noted that 'they were not able to erect a costly monument of the ordinary type to the memory of Dr. Pankhurst, but they were able to erect a far greater monument in their hearts, the monument of remembrance'.

In fact, they went further than just remembering; Pankhurst's philosophy continued to exert influence even after his death. Hardie's address referred to many of the key features of Richard's career in politics, but the context at this point was the start of the 2nd Boer War (1899–1902), and he devoted much of his speech to explaining his opposition to the conflict, linking back to Pankhurst's belief in arbitration and negotiation, and the tenet that any decision to go to war should be made by the Commons as representatives of the people:

> He asserted ... that inside the Socialist ranks there was absolute
> unanimity in declaring that, even yet, the troubles in the Transvaal
> should be submitted to reasonable arbitration and the reign of the sword
> brought to an end.[17]

On Emmeline's suggestion, a decision had been made to build a socialist hall in Richard's memory, to be named the Pankhurst Hall. The first stone was laid in St James's Road, Hightown, Salford, on 27 November 1898 by Fred Brocklehurst. The projected cost was £1,400, which was being raised by public subscription to shares of £1 each.[18] In November 1900 the first part of the hall was opened by Bruce Glasier with all the Pankhurst family in attendance. Glasier described Richard as

> one of the finest public spirits of the age. He possessed enthusiasm,
> public mindedness and chivalry to the degree of genius. He was a man
> who regarded neither kings nor lords – a republican of inborn conviction.
> He was a student – a rare lover of philosophy and literature – a thinker
> and investigator, and his career formed one of the finest traditions of
> the reform and Socialist movements in England 1898.[19]

At a further event in 1903, Sylvia Pankhurst and Walter Crane, who between them had designed the hall's decorations, were prominent in the ceremony. Crane spoke about how art could convey ideas, and educate and inspire, in the service of socialism. It was a great irony, however, that in the end the family were disappointed and angered about the hall project because the Manchester socialists decided that their society should not admit women. This was a travesty of all that Richard Pankhurst had stood for, but it was a spur to Emmeline once again to address the rights of women, and resulted in the establishment of the Women's Social and Political Union.[20]

Conclusion

Richard Marsden Pankhurst was a man out of his time. History is full of examples of people who rose to fulfil a significant role in their own day, riding a political or social wave that took them to pre-eminence. But history forgets those who were lone voices, whose ideals and actions seemed at the time to produce little effect, and who died without having achieved their aspirations. Pankhurst was a man who had excited both admiration and opprobrium in Manchester, yet had failed to make much impression elsewhere. The early promise of his youthful successes as a lawyer did not bear the expected fruit of a distinguished career and the accession to the judiciary that should have followed. His erudite and closely argued speeches and writings impressed, but lacked the moderation that might have appealed to the middle classes, and also perhaps the common touch that would have won him more working-class support. He failed in elections and did not gain the parliamentary seat he coveted. It is not surprising that there are occasional glimpses of his frustration and disappointment which suggest that he was not always the buoyant optimist most observers believed him to be.

He espoused causes that were at that time ultra-radical and unpopular: universal suffrage and the payment of MPs, free and compulsory secular education, workers' rights, international arbitration, anti-imperialism, Irish Home Rule and Socialism. Even many of those who were sympathetic to his beliefs regarded them as utopian and impractical. Some of them are still viewed in this light; notably Socialism, tainted since the twentieth century by the excesses of Communism under Stalin and other regimes.

Richard's life was one of journeys: from confirmed bachelor to family man; from non-conformist Christian to agnostic; from Liberal to Socialist. His commitment to his conscience was total; even those who found his politics abhorrent conceded that he was a man of principle. In the same way as it does today, this characteristic almost certainly held him back in his attempts to succeed in political life and in his legal career.

Nevertheless, his legacy was immensely powerful. He had forged his family, including his young and impressionable but also determined, fearless and remarkable wife, into a veritable campaigning machine for the rights and welfare of the poor and the oppressed, notably women and the working classes. Their daughter Adela judged his dominance a serious fault, leading to an oppressively earnest family life. Recording events after her father died, she recalls that when Emmeline's brother, Herbert, came to live with them 'he cheered her [Emmeline] wonderfully. They were the best of friends and there was more laughter in our house than before my father's death …' When discussing Harry, Adela is particularly damning in her view on the damage she believed was inflicted by Richard's injunctions: 'He [Harry] suffered from nervous depression, as we all did, and from the fatal belief that our parents cared nothing about us and we had no right to live, except in so far as we were of use to the Cause.' As far as she was concerned, Harry died in 1910 due to Richard's dead hand: 'Mother … believed earnestly that she was fulfilling her husband's wishes in her devotion to the Cause. None of us, really, did what we could have done for the dear boy, but for that our training, outlook and particularly our father's influence were to blame.' Indeed, her view was that Richard's power was made all the more potent by his death.[1]

Yet this inculcation of an ethos of service, though onerous to Adela, was also inspiring. In the years of their marriage, with the full support of her husband, Emmeline emerged as a political force in her own right. Her later close companion, Dame Ethel Smyth, related that Emmeline had once told her that she never sufficiently appreciated Richard when he was alive; perhaps in the hurly-burly of the moment she had not realised his profound influence and his selflessness in supporting her own development as an agitator. But Emmeline also clearly understood that her own marriage was far from the norm; she saw that in many ways the institution was inimical to women, and often told other women: 'Don't get married unless you care so much that you cannot help it.'[2]

Their daughters, with their father's injunctions to work for others, were likewise to follow a path of commitment to altruistic causes. Sylvia in particular always kept the flame burning at her father's shrine, and tried for the rest of her life to follow what she believed would have been his path. And she and her mother and sister, Christabel, were to find their wave with the foundation of the Women's Social and Political Union in 1903, and ride to victory – admittedly with some rocky hazards – in the long-standing and remarkable women's suffrage battle.

After a long estrangement, before their deaths Sylvia and Christabel corresponded about their family history. They were full of praise for their parents. In 1953 Christabel wrote to Sylvia: 'We had wonderful parents for whom we can always be thankful, whose memory is as vivid with us now as it has always been.' And further in June: 'We have had parents we could be proud of & our childhood years were peaceful & we grew old enough while Father was still with us to benefit from his example, influence and teaching and to know him for what he was.' They were unhappy about some of the things written about their parents, notably by Ray Strachey and Roger Fulford, and contemplated legal action, but Sylvia reminded Christabel in April 1954: 'I remember, too, that Father used often to say (Barrister though he was) that it is no use – when possible keep out of the law courts.' And finally: 'One thing we can always be thankful for ... our parents and their union. No Fulford can take that from us ... grieved though I am to be helpless against malice as applied to our wonderful father. To me he is just as alive as he ever was. There has never been anyone like him and I realize more and more what he went through with his family responsibilities and the public burdens he assumed ...[3]

Sylvia later on willingly took on the task of writing her father's biography, which she stated was in compliance with Emmeline's wishes, and she began to try to trace papers that might help her. She wrote to Frederick Pethick-Lawrence in 1959 explaining that the papers, letters and family Bible that Christabel had kept in her possession and used in her account *Unshackled* had been passed on the latter's death not, as they should have been, to her, but to their Aunt Bess, Richard Pankhurst's sister. She requested Fred's help in recovering them.[4] They included the precious love letters from her father to her mother, from which Christabel quoted in her book. It was perhaps because of information from Fred that Sylvia came to believe that they had been destroyed after they had reached Aunt Bess, who may have judged them too personal to risk future publication. Sylvia never did get as far as producing a full biography, although she did give us the best and most detailed account of her father's life hitherto in print in *The Suffragette Movement*.

The reputation of this paragon was not always treated with such reverence. In 1913 this humorous and not entirely sympathetic description of Pankhurst's speaking style appeared in the *Manchester City News*:

The smile was not the smile of gaiety nor of amusement. It was not the twinkle of the humorist. It was the smile of universal kindliness and goodwill such as the visage of St Francis may have worn. The voice was a natural alto, a thin piping treble, heaven knows how many octaves above the normal pitch.

It used to be amusing, in a way, to hear the Doctor, with that smile and in that voice, propounding the most blood-curdling theories of government and denouncing wrath to come on Kings and Priests and Aristocrats. You knew that he would not hurt a fly, much less a fellow creature![5]

Richard's idealisation of the working class, adopted when he was alive by the rest of his family, did not long outlive him. Even Emmeline in later years no longer believed in Richard's vision of workers full of honesty and nobility of spirit. Christabel shared Emmeline's later scepticism:

> The common people, to Father's generation, seemed almost, if not quite, a different creation ... he was tempted to think of them, or at least to hope them to be, possessed of an innate quality which would enable them, were they free and powerful enough, to reform the world and its ways ... The younger generation, speaking for myself at any rate, who regarded all sorts and conditions of men and women just as persons and not in terms of class, could see no essential difference between working people and anyone else.[6]

Yet many aspects of Richard's influence over his family did endure. When the Fabians supported the government in prosecuting war against the Boers in 1899, Emmeline resigned from their ranks because she knew that her husband would have opposed it as imperialist aggression. Christabel eventually found her niche when she joined the committee of the North of England Society for Women's Suffrage, a cause to which Richard had of course long been committed. She attributed her acceptance on this body to their devotion to his memory: 'They welcomed me benevolently for my parent's sake.'[7] And when the Suffragettes were eventually established under their official title of the Women's Social and Political Union, the campaigning and legal tactics that Emmeline led owed much to the experience of the intransigent determination not to compromise of the Women's Franchise League, and the tactics of the Boggart Hole Clough protest, both of which had been underpinned by Richard's belief in uncompromising principle, his tactical sense and his expertise in the legalities of protest.[8] Adela goes even further in suggesting that:

> Christabel was to take her father's place – dominating and inspiring my mother and providing the outlet for her wonderful personality ... She had inherited considerable political perspicuity from my father and had many historical examples to help her. She wanted the vote for the same reasons, mainly, that Mother did and 'kicking up a row' was a time-honoured method, long before her day, of moving the slow procedure of Parliamentary Government. Our father had considered similar tactics in 'free speech fights', they had been the methods used in the Irish struggle for Home Rule ...[9]

While over time Emmeline and Christabel did move away from Richard's ideals, into violent tactics and even into Conservatism, it was Sylvia who remained his devoted disciple all her life. Adela recognised this, recalling that 'Sylvia was a Socialist, bound up in my father's memory and shadowed by his death, years and years after it occurred.' Sylvia consciously remodelled herself in new situations on the lines she believed he would have taken, in the East End of London, and later as far away as Ethiopia. In a letter to Christabel in 1957 she spelled this out clearly:

> I have tried in my life to follow and to learn what I imbibed from Father and not to desert the cause to which he dedicated his life and energy – Human welfare and progress in its many aspects ... I have always tried to work for what he cared for and to be as worthy as possible to be his offspring.[10]

In 1906 Emmeline and her children decamped to live in London and continue the spectacular campaign for women's suffrage that has made such a mark on the popular imagination. Four years later, letters to the Manchester press expressed 'astonishment and sorrow' that the grave of the illustrious Doctor was in a neglected condition. Suggestions were made for a public collection towards 'putting the headstone upright and at curb level'. Others, however objected that 'each person should look after his own'. In death as in life, Richard Pankhurst was a figure who elicited both love and opprobrium.[11]

Adela, the daughter who was his stern critic, may have left us arguably the most perceptive summary of her father:

> He was a dreamer and he never came to earth ... he made vicious attacks upon the social system, denounced members of the community as exploiters, attacked religion and the churches and was then surprised and indignant because he, in turn, was attacked.[12]

But this was only half the story. While he was regarded as an impractical, even dangerous, radical in his own time, many of his views have now become mainstream, and some of his aims in political life have already been realised. He would have been gratified at the progress made by women in politics and society, at measures to empower the poor politically such as the payment of MPs, at attempts to avoid war through bodies like the United Nations. Yet it is a work in progress and modern society in all these fields still falls far short of the high ideals he espoused.

Perhaps his most notable achievement was the creation, albeit at a personal cost to all of them, of a remarkable family who continued to fight for their beliefs, whether it be against oppression or in favour of popular rights. Emmeline and Christabel have become legendary for their militant campaigning as suffragettes. Sylvia, also noted in that struggle, added anti-war activism, Socialism and serious work among the poor, which was later extended to her championing of Ethiopian freedom from Western colonialism. Adela, initially also a suffragette, made a name working for communism and trade unionism in Australia, though she later became an anti-communist and propagated Christian family values. Whatever they believed in, they were never apathetic, never uninvolved, always ardent. For them, Richard's mantra was ever true: 'If you do not work for other people, you will not have been worth the upbringing.'

In 1928, women finally achieved electoral equality with men. Emmeline died only a month beforehand, while the relatively uncontroversial Bill was making its way through parliament. The tall stone erected by the family over her grave in Brompton cemetery bore a very simple inscription, which may have surprised many to whom Richard Pankhurst was an unknown or long-forgotten figure. It demonstrates the power that he exerted over his family to the end. Even at the time of her triumph, Emmeline is memorialised on her own grave simply as the wife of Richard Pankhurst:

IN LOVING MEMORY OF
EMMELINE PANKHURST
WIFE OF
RM PANKHURST LLD
AT REST
14 JUNE 1928

Notes

Introduction

1. Richard Symonds, *Inside the Citadel. Men and the Emancipation of Women, 1850–1920* (London, 1999), pp.148, 159; Sylvia Strauss, *Traitors to the Masculine Cause. The Men's Campaigns for Women's Rights* (London, 1982), pp.144–5, 197–202.
2. L[ondon] S[chool of] E[conomics, Women's Library] 9/01/1361 Theresa Billington-Greig to Enid Goulden Bach, 1 August 1956.
3. LSE 7/TBG/B1 (box 398).
4. E. Sylvia Pankhurst, *T[he] S[uffragette] M[ovement]* (Virago, London, 1977), p.7.
5. LSE 7/TBG/2B/01.
6. TSM, p.6.
7. TSM, pp.7, 66–7.

Part 1 Life Before Emmeline

Chapter 1 Origins

1. Richard Pankhurst, 'Suffragette Sisters in Old Age: unpublished correspondence between Christabel and Sylvia Pankhurst, 1953–57', *Women's History Review*, vol. 10, no. 3 (2001), pp.486, 488.
2. TSM, p.4.
3. *S[taffordshire] A[dvertiser]*, 2 May 1857, p.7.
4. *Macclesfield Courier and Herald*, 2 May 1857, p.8.
5. TSM, p.5.
6. The censuses do not agree about Richard's exact age, but until 1881 they always indicate a birth date of either 1834 or 1835.
7. Perhaps they were unbaptised until adulthood. During a court hearing Richard was stated to have been baptised into a Baptist church in 1866; MG, 13 May 1886, p.7.
8. Pigot's *Typology of England* (1841); William White, *History, Gazetteer and Directory of Staffordshire* (Sheffield, 1851).
9. SA, 25 July 1835, p.2; 16 January 1836, p.1.
10. V. Markham Lester, *Victorian Insolvency: Bankruptcy, Imprisonment for Debt, and Company Winding-up in Nineteenth-Century England* (Oxford, 1995), p.91.
11. SA, 14 May 1842, p.3.
12. SA, 4 May 1844, p.2.

13. I am grateful to Helen Pankhurst for providing notes to me which include a copy of the letter.
14. SA, 7 September 1844, p.1.
15. SA, 21 September 1844, p.2.
16. E[stelle] S[ylvia] P[ankhurst] P[apers], International Institute of Social History, Amsterdam, 354, letters of 22 and 26 May 1865.
17. *M[anchester] G[uardian]*, 30 Nov 1850, p.6; 19 Feb 1851, p.5; 29 October 1851, p.5; MG, 19 July 1851, p.8; 29 October 1851, p.5.
18. MG, 4 Feb 1852, p.5; 21 Feb 1852, p.1; MG, 20 Oct 1852, p.5.
19. MG, 5 Nov 1853, p.12; 19 Nov 1853, p.4; 23 Nov 1853, p.8; 9 Dec 1854, p.12.
20. I am indebted to Manchester Grammar School archivists Rachel Kneale and Otto Smart for their help; the curriculum was reformed to include Science and German in the 1860s, when fees were also introduced for some pupils.
21. *M[anchester] C[ity] N[ews]*, 18 April 1903, p.6.
22. 1861 Census.
23. MG, 14 Oct 1856, p.3.
24. MG, 2 Feb 1858, p.2.
25. MG, 5 Aug 1858, p.2.
26. MG, 18 March 1859, p.3.
27. ESPP 354.
28. MG, 22 Jan 1853, p.10.
29. TSM, pp.5 and 20.
30. ESPP 354, letter from Henry Francis to Richard of 14 August 1865.
31. Christabel Pankhurst, *Unshackled* (London, 1987), p.20. Evidence that the rift was healed can be found in the death certificate of Margaret Pankhurst, 1879, as her demise was notified by her son-in-law, John Cavanah.
32. TSM, p.6. There was certainly 'a jar' when Richard espoused the cause of women's suffrage, if Lydia Becker is to be believed. See p.65.
33. TSM, pp.6, 4.
34. See p.65.
35. *City Jackdaw*, 13 April 1876, p.197.
36. *M[anchester] C[ourier]*, 1 July 1854, p.8.
37. MC, 30 June 1855, p.8.
38. Sylvia says 1858, but the record shows 1856; J[ohn] R[ylands] U[niversity] L[ibrary], OCA/20/2/1, courtesy of the University of Manchester; *The Globe*, 5 Nov 1856, p.1.
39. JRUL, OCA/4/1, pp.28, 33.
40. MC, 27 Feb 1858, p.9.
41. MG, 8 Oct 1858, p.3.
42. *Huddersfield Chronicle*, 1 October 1859, p.5.
43. CHS Fifoot, *Judge and Jurist in the Reign of Victoria* (London, 1959), pp.21–4.
44. Fifoot, p.27.
45. JRUL OCA/4/1, 2; Owens College, 227; Sylvia, p.12, refers to him as 'one of the small group of pioneers who initiated evening classes at Owens College … for the benefit of working people'.
46. E. Sylvia Pankhurst, *The Life of Emmeline Pankhurst: The Suffragette Struggle for Women's Citizenship* (London, 1935), p.17.
47. JRUL OCA/4/2, pp.cxxxii, cxxxvi.

48. ESPP 329. A letter to the *Manchester Evening News* after his death claims that he was articled to a Mr Marsden, perhaps a relative, from 1859; MEN, 7 July 1898, p.5.
49. SA 8 September 1860, p.2; *Wigan Observer*, 15 September 1860, p.1.
50. TSM, p.9.
51. MC, 21 Dec 1861, p.12.
52. ESPP 354.
53. MG, 20 Feb 1864, p.1.
54. MG, 2 April 1863, p.4.
55. MG, 30 September 1882, p.1; 3 October 1882, p.6.
56. MG, 31 January 1873, p.5.
57. MG, 20 October 1874, p.8.
58. MG, 5 June 1880, p.7; MG, 2 November 1881, p.5; MC, 1 Nov 1882, p.6; Joseph Thompson, *The Owens College* (Manchester, 1886), pp.315, 153.

Chapter 2 Man About Town

1. Roger Fulford, *Votes for Women: the Story of a Struggle* (1957), p.66.
2. Patricia W. Romero, *E. Sylvia Pankhurst, Portrait of a Radical* (Yale UP, 1987), p.18, quoting from a taped interview with Moyes.
3. TSM, pp.7–8.
4. *Manchester Faces and Places*, iv (1893), pp.33–4.
5. For the records of his lodge memberships, see United Grand Lodge of England Freemason Membership Registers, 1751–1921. I am indebted to Pam and Andy Dawes and Anthony McGarel-Groves.
6. https://eastlancashirefreemasons.org/the-interesting-life-of-manchester-mason-richard-pankhurst
7. Jasper Ridley, *The Freemasons* (London, 2008), pp.20, 32, 42, 139, 173, 206.
8. Jessica Harland-Jacobs, 'All in the Family: Freemasonry and the British Empire in the Mid-Nineteenth Century', *Journal of British Studies*, vol. 42, no. 4 (October, 2003), pp.448–482; J. How, *The Freemason's Manual: Or, Illustrations of Masonry* (London, 1862), p.78.
9. Harland-Jacobs, p.456.
10. Harland-Jacobs, p.465.
11. See https://freemasonrymatters.co.uk/index.php/the-geneva-bible-cum-prievegio-and-the-lodge-of-affability-no-317
12. How, p.83.
13. Harland-Jacobs, p.457.
14. M[anchester] C[entral] L[ibrary], M17/8/7/1; M17/8/addtnl. TSM, p.7.
15. MCL, M17/8/7/1.
16. MG, 31 March 1864, p.2.
17. TSM, p.7
18. David P. Davies, *Life and Labours of Ernest Jones* (London, 1903), p.8.
19. TSM, p.11; *Oxford Dictionary of National Biography*, entry on Ernest Jones by John Saville, 2004 online.
20. *The Times*, 28 January 1869.
21. *The Times*, 27 January 1869.
22. ESPP 343.
23. 'English Courts of Law', *Westminster Review,* v.68, 1857, pp.33–52.

24. MG, 9 Nov 1867, p.5.
25. MG, 26 Nov 1867, p.5.
26. MG, 26 Dec 1867, p.3.
27. MG, 13 May 1868, p.6.
28. MG, 9 July 1868, p.6.
29. MG, 15 Jan 1869, p.4.
30. MG, 7 Aug 1869, p.5.
31. MG, 21 September 1883, p.6.
32. MG, 14 April 1870, p.6.
33. MG, 3 June 1873, p.5.
34. MG, 12 June 1875, p.8; MEN, 18 June 1875, p.3.
35. MG, 22 June 1877, p.6.
36. MG, 29 Nov 1870, p.6.
37. MG, 10 November 1874, p.1; 18 November 1874, p.6.
38. MG, 24 October 1877, p.4.
39. MG, 4 November 1880, p.8.
40. MG, 9 November 1882, p.7.
41. Dictionary of Radical Biography, p.640.
42. *Manchester Faces and Places,* vol. iv (1893), p.33; MCL GB127.M8/2/6.
43. E. Sylvia Pankhurst, *The Life of Emmeline Pankhurst,* p.17; see Lester, *Victorian Insolvency,* pp.140–55.
44. Lester, *Victorian Insolvency,* p.114. For the NAPSS, see pp.31–2.
45. *Manchester Weekly News,* 1 May 1869, p.6.
46. MG, 21 March 1866, p.3; 26 May 1870, p.6. He and his father also engaged in the meetings of the Manchester branch around this time; MG, 7 February 1871, p.8; 11 February 1871, p.1; MG, 13 July 1872, p.9.
47. MG, 20 June 1872, p.5.
48. TSM, p.10.
49. MG, 13 April 1866, p.3.
50. MG, 4 February 1879, p.6.
51. MG, 25 February 1879, p.6.
52. For the Chamber's own, less detailed record of these debates, see MCL, GB127. M8/2/8, pp.737, 748.
53. MG, 2 November 1880, p.6.
54. MG, 23 November 1882, p.4.
55. MG, 10 November 1882, p.1.
56. MCL, GB127.M8/9/1.

Chapter 3 A Social Conscience

1. MG, 13 May 1886, p.7. See E.T. McLaren, *Dr. R. McLaren of Manchester. A Sketch* (London, 1911); I am indebted to Pam Dawes for this reference and for the advice of Emeritus Professor David Bebbington of the University of Stirling.
2. ESPP 342.
3. *Rochdale Observer,* 22 October 1870.
4. MG, 1 March 1864, p.5; 1 March 1865, p.5; 26 March 1864, p.4.
5. MG, 28 November 1871, p.1.
6. MG, 21 Dec 1872, p.1.

7. TSM, p.13.

8. Manchester Literary and Philosophical Society, Annual Report, 1898–9, p.xxxxix; MG, 10 Sept 1868, p.5; TSM, p.12 gives Richard Pankhurst the credit for reforming the operation of the institutes.

9. *Accrington Times*, October 1867, cited in Sylvia, pp.13–14; MG, 19 Oct 1867, p.7.

10. MG, 19 Nov 1867, p.5.

11. TSM, p.14, citing a speech to the Littlewood Mechanics Institute and reported in the *Glossop Chronicle*, 7 September 1867.

12. *M[anchester] E[vening] N[ews]*, 3 March 1869, p.4.

13. MG, 6 Aug 1872, p.5.

14. TSM, p.15

15. MG, 15 Aug 1872, p.5.

16. MG, 23 February 1877, p.6. By 1882 he was a Vice Director of the Institution; MG, 25 February 1882, p.5.

17. MG, 5 June 1880, p.7; Sylvia p.14.

18. For republicanism, see pp.47–54.

19. ESPP 343; MEN, 3 November 1873, p.1.

20. TSM, p.17.

21. MC, 15 November 1873, p.8.

22. MG, 8 November 1873, p.8; 12 November 1873, p.6; 14 November 1873, p.5; C.B. Dolton 'The Manchester School Board', Durham University M.Ed (1959), app.X.

23. For what follows, see Lawrence Goldman, *Science, Reform and Politics in Victorian Britain. The Social Science Association 1857–86* (Cambridge, 2002), passim.

24. See pp.31–5.

25. The following is taken from the Transactions of the NAPSS for the relevant years.

26. E. Sylvia Pankhurst, *The Life of Emmeline Pankhurst*, p.17; see also Stefan Collini, *Public Moralists: Political Thought and Intellectual Life in Britain* (Oxford, 1993), pp.58, 63, 68, 73, 94, 100, for instance.

27. Sylvia quotes his words: 'The history of England is the political Bible of the people of this country.' TSM, p.10.

28. See Richard Symonds, *Inside the Citadel, Men and the Emancipation of Women, 1850–1920* (London, 1999), pp.20, 23.

29. Collini, pp.139, 134, 131.

30. Transactions of the NAPSS, pp.476–8. Education arose again in 1869, when in discussion he argued that it should be secular and compulsory.

31. It is interesting to note that in October 1872 he attended a meeting in Manchester Town Hall that aimed to set up a system of arbitration; the main speaker, remarkably at that time, was a woman, Mrs King of London. Discussion focused on the role of women alongside men in the cause of peace and Richard supported resolutions to form a women's peace society. MG, 30 October 1872, p.7.

32. 1869 at Bristol saw a discussion on the legal management of war contraband, while in 1876 at Liverpool Richard argued that the same 'community of action' would decide on the extradition of criminals.

33. *Manchester Faces and Places*, vol. iv, p.33. He addressed the prestigious BAAS on the same subject in 1870; MEN 19 September 1870, p.2.

34. I am grateful to Alfie Jenkins of the Royal Statistical Society for the date of Pankhurst's membership, 24 November 1887; *The Times*, 6 July 1898, p.14.

35. *Transactions of the Manchester Statistical Society*, 1865–6, pp.70–87.
36. *Transactions of the Manchester Statistical Society*, 1883–4, pp.31–44.
37. MEN, 1 April 1873, p.2.
38. *Transactions of the Manchester Statistical Society*, 1887–8, pp.29–48.
39. James B. Miles, *The Association for the Reform and Codification of the Law of Nations* (Paris, 1875), pp.4,9.
40. MG, 11 August 1882, p.4; 9 December 1882, p.5.
41. *Dictionary of Radical Biography*, p.641; *Manchester Faces and Places*, iv, p.34; TSM, p.23.
42. TSM, p.24; ESPP 343; MEN, 20 January 1876, p.3.
43. MG, 16 March 1874, p.5.
44. The Peterloo Massacre occurred on 16 August 1819 in Manchester, when troops attacked an unarmed crowd resulting in many casualties; MG, 8 October 1877, p.6.
45. MEN, 28 August 1871, p.2.
46. MG, 7 October 1873, p.5.
47. TSM, p.24.
48. MEN, 2 February 1871, p.2; MG, 9 February 1876, p.1; 15 February 1876, p.1.
49. MG, 25 September 1866, p.1; 14 December 1875, p.1; 3 August 1877, p.5. As Emmeline's father, Robert Goulden, was also on the Executive Committee, it may be that they became acquainted through this institution.
50. MG, 20 August 1877, p.6.
51. TSM, p.27.
52. Sylvia claimed he believed that bargains had been struck with Russia and Turkey with the ultimate goal of seizing the whole of Asia Minor; TSM, p.25.
53. MG, 4 January 1878, p.8; he repeated his desire to see the power to declare war bestowed on parliament at a town meeting a little later; MG, 16 January 1878, p.6.
54. MG, 28 January 1878, p.8.
55. MG, 29 January 1878, p.6.
56. MG, 4 February 1878, p.6.
57. MG, 12 February 1878, p.5.
58. MG, 21 February 1878.
59. *Darlington Herald*, 1 May 1878; ESPP 343.
60. *The Times*, 1 May 1878, p.12; TSM, p.29.
61. MG, 20 July 1878, p.9.
62. TSM, p.25.
63. MG, 26 August 1878, p.8.
64. MG, 23 November 1878, p.9; MEN, 13 December 1878, p.3.
65. TSM, p.26; MEN, 12 February 1879, p.2.
66. See p.42.
67. MCL, M283/1; Gladstone's Midlothian campaign was the first modern election campaign aimed at a mass electorate.

Chapter 4 The Ultra-Radical Emerges

1. MCL, Manchester Liberal Association Minutes M283/1.
2. TSM, p.64; Joanna M. Williams, *The Great Miss Lydia Becker: Suffragist, Scientist and Trailblazer* (Barnsley, 2022), p.250.
3. MG, 10 September 1861, p.5.

4. *City Jackdaw*, 13 April 1876, p.197.
5. *City Jackdaw*, 13 April 1876, p.198.
6. On another occasion his espousal of republicanism caused a similar attempt to oust him from his position in the Union.
7. *City Jackdaw*, 13 April 1876, p.198.
8. For what follows, see Fergus A. D'Arcy, 'Charles Bradlaugh and the English Republican Movement, 1868–78', *The Historical Journal*, June 1982, vol. 25, no. 2, pp.367–83.
9. MCL, GB127.Broadsides/F1873.1.
10. MG, 29 May 1873, p.6.
11. *Liverpool Mail*, 24 January 1874, p.9.
12. MG, 28 January 1874, p.8.
13. MG, 22 October 1874, p.8.
14. His calling the Church of England a 'grotesque monster' in 1876 seems to have elicited a similar storm, and it was in this year that his tenure as secretary ended; *City Jackdaw*, 13 April 1876, p.19.
15. MG, 24 October 1874, p.7.
16. MG, 25 March 1875, p.5.
17. MG, 3 March 1876, p.5.
18. MG, 17 March 1876, p.4.
19. MC, 18 March 1876, p.5.
20. MG, 3 April 1876, p.8; this contrasts with the report which follows it of a similar Liverpool meeting, where behaviour was exemplary.
21. *City Jackdaw*, 13 April 1876, p.197.
22. MG, 8 April 1876, p.8.
23. ESPP 343.
24. MG, 3 March 1876, p.5.
25. TSM, pp.10–11. Procrustes from Greek mythology was a robber who forced his victims to lie on a bed, and either stretched them or cut off their legs to fit it.
26. MG, 21 September 1884, p.6. There was a huge demonstration against the Lords in Hyde Park also at this time; TSM, p.81.
27. MG, 2 January 1885, p.6; MG, 9 February 1885, p.6.
28. MG, 24 August 1894, p.8.
29. See TSM, pp.21–3.
30. *Manchester and Salford Co-operative Herald*, February 1876.
31. See Joanna M. Williams, *The Great Miss Lydia Becker*, pp.131, 150.
32. ESPP 343.
33. Christabel Pankhurst, *Unshackled*, p.20, is alone in claiming that he left the Church of England to become a non-conformist and therefore could not study at Oxford University. This does not fit with what we know of his background and she perhaps misunderstood some regret he once expressed that he had not been able to study at Oxford University.
34. ESPP 342; MG, 13 May 1886, p.7.
35. MG, 8 April 1871, p.4.
36. *City Jackdaw*, 13 April 1876, p.197.
37. MG, 1 August 1876, p.5; 2 Sept 1878, p.6; Joanna M. Williams, *Manchester's Radical Mayor: Abel Heywood, the Man who Built the Town Hall* (Stroud, 2017), p.168.
38. ESPP 343.

39. MG, 28 February 1877, p.8.
40. ESPP 342.
41. There is a marginal note here: 'I have since the annexed was written completed an article on its subject. But these notes have been of no use how seldom such notes are. A line of thought is like a cutting in a Railway. You can leave it when you will.'

Chapter 5 Women's Suffrage to 1880

1. *The Great Miss Lydia Becker*, p.28.
2. Helen Blackburn, *Women's Suffrage* (London, 1902), p.59; TSM, p.31 also lists Ursula Bright, Philippine Kyllmann and Mrs Steinthal.
3. TSM, p.11.
4. ESPP 342.
5. Blackburn, p.59 gives the following names: Mrs Winkworth (chair), Mrs Gloyne, Mrs Hume Rothery, Mr and Mrs Kyllmann, Mrs R.R. Moore, Miss S. Miall, Miss Wilson, Miss Becker, Miss Wolstenholm [sic], and Rev. Samuel Steinthal. They were soon joined by Liverpool campaigner Josephine Butler, lawyer Thomas Chorlton, Professor Greenbank, Mrs Mathilde Kyllmann, Mrs J.P. Thomasson, Miss Alice Wilson, and Miss M. Wilson. See M[anchester] N[ational] S[ociety for] W[omen's] S[uffrage], Annual Report, MCL, M50/1/4/1, p.14.
6. *Dictionary of Radical Biography*, p.640; see *The Great Miss Lydia Becker*, pp.45–7.
7. Christabel Pankhurst, *Unshackled*, p.19.
8. TSM, p.29.
9. Martin Pugh, *The Pankhursts* (London, 2008), p.19.
10. *The Great Miss Lydia Becker*, p.51, for example; MCL M50/1/3 Lydia Becker to Richard Pankhurst, 4 October 1868.
11. This view was supported later by the Edinburgh suffragist leader Priscilla McLaren. The career was, however, closed to women. MCL, M50/1/3 Lydia Becker to Anne Robertson, 25 October 1868; W[omen's] S[uffrage] J[ournal], August 1890, p.8.
12. MCL, M50/1/3, 25 October 1868, Lydia Becker to Anne Robertson. A woman could not so qualify at this period.
13. TSM, p.35; MC, 1 October 1883, p.5.
14. Professor June Purvis suggested this in conversation and by email. MCL, M50/1/3, 24 May 1868, Lydia Becker to Jessie Boucherett; 8 July 1868, Lydia Becker to Josephine Butler; 20 June 1868, Lydia Becker to Richard Pankhurst.
15. ESPP 340, 24 May 1868.
16. MCL, M50/1/3 7 June 1868, Lydia Becker to Sarah Jackson.
17. MCL, M50/1/3 8 July 1868, Lydia Becker to Josephine Butler.
18. ESPP 354; Henry Francis Pankhurst, will proved 1873. All the same, it was Richard who registered his father's death, and was present at the time; see Henry Francis Pankhurst, Death Certificate.
19. MCL, M50/1/3, 20 June 1868, Lydia Becker to Mary Johnson; 8 July 1868, Lydia Becker to Josephine Butler; 11 July 1868, Lydia Becker to Richard Pankhurst.
20. MCL, M50/1/3 27 May 1868, Lydia Becker to Ursula Bright.
21. R.M. Pankhurst, 'The Right of Women to Vote Under the Reform Act, 1867', *Fortnightly Review*, XXI, 1 September 1868, pp.250–4.
22. MCL, M50/1/3 14 May 1868, Lydia Becker to Ursula Bright.

23. TSM, p.39.
24. TSM, p.41.
25. 'The Right of Women to Vote under the Reform Act, 1867', p.253.
26. MCL, M50/1/3 Lydia Becker to Ursula Bright, 31 May 1868.
27. MCL, M50/1/3 Lydia Becker to Jessie Boucherett, 18 September 1868.
28. TSM, p.43.
29. For a detailed account of the arguments cited in terms of statutory and case law, as well as customary usage, see TSM, pp.44–5.
30. The Executive Committee on 30 Oct 1868 was Jacob Bright, Mrs J. Bright, Miss Becker, Mrs Butler, Thos Chorlton, Prof Greenbank, Mrs E. Kyllmann, Mrs Max Kyllmann, Miss S. Miall, Mrs R.R. Moore, Dr Pankhurst, R.D. Rusden, Rev S.A. Steinthal, Mrs J.P. Thomasson, Miss A. Wilson, Miss M. Wilson, Miss Wolstenholme. See MNSWS Annual Report, MCL, M50/1/4/1, p.14.
31. MCL, M50/1/4/3, 3rd Annual Report of the MNSWS, 23 November 1870, p.3.
32. LSE Mill-Taylor Archive, vol. XII, 29, 27 December 1867, Lydia Becker to Helen Taylor.
33. Blackburn, pp.91–4.
34. TSM, p.46.
35. Blackburn, pp.92–3.
36. Blackburn, p.95.
37. WSJ, Dec 1870, p.99.
38. Blackburn, pp.106–7.
39. WSJ, Dec 1870, p.100.
40. WSJ, Dec 1871, pp.126–7.
41. WSJ, Dec 1872, p.157.
42. See *The Great Miss Lydia Becker*, pp.218–223.
43. See pp.80–2.
44. For details of their courtship, see pp.86ff.
45. eg MCL, M50/1/4/13, p.26; M50/1/4/16, p.24.

Chapter 6 Married Women's Property

1. Remarkably, up to 1,000 women nationwide voted in the general election of 1868; see pp.66–9.
2. Joan Perkin, *Women and Marriage in 19th century England* (London, 1989), p.295.
3. Perkin, p.296.
4. Perkin, pp.298–302.
5. *The Times*, 4 Aug 1870, p.12.
6. See p.5.
7. Lawrence Goldman, *Science, Reform and Politics in Victorian Britain. The Social Science Association 1857–1886* (Cambridge, 2002), p.126
8. For this and what follows, see Lee Holcombe, *Wives and Property* (Toronto, 1983), pp.128–147.
9. Holcombe, pp.125–4, provides a detailed list of all the committee members, along with biographical details.
10. MCL, M50 1/3, 20 May 1868, Lydia Becker to Elizabeth Wolstenholme; Lydia Becker to Richard Pankhurst.

11. Holcombe, p.144.
12. Holcombe, p.177.
13. Holcombe, p.166.
14. Holcombe, p.179.
15. MG, 23 September 1871, p.8.
16. Holcombe, p.186.
17. Holcombe, p.196.
18. Holcombe, p.198.
19. Holcombe, p.202, see pp.203–4 for details of the Act's provisions.
20. *The Times*, 1 January 1883, p.7.

Part 2 Marriage, Children and Elections, 1879–93

Chapter 7 An 'ideal marriage'

1. This was Christabel's description in a letter to Sylvia of 25 May 1953; Richard Pankhurst, 'Suffragette Sister in Old Age: unpublished correspondence between Christabel and Sylvia Pankhurst, 1953–57', *Women's History Review*, vol. 10, no. 3 (2001), p.486.
2. TSM, p.55.
3. E. Sylvia Pankhurst, *The Life of Emmeline Pankhurst*, p.11.
4. See pp.39–44.
5. His father died in 1873.
6. There are rumours that the letters were buried under Emmeline's statue in Victoria Tower Gardens in March 1930, for which information I am indebted to Professor June Purvis. However, Sylvia ascertained in the 1950s that they passed on Christabel's death to Richard's sister, Bess, and seems to have been informed by Frederick Pethick-Lawrence that they had been at some point destroyed; Pethick-Lawrence Papers, Trinity College, Cambridge, PETH 9/83, 9/86. See also *Unshackled*, pp.21–2.
7. For details of Emmeline's background, see pp.89–93.
8. E. Sylvia Pankhurst, *The Life of Emmeline Pankhurst*, p.18.
9. TSM, p.103.
10. MC 20 December 1879, p.7.
11. TSM, p.53; ESPP 352 (ACLL cards).
12. National Library of Australia, Pankhurst-Walsh Papers, 22/66, 'Philosophy of the Suffragette Movement', p.6.
13. Emmeline herself recounted this in her ghosted autobiography, *My Own Story* (London, 1914), pp.2–3.
14. Pugh, pp.9–10.
15. Emmeline Pankhurst, *My Own Story* (London, 1914), p.9: also see *The Great Miss Lydia Becker*, p.91.
16. TSM, p.54.
17. *Votes for Women*, 31 December 1908, p.230.
18. Pugh, p.11.
19. *Unshackled*, pp.17–18
20. E. Sylvia Pankhurst, *The Life of Emmeline Pankhurst*, p.15.
21. As Olive Banks in *Becoming a Feminist: The Social Origins of 'First Wave' Feminism*, (Brighton, 1986), pp.26–9 noted happened for other women.

22. Pugh, p.15.
23. Pugh, p.22.
24. Probate record of Margaret Pankhurst; Census 1881.
25. 'Suffragette Sisters in Old Age', p.512.
26. LSE Women's Library 9/01/1360.
27. Or it may have emerged later when she was on the Chorlton-on-Medlock Board of Health and the inmates of the workhouse seem to have used the term for her; *Unshackled*, p.34.
28. Sylvia Pankhurst in Margot Oxford, ed., *Myself When Young* (London, 1938), p.260.
29. Pankhurst-Walsh Papers, MS2123, 22/66, 'The Philosophy of the Suffragette Movement', p.7; 'My Mother', p.5.
30. For what follows, see TSM, pp.57–8; 66–8.
31. MG, 29 May 1880, p.8, 6 November 1880, p.9.
32. Emmeline Pankhurst, *My Own Story*, p.14.
33. ESPP 127; 'My Mother', p.2.
34. Pankhurst-Walsh Papers, MS2123, 22/66, 'The Philosophy of the Suffragette Movement', pp.15–16.
35. Verna Coleman, *Adela Pankhurst, the wayward suffragette, 1885–1961* (Melbourne, 1996), location 276.
36. Pankhurst-Walsh Papers, MS2123, 22/66, 'The Philosophy of the Suffragette Movement', p.7; 16/50, 'My Mother', pp.5–6.
37. MEN, 29 September 1883, p.3; see p.108.

Chapter 8 Parliamentary Candidate

1. MG, 23 August 1881, p.1; 3 September 1881, p.9.
2. MG, 23 July 1883, p.8.
3. *The Times*, 11 September 1883, p.5.
4. TSM, pp.60–5.
5. *The Times*, 13 September 1883, p.4.
6. The fictional *Phineas Finn* by Anthony Trollope illustrates this clearly.
7. The *Observer*, 16 September 1883, p.5; *The Times*, 17 September 1883, p.7.
8. MG, 18 September 1883, p.8.
9. MG, 20 September 1883, p.8; *The Times*, 20 September 1883, p.10; See Joanna M. Williams, *Manchester's Radical Mayor*, p.219.
10. *The Times*, 21 September 1883, p.8.
11. MG, 21 September 1883, p.6.
12. MG, 26 September 1883, p.5.
13. TSM, p.62.
14. Ibid.
15. Quoted in MG, 22 September 1883, p.8.
16. MG, 22 September 1883, p.5.
17. Pugh, *The Pankhursts*, p.27.
18. MG, 25 September 1883, pp.6, 5; 24 September 1883, p.6; *The Times*, 25 September 1883, p.6.
19. Joanna M. Williams, *The Great Miss Lydia Becker*, p.250.
20. MG, 27 September 1883, p.6.
21. *The Times*, 28 September 1882, p.7.
22. TSM, pp.62–3.

23. MG, 24 September 1883, p.6.
24. Speech at Miles Platting, reported in MG, 26 September 1883, p.6.
25. MG, 27 September 1883, p.6.
26. MG, 27 September 1883, p.7; 28 September 1883, p.7.
27. MG, 28 September 1883, p.5.
28. MG, 28 September 1883, p.8.
29. MG, 29 September 1883, p.8.
30. MEN, 29 Sept 1883, p.3.
31. MG, 29 September 1883, p.8; *The Standard*, 1 October 1883, p.3.
32. Cited in MG, 29 September 1883, p.5.
33. MG, 2 October 1883, p.1.
34. MG, 3 October 1883, p.8.
35. MG, 4 October 1883, p.5.
36. *The Times*, 5 October 1883, p.8.
37. Voting was secret from 1872 onwards.
38. MG, 5 October 1883, p.8.
39. MG, 25 September 1883, p.1.
40. See for instance MG, 2 October 1883, p.5.
41. Pugh, *The Pankhursts*, p.29.
42. MG, 5 October 1883, p.8. Indeed, there was now speculation in London that Parnell, leader of the Irish nationalists, might find him a seat in an Irish borough; MG, 5 October 1883, p.5.
43. MG, 12 October 1883, p.6.
44. MG, 9 October 1883, p.8.
45. MG, 2O November 1883, p.7.
46. Manchester Rate Book, 17 August 1885.
47. *Slater's Directory of Manchester*, January 1886, p.305; Pugh, p.30; Patricia W. Romero, *E. Sylvia Pankhurst, Portrait of a Radical*, p.5.
48. E. Sylvia Pankhurst, *The Life of Emmeline Pankhurst*, p.19.
49. MG, 9 October 1883, p.5.
50. MG, 15 October 1883, p.6; 27 October 1883, p.7.
51. MG, 15 November 1883, p.8; 6 December 1883, p.8.
52. MG, 31 December 1883, p.3.

Chapter 9 London Adventure

1. He was still active in the MNSWS at this time; on 17 February 1885 they held a 'great meeting' in the Free Trade Hall in Manchester at which Richard proposed that petitions in favour of women's votes be presented to both Houses of Parliament; WSJ, 2 March 1885, p.42.
2. MG, 27 October 1884, p.5; 7 November 1884, p.8.
3. The implied suspicion was that there had been a shady deal, thought to concern the redistribution of seats in favour of the Conservatives to balance up the votes of Liberal-leaning workers.
4. MG, 29 November 1884, p.8.
5. MG, 29 May 1885, p.6; 8 January 1885, p.5; 9 January 1885, p.5.
6. MG, 21 May 1885, p.8; *The Times*, 29 May 1885, p.7.
7. *The Times*, 11 July 1885, p.13.

8. MG, 18 September 1885, p.7; 21 September 1885, p.3.

9. ESPP 333.

10. MG, 19 September 1885, p.5; *The Times*, 30 September 1885, p.6.

11. MG, 3 October 1885, p.8.

12. *The Times*, 17 October 1885, p.7.

13. MG, 26 October 1885, p.5; *South London Press*, 7 November 1885, p.14.

14. TSM, p.71.

15. *South London Press*, 14 November 1885, p.6.

16. TSM, p.72, citing evidence from the court records and the London press.

17. TSM, p.72; Bright's support was recorded in the *South London Press* on 7 November 1885, p.7.

18. MG, 28 October 1885, p.6.

19. *Observer*, 8 November 1885, p.2.

20. TSM, p.73.

21. MG, 13 May 1886, p.7.

22. TSM, pp.74–5.

23. *South London Press*, 21 November 1885, p.7.

24. *South London Press*, 28 November 1885, p.4.

25. MG, 24 November 1885, p.5.

26. *South London Press*, 31 October 1885, p.7.

27. The same organ went on to state that the Tories, aided and abetted by the clergy, had run their contest 'in an ungenerous spirit'.

28. *The Times*, 27 November 1885, p.9.

29. MG, 1 January 1886, p.6.

30. ESPP 339; MG, 5 March 1886, p.8.

31. *The Times*, 5 December 1885, p.3.

32. TSM, p.75.

33. MG, 11 December 1885, p.6.

34. MG, 1 February 1886, p.6. Pankhurst was still at this time invested in the mainstream Liberal Party. In February 1886 he was elected as a vice-president of the newly formed South-West Manchester Liberal Association; MG, 18 February 1886, p.7.

35. MG, 13 May 1886, p.7; TSM, p.76.

36. MG, 15 May 1886, p.9.

37. TSM, p.77.

38. MG, 10 June 1886, p.5.

39. *The Times*, 26 June 1886, p.5; TSM, p.75.

40. TSM, p.79.

41. *The Times*, 1 July 1886, p.10; MG, 1 July 1886, p.8.

42. *The Times*, 27 March 1891, p.8; 30 October 1891, p.8; see pp.144–5.

43. I am grateful to Professor June Purvis, who provided a copy of a letter in her Private Suffrage Collection from Richard, written on 1 September 1885 on Outer Temple Legal Club notepaper, and with the postscript that 'The above address finds me'.

44. *The Times*, 19 December 1887, p.12.

45. MG, 12 January 1886, p.6.

46. MG, 24 March 1887, p.7; *The Times*, 22 March 1887, p.11; *Leeds Times*, 30 April 1887, p.7.

47. *Manchester Faces and Places*, iv, p.34.

48. *The Times*, 16 June 1888, p.5.
49. MG, 11 September 1888, p.8; 13 September 1888, p.6.
50. MG, 23 August 1889, p.6.
51. *The Times*, 21 September 1889, p.12.
52. *The Times*, 14 November 1889, p.11.
53. MG, 20 May 1890, p.12.
54. MG, 15 October 1890, p.7; 4 December 1890, p.7.
55. MG, 7 May 1891, p.7; 11 July 1891, p.7.
56. MG, 1 August 1891, p.8.
57. MG, 26 March 1892, p.9; 28 March, p.6.
58. MG, 21 September 1892, p.7; 23 September 1892, p.8.
59. MG, 14 October 1892, p.7.
60. MG, 17 May 1893, p.7.
61. MG, 20 September 1893, p.3.
62. TSM, pp.83–4.
63. *Unshackled*, p.27.
64. See p.133; TSM, p.89.
65. TSM, p.4.
66. Quoted in Coleman, *Adela Pankhurst*, location 259.
67. TSM, p.90; Diane Atkinson, *Rise up Women!* (London, 2018), pp.14–15.
68. Cady Stanton also wrote a feminist version of the Bible, editing out 'immoral' sections and some of St Paul's Epistles.
69. *Unshackled*, p.29.
70. TSM, pp.90–1.
71. David Mitchell, *Queen Christabel* (London, 1977), p.17.
72. *Unshackled*, pp.24–5.
73. For these events, see p.133.

Chapter 10 'The four pillars of my house'

1. TSM, p.67.
2. ESPP 342.
3. John Tosh, *A Man's Place* (London, 1999), p.110.
4. 'My Mother', pp.5–6.
5. *Unshackled*, p.36.
6. TSM, p.67.
7. *Unshackled*, p.24.
8. Coleman, *Adela Pankhurst*, location 187; 'My Mother', p.10.
9. Frank also had the name Robert, after his maternal grandfather; Harry was not given that name because by the time of his birth Richard and Emmeline were no longer on speaking terms with Robert Goulden; p.108; see Pethwick-Lawrence Papers, PETH 9/80, letter from Sylvia Pankhurst to Frederick Pethick-Lawrence, 10 July 1959.
10. Richard Pankhurst, *Sylvia Pankhurst, Artist and Crusader* (London, 1979) p.11. It is perhaps doubtful how mellifluous this rendition could have been as Richard was reputedly tone deaf.
11. TSM, p.68.
12. LSE, *Woman's Herald*, 7 February 1891, pp.241–2.
13. TSM, p.4.

14. TSM, p.106.
15. TSM, p.102.
16. *Unshackled*, pp.34–5.
17. 'My Mother', p.4.
18. LSE, The Women's Library, Jill Craigie Collection, Christabel Pankhurst to Richard Marsden Pankhurst; cited in June Purvis, *Emmeline Pankhurst: a Biography* (London, 2002), p.22.
19. 'My Mother', pp.8–9; TSM, pp.107–8.
20. Adela Pankhurst to Helen Moyes, quoted in Helen Moyes, *Woman in a Man's World* (Sidney, 1971), p.38.
21. TSM, p.67.
22. *Unshackled*, p.29.
23. TSM, pp.107, 106.
24. TSM, p.102.
25. TSM, p.177.
26. *Unshackled*, p.31.
27. TSM, pp.109–10; 'My Mother', p.21.
28. *Unshackled*, p.27.
29. TSM, p.324.
30. TSM, pp.88, 103.
31. 'My Mother', p.7; Coleman, *Adela Pankhurst*, location 196.
32. Coleman, *Adela Pankhurst,* locations 334 and 343.
33. 'My Mother', p.13; Coleman, *Adela Pankhurst*, location 396.
34. 'My Mother', p.8.
35. TSM, p.147.
36. 'My Mother', pp.17 and 27; see also June Purvis, 'Emmeline Pankhurst (1858–1928), Suffragette Leader and Single Parent in Edwardian Britain', *Women's History Review*, 20:1 (2011), pp.92–3; Coleman, *Adela Pankhurst*, location 549.
37. *Unshackled*, p.28.
38. National Library of Australia, Pankhurst-Walsh Papers MS2123, folder 83, 'The Story of My Life', p.2.
39. 'My Mother', p.3.
40. TSM, pp.98, 90.
41. Sylvia Pankhurst in Margot Oxford, ed., *Myself When Young*, p.259.
42. LSE *Woman's Herald*, 7 February 1891, pp.241–2.

Chapter 11 London Campaigns and the Emergence of Emmeline

1. TSM, p.80; ESPP 333.
2. Holton, *Suffrage Days* (London, 1996), p.73.
3. The story of the trampling has been questioned, but what is clear is that he died at the event and was an innocent onlooker.
4. Anne Taylor, *Annie Besant* (Oxford 1992), p.195.
5. TSM, pp.80–1; Diane Atkinson, *Rise up Women!* (London 2018), pp.14–15; see also *The Great Miss Lydia Becker*, pp.249–55.
6. Confusingly, the official title of the College Street group was the Central Committee of the National Society for Women's Suffrage; that of the Parliament Street group was the Central National Society for Women's Suffrage.
7. See pp.83–4.

8. The resolution was again supported at a public meeting in the Prince's Hall that evening. See ESPP 341, Report of the WFrL Executive Committee, 1889–90.

9. LSE Women's Library, Autograph letters, 9/13/14.

10. ESPP 341, Report of the Executive Committee, 1889–90.

11. Maureen Wright, *Elizabeth Wolstenholme Elmy and the Victorian Feminist Movement*, (Manchester, 2011), p.137, explains that Elizabeth Wolstenhome Elmy's letter to Scatcherd of 12 July talks about a meeting relocated due to Emmeline's confinement.

12. Sandra Stanley Holton, '"To Educate Women into Rebellion": Elizabeth Cady Stanton and the Creation of a Transatlantic Network of Radical Suffragists', *American Historical Review*, October 1994, p.1129.

13. I am indebted for this information to Janet Douglas, who shared with me her researches on Alice Scatcherd.

14. ESPP 341, Annual Report 1889–90.

15. Purvis, *Emmeline Pankhurst*, p.52; TSM, pp.94–7.

16. Wright, *Elizabeth Wolstenholme Elmy*, p.137.

17. Sylvia Pankhurst's papers in Amsterdam include a correspondence of 1890 between Richard and Sir Charles discussing the import of the MWP Acts; ESPP 335.

18. Holton, *Suffrage Days*, pp.72–3, 77.

19. TSM, p.92.

20. Holton, *Suffrage Days*, pp.73–4; BL Add MS 49610, no. 235.

21. Wright, *Elizabeth Wolstenholme Elmy*, p.141; the Elmys' factory had burnt down.

22. ESPP 341, WFrL Annual Report, 1889–90.

23. Maroula Joannou and June Purvis, eds., *The Women's Suffrage Movement* (MUP, 1998), p.21; SS, *Suffrage Days*, pp.77–8; M. Wright, pp.143–5, 101; ESPP 341, Report of the Executive Committee, 1889–90.

24. Pugh, *The Pankhursts*, pp.54–5; Joannou and Purvis, p.25.

25. MG, 22 April 1891, p.5.

26. MCL, M50/2/1/141, May 1891.

27. David Mitchell, *Queen Christabel*, p.22, citing a leaflet in the LSE, McIlquham Papers.

28. ESPP 341.

29. LSE, Fabian Society, *Special Report of the Proceedings of the Three Days Conference*, minutes, 9–11 June 1886.

30. Sylvia Pankhurst in *Myself When Young*, p.267.

31. See pp.144–5.

32. ESPP 341.

33. When Ursula Bright attended the World Congress of Representative Women in Chicago, in 1893, she mentioned also equal wages, access to public office, and equalities in contract law; see Sandra Stanley Holton, 'From Anti-Slavery to Suffrage Militancy: The Bright Circle, Elizabeth Cady Stanton and the British Women's Movement', in *Suffrage and Beyond: International Feminist Perspectives,* (New Zealand, 1994), p.1132.

34. TSM, p.97.

35. ESPP 341, letters from Mary Cozens; TSM, p.96.

36. *The Times*, 27 April 1892, p.9.

37. TSM, p.90 describes him from her child's perspective 'with his red tie and bristling moustache, and the truculent manner which belied his kindly nature, dashed in and out in a state of perpetual excitement ...'

38. *The Times*, 27 April 1892, p.9.

39. Joannou and Purvis, p.29; Holton, *Suffrage Days*, pp.85–6; ESPP 337, 14 May 1892, Mr Levy to Richard Pankhurst.
40. LSE Women's Library 7JCC 01/02, folder 2.
41. At the Fabian conference in 1886 Richard had given a lecture on 'The situation from the earlier Radical point of view'; see Edward R. Pease, *The History of the Fabian Society* (Project Gutenberg, 2004), cap. III, www.gutenberg.org.
42. Pugh, *The Pankhursts*, pp.54–6. They did, however, rejoin the Manchester women's suffrage society and attended its AGM on 20 November 1894; MG, 21 November 1894, p.6.
43. Holton, *Suffrage Days*, p.87 and 'To Educate Women into Rebellion', p.1134.
44. TSM, p.97. Scatcherd was wealthy and donated £50 every year to the funds; Joannou and Purvis, p.19.
45. Joannou and Purvis, pp.25, 27, 30, 31.

Part 3: Final Years in the North, 1893–98

1. A copy of John Smedley's handbook explaining in detail the aims and functions of hydropathic treatments can be found at https://iiif.wellcomecollection.org/pdf/b20398700
2. TSM, pp.111–3. Adela, writing more about a later incarnation of the store in Manchester, claimed that 'if "Emerson's" had succeeded, Mother and all the rest of us in town would, whatever our natural bent, have been compelled to give ourselves up to it, in order that the funds for politics might be forthcoming ...' Indeed, she had to leave school before she was 16 to work in the enterprise's third incarnation in Manchester; 'My Mother', p.6.
3. MG, 20 October 1886, p.8; 29 October 1886, p.8.
4. For what follows, see TSM, pp.113–17.

Chapter 12 The Family in the North

1. 'My Mother', p.13.
2. The house was rented at a hefty £60 a year, with a rateable value of £50; see the Manchester Rate Books, 1897.
3. *Unshackled*, p.31.
4. 'The Philosophy of the Suffragette Movement', p.9.
5. TSM, pp.121–4.
6. 'My Mother', p.15.
7. Pugh, *The Pankhursts*, p.62.
8. TSM, p.140.
9. TSM, pp.139–41.
10. 'My Mother', pp.22–3; Purvis, *Emmeline Pankhurst*, p.48; Coleman, *Adela Pankhurst*, p.21.
11. Adela, on the other hand, did teach for a while later on.
12. I am grateful to Professor June Purvis for the details of Christabel's achievement; see June Purvis, *Christabel Pankhurst: a biography* (London, 2018), p.109.
13. MG, 14 June 1887, p.6.
14. MG, 6 March 1891, p.7.
15. For what follows, see TSM, pp.119–128.

16. Jeffrey Hill, 'Manchester and Salford Politics and the Early Development of the Independent Labour Party', *International Review of Social History*, vol. 26, no. 2 (1981), p.193.
17. K.O. Morgan, *Keir Hardie, Radical and Socialist* (London, 1975), p.64.
18. *Sheffield Daily Telegraph*, 29 June 1894, p.5.
19. *Yorkshire Post*, 3 July 1894, p.4.
20. *Sheffield Daily Telegraph*, 3 July 1894, p.5.
21. *L[abour] L[eader]*, 7 July 1894, p.9.
22. *Yorkshire Evening Post*, 5 July 1894, p.4.
23. *Sheffield Daily Telegraph*, 6 July 1894, p.5. Perhaps the Pankhursts found this incident especially distressing as they had lost their own small son, Frank.
24. TSM, p.120.
25. TSM, p.119.
26. 'The Philosophy of the Suffragette Movement', p.13.
27. ESPP 323, Ursula Bright to Emmeline Pankhurst, 10 July 1894. See for instance MG, 19 September 1894, p.6; 2 November 1894, p.6.
28. MG, 12 November 1894, p.5.
29. MG, 12 November 1894, p.5; *Clarion*, 15 December 1894, p.6.
30. TSM, p.120.
31. *Unshackled*, p.32.
32. LSE ILP/4/1895/10.
33. TSM, p.126.
34. TSM, p.127.
35. *Clarion*, 25 April 1896, p.134.
36. University of Liverpool Special Collections and Archives, John Bruce Glasier Papers, GP/2/1/3, 4, 5, 6.
37. MG, 1 June 1896, p.10.
38. TSM, p.128.
39. MG, 22 October 1894, pp.5 and 6; *Clarion*, 20 October 1894, p.4.
40. TSM, pp.124–6; MG, 31 January 1890; 3 February 1890, p.6. For more information, see https://library.chethams.com/blog/ancoats
41. See TSM, pp.128–32.
42. MG, 20 February 1895, p.7.
43. This was not the only time Pankhurst led representations to the guardians; he and others approached the Manchester board on 6 March; MG, 7 March 1895, p.8.
44. MG, 11 March 1895, p.8.
45. TSM, p.131.
46. *Clarion*, 20 April 1895, p.124; ILP online records, https://microform.digital/boa/collections/60/independent-labour-party-records-1893-1960, 1894–5 Annual Report, image 49.
47. ILP online records, https://microform.digital/boa/collections/60/independent-labour-party-records-1893-1960, 1895–6 NAC minutes, image 6.

Chapter 13 ILP Candidate – the Gorton election of May 1895

1. LSE ILP/4/1895/10; TSM, pp.133–6. He had, in fact agreed to stand as the ILP candidate for Chorley, Lancashire, in May, but it seems that this came to nothing.

It was a safe Conservative seat, and in the event remained unopposed; *The Times*, 31 May 1895, p.7; MG, 12 July 1895, p.9.

2. MG, 15 June 1895, p.8.

3. See for instance the letters in MG, 9 July 1895, p.4; 10 July 1895, p.4; ILP online records, 1895–6 NAC minutes, image 26.

4. *The Times*, 8 July 1895, p.10; MG, 8 July 1895, p.4.

5. LSE ILP/4/1895/116.

6. MG, 11 July 1895, p.4.

7. Pugh, *The Pankhursts*, p.71; Purvis, *Emmeline Pankhurst*, p.45.

8. MG, 12 July 1895, p.4; ESPP 336.

9. MG, 2 May 1894, p.7.

10. TSM, p.134.

11. Ibid.

12. *Clarion*, 29 June 1895, p.204; MG, 8 July 1895, p.1.

13. TSM, p.136.

14. Elections were held over a period at that time.

15. MG, 22 July 1895, p.6.

16. TSM, p.136.

17. ILP online records, 1895–6 Annual Report, images 86–7.

18. Stefan Collini, *Public Moralists*, p.129.

19. TSM, p.136.

20. Pugh, *The Pankhursts*, p.71.

21. *Unshackled*, pp.34–5.

22. MG, 17 February 1896, p.3.

23. ILP online records, 1896 Annual Report, image102; *Clarion*, 11 April 1896, p.118.

24. ILP online records, NAC Minutes, 2 January 1896, images 52–55; 22 April 1896, images 88, 97, 98.

25. MG, 10 November 1893, p.3; 8 April 1896, p.6; 13 February 1896, p.9.

26. MG, 21 March 1896, p.4.

27. MG, 17 October 1896, p.4.

28. TSM, p.8.

29. MG, 24 April 1896, p.5; *Clarion*, 28 April 1894, p.3.

30. For this account, see Pugh, *The Pankhursts*, pp.72–4; Purvis, *Emmeline Pankhurst*, pp.46–8; TSM, pp.136–9.

31. MG, 6 July 1896, p.5.

32. MG, 4 May 1896, p.9.

33. Ibid.

34. MG, 23 May 1896, p.7; *Clarion*, 6 June 1896, p.182.

35. *Clarion*, 2 May 1896, p.140.

36. MG, 4 June 1896, p.7.

37. MG, 13 July 1896, p.10.

38. Fred's claim to illness is supported by the fact that he went abroad for health reasons soon after his release; ILP online records, 1896–7, Annual Report, image 121.

39. MG, 22 June 1896, p.10; Andrew Rosen, *Rise up Women!: the Militant Campaign of the Women's Social and Political Union 1903–1914* (London, 2012), p.20.

40. University of Liverpool, GP/2/1/4, 21 June 1896.

41. MG, 30 June 1896, p.5; MG, 4 July 1896, pp.6, 8.

42. ILP online records, NAC Minutes, 3 July 1896, images 105–6.
43. University of Liverpool, GP/2/1/4.
44. MG, 4 July 1896, p.8.
45. MG, 11 July 1896, p.5.
46. ILP online records, NAC Minutes, 3 July 1896, images 105–10.
47. MG, 6 July 1896, p.5. Mundella died of a stroke shortly afterwards, so perhaps he was unable to fulfil this commitment.
48. University of Liverpool, GP/2/1/4.
49. TSM, p.136.
50. TSM, p.137.
51. MG, 24 September 1896, p.7; 3 October 1896, p.5. ILP online records, NAC Minutes, 1 October 1896, image 117.
52. University of Liverpool GP/2/1/4.
53. TSM, p.139.
54. See p.152.
55. MG, 3 May 1897, p.6.
56. MG, 1 September 1896, p.6; *The Times*, 2 September 1896, p.3; MG, 2 September 1896; *The Times*, 4 September 1896 p.4; MG, 5 September 1896, p.5; *Leeds Mercury*, 2 September 1896, p.7; TSM, p.141; Purvis, *Emmeline Pankhurst*, p.49.
57. ILP online records, 1896–7 Annual Report, image 119.
58. *Clarion*, 5 December 1896, p.388.

Chapter 14 Maintaining the Family Income

1. Pethick-Lawrence Papers, PETH/9/72, letter of 25 June 1957; 'My Mother' pp.5–6; *Unshackled*, p.25.
2. *Unshackled*, p.27.
3. MG, 8 Jan 1895, p.4; 14 January 1897, p.9.
4. MG, 18 February 1891, p.7.
5. MG, 27 September 1883, p.66; November 1883, p.7.
6. David E. Owen, *The Manchester Ship Canal* (Manchester 1983), pp.40–3.
7. MG, 7 February 1893, p.12.
8. MG, 29 August 1893, p.9.
9. ESPP 342.
10. TSM, p.142.
11. Owen, p.63.
12. MG, 7 June 1894, p.8; 22 June 1894, p.6.
13. MG, 14 September 1894, p.8.
14. MG, 10 June 1895, p.6.
15. MG, 30 September 1895, p.6.
16. MG, 19 November 1895, p.5.
17. MG, 16 March 1894, p.7.
18. MG, 11 July 1895, p.12.
19. Pugh, *The Pankhursts*, p.75; Owen, p.117.
20. MG, 15 October 1896, p.9; 7 January 1897, p.3.
21. MG, 12 November 1896, p.9.
22. MG, 19 February 1896, p.3.

23. MG, 30 September 1896, p.7.
24. TSM, p.139.

Chapter 15 The Final Years

1. MG, 7 October 1890, p.12; ESPP 331.
2. MG, 25 February 1897, p.7.
3. LSE ILP/4/1897/29, letter from Richard Marsden Pankhurst to Tom Mann. The farmhouse was apparently divided into two and the Pankhursts occupied one part, the farmer's family, named Whittaker, the other. I am very grateful to Allan Edgar for showing me a letter from a Whittaker descendant that gives this information.
4. Purvis, *Emmeline Pankhurst*, p.49; TSM, p.146. TSM suggests that Emmeline decided on the move to Mobberley because of worries for Richard's health.
5. MG, 21 May 1897, p.12.
6. MG, 25 August 1897, p.7.
7. ILP online records, NAC Minutes, 5 January 1897, image 134.
8. ILP online records, 1897 Annual Report, image 180; NAC Minutes, 12 April 1898, images 24–5; 5 May 1898, images 27, 33; *Labour Leader*, 16 April 1898, p.125.
9. MG, 24 May 1897, p.10.
10. *Clarion*, 19 June 1897, p.199.
11. MG, 19 July 1897, p.5; 29 July 1897, p.9.
12. MG, 12 October 1897, p.12.
13. MG, 30 October 1897, p.10.
14. *Clarion*, 11 December 1897, p.398. I am grateful to Alistair MacLeod for the reference about where the cyclists came from.
15. MG, 8 November 1894, p.5.
16. MG, 19 February 1897, p.3; 10 March 1897, p.11; 11 March 1897, p.3; 12 March 1897, p.3; 17 March 1897, p.4; 18 March 1897, p.4; 19 March 1897, p.4.
17. MG, 31 May 1897, p.12. This campaign foreshadowed a more famous one in the 1930s.
18. MG, 15 October 1897, p.9.
19. MG, 11 November 1897, p.9.
20. MG, 13 September 1897, p.10.
21. TSM, p.145; Purvis, *Emmeline Pankhurst*, p.50; Pugh, *The Pankhursts*, p.76.
22. MG, 25 September 1897, p.5.
23. Purvis, *Emmeline Pankhurst*, p.50.
24. MG, 15 September 1897, p.5.
25. MG, 19 October 1897, p.4.
26. MG, 9 November 1897, p.5.
27. *The Times*, 6 May 1898, p.15.
28. TSM, p.148.
29. For what follows, see TSM, pp.146–153.
30. It was Harry's ninth birthday on 7 July, two days after his father's death; it is not recorded that anyone paid much attention to the fact.
31. LSE, ILP/4/1898/52.
32. TSM, p.146. The accounts seem to suggest that Richard himself was not aware of the cause of his pain, but that the doctor chose to spare him the worry it might cause him.
33. E. Sylvia Pankhurst, *Emmeline Pankhurst*, pp.40–1.

34. *Unshackled*, p.35
35. *Clarion*, 9 July 1898, p.220.
36. MEN, 5 July 1898, p.4.
37. TSM, p.66.
38. MCN, 16 July 1898; *Manchester Weekly Times*, 15 July 1898, p.2; *Altrincham, Bowdon and Hale Guardian*, 13 July 1898, p.5; *Clarion*, 16 July 1898, p.229.
39. Brocklehurst does refer to the interment of 'the ashes of their dead friend', but this may be just a reference to the Prayerbook words used in the traditional burial service; the records of Manchester Crematorium were destroyed in the Second World War, so it is impossible to check; MG, 11 July 1898, p.12.
40. University of Liverpool, GP/2/1/6.
41. University of Liverpool, GP/1/1/319.
42. MC, 11 July 1898, p.7.
43. Purvis, *Emmeline Pankhurst*, p.53; *Labour Leader*, 9 July 1898, p.228. Hardie wrote: 'Had it been possible to have got back the same evening I wd have gone but Mrs H requires consideration first at present'; LSE ILP/4/1898/145.
44. Whitman's poem, *Virginia's Woods*, is about the woodland grave of a fallen soldier. The line reads: 'Bold, cautious, true, and my loving comrade'; the need for a slight adaptation is clear!
45. MEN, 9 July 1898, p.4.

Chapter 16 Legacy

1. *The Times*, 6 July 1898, p.14.
2. *Clarion*, 9 July 1898, p.220.
3. MG, 10 April 1899, p.10.
4. MEN, 6 July 1898, p.4.
5. Proceedings of The Manchester Literary and Philosophical Society, Annual Report of the Council, pp.xxxviii–xl.
6. ILP online records, NAC Minutes, images 47–8; MG, 9 July 1898, p.10; 11 July 1898, p.12.
7. ILP online records, Annual Report, 1898–9, images 213–4.
8. ESPP 331. I am very grateful to Professor June Purvis for providing me with a copy of the shares list from her Private Suffrage Collection.
9. MG, 12 July 1898, p.11; 13 July 1898, p.5; MG, 15 July 1898, p.9.
10. For Thompson see pp.115–6.
11. MEN, 16 July 1898, p.2. See Purvis, *Emmeline Pankhurst*, pp.54–5.
12. See Purvis, *Emmeline Pankhurst,* pp.54–5. It is interesting to note that Sir Charles Dilke, whom the Pankhursts had supported in the time of his deep trouble over a divorce scandal, rendered only a measly £1; List of Subscriptions issued by the Executive Committee on 17 August 1898. I am hugely grateful to Professor June Purvis for her generosity in sending me a copy of this document from her Private Suffrage Collection.
13. MG, 19 August 1898, p.5; *Clarion*, 17 September 1898, p.199. I am grateful to Pam Dawes for the information about Snazelle, from whom the word 'Snazzy' is thought to have been derived!
14. See June Purvis, 'Emmeline Pankhurst (1858–1928), Suffragette Leader and Single Parent in Edwardian Britain', pp.95–6.
15. ILP online records, Annual Report, 1898–9, image 214; MG, 16 July 1898, p.7; 23 July 1898, p.10; 25 July 1898, p.12; *Clarion*, 3 September 1898, p.267.

16. MG, 17 October 1898, p.9; *Clarion*, 22 October 1898, p.338; 17 December 1898, p.404.
17. MG, 23 October 1899, p.12.
18. *Clarion*, 3 December 1898, p.391; 19 November 1898, p.372.
19. ILP News no. 44, vol. iv, November 1900, p.2.
20. MCN, 10 October 1903, p.7; Purvis, *Emmeline Pankhurst,* pp.54–5, 66–7; TSM, p.167. The Hall later became a cinema.

Conclusion

1. 'My Mother', pp.24–5, 30, 35, 46–7.
2. Ethel Smyth, *Female Pipings in Eden* (London, 1924), p.242; ESPP folder 35, a draft of Sylvia's *The Suffragette Movement,* cited in F. Andrew Rosen, *Rise up Women!* (London, 1974), pp.207–8.
3. LSE Women's Library, 7JCC 01/12 FOLDER 1, letters from Christabel to Sylvia, 5 May 1953, 17 June 1953, 22 April 1954, 3 August 1957.
4. Pethick-Lawrence Papers, PETH 9/82, 9/83, 9/86, all from Sylvia to Frederick Pethick-Lawrence, 1959.
5. MCN, 12 April 1913.
6. *Unshackled*, p.32.
7. David Mitchell, *Queen Christabel*, p.43.
8. Sandra Stanley Holton, 'From Anti-Slavery to Suffrage Militancy', p.213.
9. 'The Philosophy of the Suffragette Movement', pp.20–22.
10. Ibid., p.16; Richard Pankhurst, 'Suffragette Sisters in Old Age', p.507.
11. MCN, 23 April 1910, p.6; 30 April 1910, p.6; 7 May 1910, p.9.
12. 'My Mother', p.5.

Select Bibliography

Published Works

Abrams, Fran, *Freedom's Cause. Lives of the Suffragettes* (London, 2003)

Atkinson, Diane, *Rise up Women!* (London, 2018)

Banks, Olive, *Becoming a Feminist: The Social Origins of 'First Wave' Feminism* (Brighton, 1986)

Blackburn, Helen, *Women's Suffrage* (London, 1902)

Caine, Barbara, *English Feminism, 1780–1980* (Oxford, 2002)

Caine, Barbara, *Victorian Feminists* (Oxford, 1992)

Coleman, Verna, *Adela Pankhurst, the wayward suffragette, 1885–1961* (Melbourne, 1996)

Collini, Stefan, *Public Moralists: Political Thought and Intellectual Life in Britain* (Oxford, 1993)

D'Arcy, Fergus A., 'Charles Bradlaugh and the English Republican Movement, 1868–78', *The Historical Journal*, June 1982, vol. 25, no. 2, pp.367–83

Davies, David P., *Life and Labours of Ernest Jones* (London, 1903)

Dictionary of Radical Biography

'English Courts of Law', *Westminster Review,* v.68, 1857, pp.33–52

Fifoot, C.H.S., *Judge and Jurist in the Reign of Victoria* (London, 1959)

Fulford, Roger, *Votes for Women: the Story of a Struggle* (1957)

Goldman, Lawrence, *Science, Reform and Politics in Victorian Britain. The Social Science Association 1857–86* (CUP, 2002)

Goldman, Lawrence, *Science, Reform and Politics in Victorian Britain. The Social Science Association 1857–1886* (Cambridge, 2002)

Harland-Jacobs, Jessica, 'All in the Family: Freemasonry and the British Empire in the Mid-Nineteenth Century', *Journal of British Studies,* vol. 42, no. 4 (October, 2003), pp.448–482

Hill, Jeffrey, 'Manchester and Salford Politics and the Early Development of the Independent Labour Party', *International Review of Social History*, vol. 26, no. 2 (1981)

Holcombe, Lee, *Wives and Property* (Toronto, 1983)

Holton, Sandra Stanley, *Suffrage Days* (London, 1996)

How, J, *The Freemason's Manual: Or, Illustrations of Masonry* (London, 1862)

Joannou, Maroula, and Purvis, June, eds., *The Women's Suffrage Movement* (MUP, 1998)

Lester, V. Markham, *Victorian Insolvency: Bankruptcy, Imprisonment for Debt, and Company Winding-up in Nineteenth-Century England* (Oxford, 1995)

Manchester Faces and Places, vol. iv (1893)

Manchester Literary and Philosophical Society, Annual Report, 1898–99

Mayhall, Laura E. Nym, *The Militant Suffrage Movement. Citizenship and Resistance in Britain, 1860–1930* (Oxford, 2003)

McLaren E.T., *Dr. R. McLaren of Manchester. A Sketch* (London, 1911)

Miles, James B., *The Association for the Reform and Codification of the Law of Nations* (Paris, 1875)

Mitchell, David, *Queen Christabel* (London, 1977)

Mitchell, David, *The Fighting Pankhursts* (London, 1967)

Morgan, K.O., *Keir Hardie, Radical and Socialist* (London, 1975)

Moyes, Helen., *Woman in a Man's World* (Sidney, 1971)

Owen, David E, *The Manchester Ship Canal* (Manchester, 1983)

Oxford Dictionary of National Biography

Oxford, Margot, ed., *Myself When Young* (London, 1938)

Pankhurst, Christabel, *Unshackled* (London, 1987)

Pankhurst, E. Sylvia, *The Life of Emmeline Pankhurst: The Suffragette Struggle for Women's Citizenship* (London, 1935)

Pankhurst, E. Sylvia, *The Suffragette Movement* (London, 1977)

Pankhurst, Emmeline, *My Own Story* (London, 1914)

Pankhurst, Richard Marsden, 'The Right of Women to Vote Under the Reform Act, 1867', *Fortnightly Review,* XXI, 1 September 1868, pp.250–4

Pankhurst, Richard, 'Suffragette Sisters in Old Age: unpublished correspondence between Christabel and Sylvia Pankhurst, 1953–57', *Women's History Review,* vol. 10, no. 3 (2001), pp.483–538

Pankhurst, Richard, *Sylvia Pankhurst, Artist and Crusader* (London, 1979)

Perkin, Joan, *Women and Marriage in 19th century England* (London, 1989)

Pigot's Typology of England (1841)

Proceedings of The Manchester Literary and Philosophical Society, Annual Report of the Council

Pugh, Martin, *The Pankhursts* (London, 2008)

Purvis, June, 'Emmeline Pankhurst (1858–1928), Suffragette Leader and Single Parent in Edwardian Britain', *Women's History Review*, 20:1 (2011)

Purvis, June, *Christabel Pankhurst: A Biography* (London, 2018)

Purvis, June, *Emmeline Pankhurst: A Biography* (London, 2002)

Ridley, Jasper, *The Freemasons* (London, 2008)

Romero, Patricia W., *E. Sylvia Pankhurst, Portrait of a Radical* (Yale, 1987)

Rosen, Andrew, *Rise up Women!: the Militant Campaign of the Women's Social and Political Union 1903–1914* (London, 2012)

Slater's Directory of Manchester, January 1886

Smyth, Ethel, *Female Pipings in Eden* (London, 1924)

Stanley Holton, Sandra, '"To Educate Women into Rebellion": Elizabeth Cady Stanton and the Creation of a Transatlantic Network of Radical Suffragists', *American Historical Review,* October 1994, pp.1112–1136

Stanley Holton, Sandra, 'From Anti-Slavery to Suffrage Militancy: The Bright Circle, Elizabeth Cady Stanton and the British Women's Movement', in *Suffrage and Beyond: International Feminist Perspectives* (New Zealand, 1994), pp.213–33

Stanley Holton, Sandra, *Suffrage Days* (London, 1996)

Strauss Sylvia, *Traitors to the Masculine Cause. The Men's Campaigns for Women's Rights* (London, 1982)

Symonds Richard, *Inside the Citadel. Men and the Emancipation of Women, 1850–1920* (London, 1999)

Taylor, Anne, *Annie Besant* (Oxford, 1992)

Thompson, Joseph, *The Owens College,* (Manchester, 1886)

Thompson, Laurence, *The Enthusiasts. A biography of John and Katharine Bruce Glasier* (London, 1971)

Tosh, John, *A Man's Place* (London, 1999)

Transactions of the Manchester Statistical Society, 1865–66, 1883–84, 1887–88

White, William, *History, Gazetteer and Directory of Staffordshire* (Sheffield, 1851)

Williams, Joanna M., *Manchester's Radical Mayor: Abel Heywood, the Man who Built the Town Hall* (Stroud, 2017)

Williams, Joanna M., *The Great Miss Lydia Becker: Suffragist, Scientist and Trailblazer* (Barnsley, 2022)

Wright, Maureen, *Elizabeth Wolstenholme Elmy and the Victorian Feminist Movement,* (Manchester, 2011)

Newspapers

Accrington Times
Altrincham, Bowdon and Hale Guardian
City Jackdaw
Huddersfield Chronicle
ILP News
Labour Leader
Leeds Times
Liverpool Mail
London Daily News
Macclesfield Courier and Herald
Manchester and Salford Co-operative Herald
Manchester City News
Manchester Courier
Manchester Evening News
Manchester Guardian
Manchester Weekly News
Sheffield Daily Telegraph
South London Press
Staffordshire Advertiser
The Clarion
The Observer
The Times
Votes for Women
Woman's Herald
Women's Suffrage Journal
Yorkshire Evening Post

Online Sources

Census 1861, 1871, 1881, 1891
Death Certificates – Margaret Pankhurst, Henry Francis Pankhurst, Richard Marsden Pankhurst
https://eastlancashirefreemasons.org/the-interesting-life-of-manchester-mason-richard-pankhurst
https://iiif.wellcomecollection.org/pdf/b20398700
https://library.chethams.com
ILP online records, https://microform.digital/boa/collections/60/independent-labour-party-records-1893-1960
Pease, Edward R., *The History of the Fabian Society* (Project Gutenberg, 2004), cap. III, www.gutenberg.org
Probate Records – Margaret Pankhurst, Henry Francis Pankhurst
www.freemasonrymatters.co.uk

Unpublished Sources

International Institute of Social History, Amsterdam: Estelle Sylvia Pankhurst Papers
London School of Economics, The Women's Library: Jill Craigie Collection; Autograph letters; Independent Labour Party Papers
Manchester Central Library: Women's Suffrage Collection
National Library of Australia, Pankhurst-Walsh Papers
Trinity College, Cambridge Library: Pethwick-Lawrence Papers
University of Liverpool Special Collections and Archives: John Bruce Glasier Papers
University of Manchester, Owens College Archive
United Grand Lodge of England Freemason Membership Registers, 1751–1921

Index

Afghanistan 44, 97
American Civil War 19, 36–7, 90
Angel Meadow 105–106, 159, 173
Anstey, Thomas Chisholm 66, 68
Athenaeum 8, 10, 17, 26, 46, 50, 90, 106, 147, 191
Attercliffe election 154

Balfour, Arthur 115–16
Ballot Act 38
Bamford, Samuel 38
Bazley, Sir Thomas 7, 38, 49
Becker, Lydia 45, 55, 60–78, 79–80, 83, 91, 103, 138, 214–15
Besant, Annie 135, 138, 232
Billington-Greig, Theresa xiv– xv, 93
Blatchford, Robert 143, 151, 157, 194, 198
Bloody Sunday 137
Bodichon, Barbara Leigh Smith 31, 60
Boggart Hole Clough 167, 169, 172–6, 183, 192, 204
Boucherett, Jessie 63, 71, 79–80
Bradlaugh, Charles xv, 48, 115, 138
Brierley, Ben 103
Bright, Jacob 38, 41, 48, 60, 62, 70–5, 80, 82–4, 96, 110, 113, 124, 138, 146, 198
Bright, John 51, 103, 195
Bright, Ursula 62, 80, 84, 124, 139–46, 154, 198, 222
British Association for the Advancement of Science 32, 45, 211
Brocklehurst, Fred 165, 170–4, 176, 188, 191, 193, 199–200, 228
Brooklands Cemetery 184, 190–1
Brougham, Lord 32, 66, 78

Burns, John 137–8
Burrows, Herbert 138, 144
Butler, Josephine 63, 65, 79–80, 137, 140, 214–15

Cady Stanton, Elizabeth 124, 140, 220
Carnarvon, Lord 40
Chamberlain, Joseph xv, 28, 102
Chancery Court of the County Palatine of Lancaster 12, 22, 34, 108, 121, 188
Chartists 18–19, 191
Chesters Thompson, Stephen 115, 117, 177, 198
Chorlton v Lings 69
Chorlton-on-Medlock 6, 68, 104, 116, 159, 161, 165, 174, 191, 192, 217
Christianity 35, 55–9, 116, 132
Christie, Professor RC 9, 10, 183
Church of England 31, 36, 47, 50, 53, 57, 97, 191, 213
Churchill, Lord Randolph 114
Clarion Cycling Club 151, 168, 184, 191
Co-operation 18, 54–5
College Street group 138, 146, 221
Commercial law 24, 26, 32, 35
Conservatives 36, 41, 44, 49, 83, 98, 110, 112, 115, 138, 165, 166, 218
Crane, Walter 130, 200
Cromwell, Oliver 19, 96, 113

Davitt, Michael 103, 106
Delves School, The 3
Dickens, Charles 10, 19–20, 34
Dilke, Sir Charles xv, 63, 70, 141, 222, 228
Disley 149–50

Disraeli, Benjamin Lord Beaconsfield
    39–41, 43–4, 47, 49, 51–52, 74, 83, 97

Eastern Question 39, 42–3
Education Act 30, 38
Emersons 122–3, 131, 147
Engels, Friedrich 18

Fabian Society 143, 144, 153, 157, 185,
    204, 223
Fairbairn, Sir William 7, 12
Fawcett, Henry 63, 96
Fawcett, Millicent 80, 138, 142, 146
Fenians 18, 90, 103
Fenwick Miller, Florence 131, 139–41
Forsyth, William 75
Fraser, Bishop of Manchester 47
Free Trade Hall, Manchester 7, 39, 42, 62,
    67, 155, 199, 218

Gaskell, Elizabeth 77
Gladstone, William 23, 32, 34, 38, 83, 100,
    103, 107, 113–14, 163, 195, 212
Glasier, Bruce 157–8,170–2, 174, 185, 192,
    199–200
Glasier, Katharine 157–8, 192, 199
Gorton 159, 162, 164–6, 185, 198
Goulden, Herbert 190, 202
Goulden, Jane (née Craine) 90
Goulden, Mary 108, 173
Goulden, Robert 89–91, 108, 212, 220

Haldane, Richard Lord 139, 143
Hall, Leonard 160, 164, 169–72, 174, 184,
    192–3
Hamilton, Colonel 111–17
Harker, John 169, 173
Heywood, Abel 41, 44, 56, 97, 99, 102
House of Lords 23, 38, 52–4, 71, 78, 81–4,
    97, 110, 143, 163, 167, 171, 213
Hyndman, Henry 137–8, 153, 157, 169

Independent Labour Party (ILP) 151, 153–
    60, 162–9, 170–1, 173–6, 182, 184–5,
    188, 190–2, 194, 196–7, 199, 224
India 25, 40, 44, 51–2, 98, 100, 105
Inns of Court 10

International Arbitration Association 111
International Association for the
    Reform and Codification of the Law of
    Nations 37
Irish xiii, 18, 27, 38, 84, 90–1, 98–9, 103,
    105– 107, 113–15, 117, 151, 158, 163,
    194, 201, 204, 218
Isle of Man 8, 65, 98

Jones, Ernest 17–19, 38

Keir Hardie, James xii, 131, 151, 153–5,
    157, 160, 162–7, 170–4, 184, 192, 199,
    228

Labour Church 168, 185, 191
Land nationalisation 97, 168
Land reform 18, 38, 54, 104
Law Amendment Society 31, 78
Law of Bankruptcy 4, 11, 23, 35, 104, 177,
    191, 194
Liberals 30, 32–4, 36, 38–45, 48–9, 51–2,
    56–7, 60, 62–3, 72, 74, 80, 83, 90, 97–
    107, 109, 110–13, 115, 117, 138, 140,
    143, 152, 154, 162–3, 165–6, 186, 195,
    201, 218–19
Liberation Society 56–7, 111
Liebknecht, Wilhelm 158, 169
Lincoln's Inn 12, 118
Lloyd Garrison, William 123, 140
Local Government Act 1894 70, 145

Manchester Ancoats Brotherhood 158–9,
    174, 195
Manchester and Salford Industrial
    Co-operative Society 22
Manchester Arts Club 167, 191, 193, 197
Manchester Brasenose Club 14, 16,
    49, 197
Manchester Chamber of Commerce
    23–31, 35–6, 104, 178, 191, 194
Manchester Corporation 22–3, 94, 108,
    119, 121, 168, 171, 178, 180–1, 186–9,
    191, 193
Manchester Council 5, 24, 71, 173, 175,
    180, 191, 196
Manchester Cremation Society 183

Manchester Grammar School 2, 6, 9, 12, 50, 147, 208
Manchester High School 150, 152
Manchester Law Students Society 10, 23, 167, 174, 191
Manchester Literary and Philosophical Society 147, 183, 196
Manchester Mechanics Institution 29–30, 47
Manchester National Society for Women's Suffrage (MNSWS) 70–6, 79, 145, 215, 218
Manchester Radical Association 109–10
Manchester Republican Club xv, 47–52
Manchester School Board 30, 56, 155, 191
Manchester School of Art 28
Manchester Ship Canal 26, 98, 104, 119, 162, 178–81, 184, 186, 197–8
Manchester Statistical Society 36–7, 167, 186, 191
Manchester Sunday School Union 28, 56
Manchester Town Hall 12, 24, 28, 50, 82, 105–107, 115, 152, 156, 195, 211
Mann, Tom 158, 165, 170–1, 175, 183, 185, 199, 227
Married Women's Property Act 79–84
Martyn, Caroline 158, 170
Marx, Eleanor 158
Marx, Karl xii, 18, 165
Mason, Hugh 102, 105
Masons 15–16
McIlquham, Harriet 139–40, 143
McLaren, Dr 27–8, 55
McLaren, Priscilla 80, 138, 214
Mill, John Stuart 33, 57, 60, 66–7, 79, 81, 112, 165
Mobberley 183–4, 188m, 227
Morris, William 122–3, 138, 143, 191
Municipal Corporations Act 70–1

National Association for the Promotion of Social Science 24, 30–5, 37, 61, 78–83, 194, 211
National Education League 28
National Reform Union 38, 42–5, 195
National Union of Dock Labourers 175, 179
National Union of Women's Suffrage Societies 146
Non-conformist xiii, 4, 7, 16, 33, 38, 46, 53, 55, 57, 201, 213
North of England Society for Women's Suffrage 204
Northern Circuit 12, 18, 171

Ottoman Empire 39
Owens College 9, 11–13, 28, 30, 50, 155, 191, 197, 208

Pankhurst Hall 200
Pankhurst, Adela xiv, 87, 89–90, 94–5, 126–9, 133–5,149–52, 155, 174,177, 188, 190, 202, 204–206, 223
Pankhurst, Christabel xii–xiii, 2, 7–8, 22, 62, 87–9, 92, 95, 118, 124, 127, 129–34, 146, 150–2, 156, 158, 164, 166, 178, 188–9, 191, 202–206, 214, 216
Pankhurst, Elizabeth (Bess) 8, 94, 203, 216
Pankhurst, Emmeline (née Goulden) xiii–xiv, 9, 63–4, 75, 86–95, 96, 99, 103, 108, 110–11, 113, 118, 122–5, 126–31, 133, 135–6, 138–46, 147, 149–61, 163–5, 167–77, 179, 181, 183–93, 195–6, 198–200, 202–206, 212, 216, 220, 222, 227
Pankhurst, Francis James 2–3
Pankhurst, Frank 95, 122, 125, 127, 133–4, 220
Pankhurst, Harriet 3, 8
Pankhurst, Harry xiv, 127, 129, 133–5, 139–40, 152, 188, 190, 199, 202, 220, 227
Pankhurst, Henry Francis 2–8, 12, 21, 65, 123, 127, 133, 190, 214
Pankhurst, John Calvin 4, 6–8
Pankhurst, Margaret 2–5, 7–8, 65, 190, 208
Pankhurst, Richard Keir 93
Pankhurst, Richard Marsden
    Early life 4–13
    Law career 17–23, 118–22, 177–82
    Marriage 86–95
    Fatherhood 126–36, 149–52
    Views on religion 55–9
    Liberalism 37–44, 98–107
    Women's suffrage 60–76
    Married women's property 77–84

Parliamentary candidate 96–108, 111–15, 162–5
   Republicanism 47–54
   Socialism 152–8
   Death 188–90
Pankhurst, Sylvia xii–xv, 3, 6–9, 11, 14–17, 22–4, 28, 30–1, 33, 37–8, 49, 61–5, 67, 69, 71, 86–90, 92–5, 96, 103, 108–9, 122, 124, 126–35, 139–41, 143, 146, 149–53, 157–60, 164–5, 177, 179, 182, 188–90, 200, 202–203, 205–206, 208, 211–12, 216
Parliament Street group 138–9, 142, 146, 221
Parnell, Charles Stuart 103, 105, 114, 218
Patent Law Reform Association 24
Paxton Hood, Reverend Edwin 96, 113
Peak and District Preservation Committee 185–6
Permissive Bill 34
Persons campaign 66–9
Poor Law 5, 159–60, 162, 185–6

Queen Victoria 48, 52, 80, 135
Queen's Bench 113, 117, 119

Rochefort (Dufaux), Noémie 91–2, 188
Rochefort, Henri 91, 93, 124
Rollit Bill 117, 143–5
Roscoe, Professor Henry E. 12, 147, 187
Rotherhithe 111–17, 119, 177, 198
Rowley, Charles 158
Royal Manchester Institution 28
Royal Titles Bill 51
Russo-Turkish War 42, 137

Salisbury, Marquess of (Lord) 71, 115, 155
Scatcherd, Alice (Cliff) 138, 140–2, 146, 192, 198, 223
Scott, CP 198
Selborne, Lord Chancellor 84
Selden Society 118
Sexton, James 175–6, 179
Shaw, George Bernard 144–5, 159, 199

Slavery 19, 37, 78, 90, 123–4, 146, 185
Social Democratic Federation 153, 155, 157, 174, 185
Socialism 18, 33, 108, 134–5, 138, 143, 152–5, 159, 167–9, 180, 184, 193–4, 196, 200–201, 206
Southport 149, 151, 184, 197
Sowler, Thomas 116–17
Sowler, Harry 198
Stanton Blatch, Harriet 124, 140–1, 145
Stead, WT 137–8
Suffragettes, *see* Women's Social and Political Union

Taylor, Helen 112
Tillett, Ben 154, 165, 172, 175

Union Chapel Essay and Discussion Society 27, 55
Union of Lancashire and Cheshire Mechanics Institutes 29, 47
Victoria Park 135, 150

Victoria University of Manchester 12, 30, 152, 183, 187

Waugh, Edwin 17
Wolstenholme Elmy, Elizabeth 31, 60, 75, 78–80, 82, 84, 140–1, 143–4, 215, 222
Women, Bill for the Removal of the Electoral Disabilities of 70, 74–5, 86, 139
Women's Emancipation Union 143–4
Women's Franchise League 138–46, 154
Women's Liberal Federation 138, 140
Women's Social and Political Union xii, xiv, 7, 62–3, 146, 157, 200, 202, 204, 206
Women's suffrage xii, 38, 55, 60–76, 78–9, 83, 86, 91, 95, 103, 124, 138–9, 141–2, 144–6, 152–3, 202, 204–205, 208, 221, 223
World Congress of Representative Women, Chicago 145, 222